GREGORY OF NYSSA

Gregory of Nyssa presents new translations of key selections of Gregory's writings, with an informative introduction and extensive notes and commentary to illuminate Gregory's writings and to illustrate how educated Christians tried to recommend and explore their faith in the face of a paganism that was still alive.

Anthony Meredith presents a diverse range of Gregory's writings – his contribution to the debates of the period about the nature of God in argument with a form of extreme Arianism, his discussion of the nature and work of the Holy Ghost, against the so-called 'Spirit fighters', his defence of the humanity of Christ against those who denied it, notably Apolinarius, and his preoccupations with philosophical questions, above all the nature of fate.

Gregory of Nyssa provides a concise and accessible introduction to the thought of this early church father.

Anthony Meredith S. J. is Lecturer in Early Christian Doctrine at Heythrop College, University of London and is a curate at Farm Street Church in the West End of London. He is the author of *The Cappadocians* (1995).

THE EARLY CHURCH FATHERS
Edited by Carol Harrison
University of Durham

The Greek and Latin fathers of the Church are central to the creation of Christian doctrine, yet often unapproachable because of the sheer volume of their writings and the relative paucity of accessible translations. This series makes available translations of key selected texts by the major fathers to all students of the early church.

Already published:

MAXIMUS THE CONFESSOR
Andrew Louth

IRENAEUS OF LYONS
Robert M. Grant

AMBROSE
Boniface Ramsey O.P.

ORIGEN
Joseph W. Trigg

GREGORY OF NYSSA

Anthony Meredith S. J.

London and New York

First published 1999
by Routledge
2 Park Square, Milton Park, Abingdon, Oxon, OX14 4RN

Simultaneously published in the USA and Canada
by Routledge
270 Madison Ave, New York NY 10016

Transferred to Digital Printing 2005

© 1999 Anthony Meredith S. J.

The right of Anthony Meredith to be identified as the Author of this
Work has been asserted by him in accordance with the Copyright,
Designs and Patents Act 1988

Typeset in Garamond by RefineCatch Limited, Bungay, Suffolk

British Library Cataloguing in Publication Data
A catalogue record for this book is available from the British Library

Library of Congress Cataloguing in Publication Data
A catalogue record for this book has been requested

ISBN 0–415–11839–5 (hbk)
ISBN 0–415–11840–9 (pbk)

TO MY SISTER

CONTENTS

CONTENTS

ABBREVIATIONS

CWS	Classics of Western Spirituality
ET	English Translation
GNO	Werner Jaeger, *Gregorii Nysseni Opera*
JTS	*Journal of Theological Studies*
PG	J.-P. Migne, *Migne's Patrologia Graeca*
PGL	Patristic Greek Lexicon (edited by G. W. H. Lampe, Oxford, 1961)
PL	J.-P. Migne (ed), *Patrologia Latina*
SC	*Sources Chrétiennes*
SP	*Studia Patristica*
TRE	*Theologische Realenzyklopädie*

1

INTRODUCTION

LANDSCAPE

Gregory of Nyssa was born in about 335 AD in the Roman province of Cappadocia, a somewhat barren region to the north east of modern Turkey. It had been annexed by the emperor Tiberius (14–37 AD) in AD 17 on the deposition of the last native king, Archelaus, in that year. Initially governed by a prefect, like Judaea in the time of Christ, it rose in status in AD 72 and enjoyed the advantages of being a consular province, and so it remained until its division by the emperor Valens in 371/2 – an event fraught with considerable consequences both for Gregory himself and for his friend and namesake, Gregory of Nazianzus.

As to Cappadocia's religious history prior to the advent of the Christian gospel, we are remarkably ill-informed. A reference in Gregory of Nazianzus' oration 18:5 on the death of his father rather suggests that there existed in Cappadocia a sect named Hypsistarians, to which his father belonged[1]. It appears to derive from the appellation of God as *Highest* and may well represent an attempt to offer an understanding of God which would please Jews and Pagans alike – a sort of fashionable syncretism which could be applied to Adonai and Zeus indifferently. If this is the case, it suggests that there existed forces in Cappadocia, well before the arrival of Christianity, which favoured a generous attitude to the surrounding culture.

The Cappadocians mentioned in the second chapter of Acts were the first Christians there, and we must assume from the opening verse of 1 Peter that the faith continued there perhaps a hundred years later. Further, in his *Ecclesiastical History* 6.11, Eusebius mentions a certain Alexander who previously had been bishop in the land of the Cappadocians and subsequently became bishop of

1

Jerusalem, in which place he ordained Origen. Clearly there was some form of organized Church in Cappadocia well before the middle of the third century, before the arrival from Caesarea sometime in the 250s of the 'Apostle of Cappadocia', Gregory the Wonderworker.

Even the graphic and laudatory account of his pioneering exploits left to us by Gregory of Nyssa,[2] should not be allowed to obscure the importance of the conversion of Cappadocia prior to the arrival of Gregory Thaumaturgos. Even so, what he actually discovered when he arrived in Cappadocia is hard for us at this distance of time to reconstruct, above all because of the paucity of our evidence. Yet Gregory Thaumaturgos is interesting and important for two reasons: (1) He brought with him the teachings and theology of his master, Origen, who died not long after 254 in the aftermath of the Decian persecution (250–251). Origen's influence, everywhere present in the writings of Gregory of Nyssa, is doubtless due in no small measure to Gregory Thaumaturgos;[3] (2) Gregory (the Wonderworker) was responsible for the conversion to the faith of Macrina the Elder, the paternal grandmother of Gregory of Nyssa. In the course of his letters, Basil often refers with great respect to this same Macrina the Elder.[4]

Gregory of Nyssa himself came from a large family[5] of ten children, five boys and five girls. Of his five sisters we know the name of only one for certain, Macrina the Younger. (The Theosebeia, mentioned by Gregory of Nazianzus in his *Letter* 197.6 as being a σύζυγος was in all probability Gregory of Nyssa's wife, not his sister.) Her influence upon her brother was considerable. He wrote her *Life* and used her deathbed as the setting for his dialogue *On the Soul and Resurrection*, his own version of Plato's *Phaedo*. Socrates becomes Macrina, talking to her brother about the nature of the soul and of its destiny after death, and about the relationship between the Platonic belief in the natural immateriality of the soul with the Christian belief in the resurrection of the body.

We know the names of all but one of the boys of the family – Basil, Peter (later bishop of Sebaste in Armenia), Naucratias (killed by a boar), Gregory himself and the missing fifth brother. The family was distinguished and propertied, Christian and cultivated.[6] Basil certainly enjoyed the benefit of an extensive university education under the most celebrated 'rhetors' or professional teachers of the day – Libanius, in Constantinople[7] and Himerius at Athens, where he spent the years from 351–356 in the company of his soul friend, Gregory of Nazianzus.

2

On the face of it Gregory's own education was far less cosmopolitan. Apparently he attended none of the great universities of the day, and was entirely dependent upon Basil for his cultural and philosophical training. In a letter to the sophist, Libanius (number 13), Gregory mentions Basil as the pupil of Libanius and as his own 'father and master'. This being the case it must be admitted that Basil did a very competent job in training his younger brother. Gregory may have lacked some of his great brother's flair as a leader, and his political sense in the difficult years prior to the second ecumenical council of Constantinople, but he is in no way inferior to him either in his use of sophisticated language or in his powers of speculative thought and spiritual insight. What is surprising is the fact that, although he lacked the training and expertise of Basil, he moved so much more sympathetically in the thought world of his day.

On several occasions in his treatises Basil expresses his unease with the pointlessness of much contemporary education – an attitude we never find in his younger brother, except when he wishes to attribute heretical opinions to the influence of Aristotle.[8] We must assume not only that he had a subtler mind, but that he had at his disposal sources of information, in the shape of a library, which enabled him to supplement his own less elaborate education, although any attempt to reconstruct its possible contents is doomed to failure from lack of evidence. Indeed, one of the peculiarities of Gregory from our point of view is the almost total absence in him of reference to, or direct citation from, his non-Christian sources – a marked contrast with Augustine in the West, who seems at times to be eager to display his pagan culture, above all in the *City of God*.

In another significant respect Gregory differed from his brother. Basil was not only a monk himself, he also finds a place as one of the greatest of all monastic legislators, whose influence stretches well beyond Cappadocia. He left behind him two sets of *Rules*, *Longer* and *Shorter*, together with a collection of aphorisms, known as the *Moralia*. As far as our sources go, we can be fairly certain that despite his evident sympathy for and understanding of the monastic and ascetic life, Gregory of Nyssa was never a monk himself. At some point he married,[9] a move he seems to have regretted, and was therefore barred from a monastic vocation. His wife's name was probably Theosebeia. It also appears from a letter written to him by his friend, Gregory of Nazianzus, that at some period between 362 and 371, he became a teacher of public speaking (rhetor) and, further, was much in love with his chosen profession: 'You had rather be thought of as a rhetor than as a Christian' (*Letter* 11) wrote Gregory Nazianzus. It is slightly ironical to find the most rhetorically self-conscious of all the Cappadocians criticizing his friend and namesake for just this particular weakness, especially when his own letter contains two quotations from Hesiod and from Euripides, writers never cited by Gregory of Nyssa himself.

Be that as it may, other forces were at work, which brought this elegant and retired life to an end. In 372 the emperor Valens, no friend of Basil, divided the province of Cappadocia in half, giving it two capitals, at Caesarea (modern Kayseri) and Tyana. This meant in practice that Basil's sphere of influence was greatly reduced and, in order to compensate for this reduction in authority, he created at least two new dioceses at Sasima and Nyssa, to which he appointed his friend and his brother respectively. It can hardly be said that either appointment was 'happy'.

Gregory of Nazianzus spent practically no time in his see, which was exceedingly minute, though his possession of it was used against him at the council of Constantinople in 381. In 380 the strongly pro-Nicene Spaniard, Theodosius, became emperor in place of the Arian Valens, and shortly afterwards had Gregory made archbishop of Constantinople, in place of the Arian Demophilus, a position he was not long allowed to enjoy. Gregory had contravened, it was maliciously alleged, canon 15 of Nicaea, which had forbidden translation from one bishopric to another, and he was forced to resign. Even then he did not return to Sasima, a place he evidently regarded with great disgust, as he himself tells us in his *Poem about His Life* (at PG 37.1059, lines 439–445). Instead, he spent the remaining years of his life administering the see of Nazianzus, orphaned by the death of his father in 374. Gregory of Nyssa was hardly more successful as a bishop. Basil has little but pity and contempt for his younger brother's inadequacies in his new post.[10]

Fortunately his brother's strictures could not reach beyond the grave and Basil's death in January of 379 may not have been wholly unwelcome to Gregory. We know nothing of his activities at the council of the 150 Fathers held at Constantinople in 381; but evidently his abilities and orthodoxy made a deep impression on both the emperor and on the other Fathers. Three facts reinforce this impression. He was chosen to deliver the funeral oration on Meletius, bishop of Antioch, the first president of the council, who had died in the course of the first session. Then, after the close of the council, he was selected to be one of the promoters of the orthodox teaching, above all on the deity of the Holy Ghost, in the Roman province of Pontus.[11] Finally, at a slightly later date, he was selected to deliver funeral orations on the emperor's little daughter, Pulcheria, and his wife F(P) Flaccilla.[12] These three assignments indicate the high regard in which Gregory's rhetorical abilities were held in both religious and secular circles.

The period up to 386, following Basil's death, was filled with intense, literary activity. It is to these seven years that we must date his elaborate reply to the extreme Arian, Eunomius. Further, he produced a continuation (and partial correction) of his brother's commentary *Homilies on the Six Days of Creation* (*In Hexameron*) with his own work of the same name and his *On the Making of Man*, each with their characteristic Gregorian search for order and connexion (εἱρμός and ἀκολουθία) in the divine activity. Finally, we have also his deathbed dialogue with Macrina, called *On the Soul and Resurrection*, which is surely intended to remind us of the death of Socrates, movingly recorded in Plato's dialogue, the *Phaedo*.

All these great works illustrate two sides of Gregory's character. He was clearly a man deeply devoted to his family, above all to his brother and sister. Yet this very devotion was certainly not uncritical, and this critical spirit found particular expression in his subtle corrections and modifications of his brother's writings. For although Basil knew much about contemporary science and philosophy – a fact which is evident by a cursory reading of his nine *Homilies on the Six Days of Creation* – he adopts a distinctly guarded, if not actually hostile, stance towards it. For him it is 'the vain learning of this world'. Gregory, on the other hand, despite his more limited and apparently inferior learning and formal education, is more sympathetic than is his brother to 'culture' and, above all, to philosophy.

Two illustrations will help to underline this point. At an earlier stage in his life, while Basil was still alive, Gregory undertook the important task of giving a theoretical justification of the monastic life, for which his brother had composed his two sets of *Rules*. This Gregory did in his earliest known writing *On Virginity*, in the course of which he offered an account of the principles on which the consecrated life rests. Part of the strength and complexity of this fascinating work results from the fact that it is never quite clear for whom precisely it was meant. Nor is it clear whether by virginity, Gregory means the physical condition of being a virgin, or the state of interior disposition of purity of heart and self mastery as Gregory, on occasion, suggests, for example in chapters 7 and 15. In the

5

former case it is restricted to the religious, in the latter it is potentially open to everyone. Even so, as an exploration of the principles upon which the practice must rest, it is a very valuable exercise.

Second, in their respective accounts of the exegesis of Genesis 1, Basil is remarkable for his knowledge of the various abstruse physical theories that the astronomers and cosmologies of the day offered to account for the beginning and structure of the physical universe. Gregory is clearly far more interested in trying to discover within the scriptural narrative the inner connection of events, the 'akolouthia'.[13] For Gregory, Moses' account of the order of creation is itself dominated by a belief in the progressive development of the universe; and the work of the exegete is to discover this order – 'taxis'.

Gregory's belief in the ordered nature of reality implies an unwillingness to believe in sudden eruptions of the divine into the world, and a lack of stress on the miraculous, supernatural element in religion. Both nature, and the growth of the individual towards perfection and towards God, are conceived in an ordered and orderly fashion. But it also reflects something of the Stoic belief in the same principle and in the omnipresence of a detectable order in the world system. Something of Gregory's insistence on the omnipresence of God in the world and his interpretation of psalm 138/9 illustrates his debt to a form of Stoicising Platonism, which believed in the existence of a universal, spiritual principle, the soul of the world.

BACKGROUND 1

Gregory's interest in, and influence by, the classical world of late antiquity was by no means restricted to rhetoric and fine writing, to which reference has already been made. In his work *On the Christian Discipline*[14] he observes that he had been criticized by some people for having abandoned 'the grace that comes from above' in favour of secular learning and logic. Despite his rejection of this accusation, it is clear that he was deeply influenced by this culture, although the actual extent of this is hard to assess.

On the one hand, it is indeed true that *verbatim* quotations from classical writers are few in number. One unacknowledged passage from Plutarch occurs in a very unexpected place, although it may have been lifted from Eusebius' gigantic compilation *Preparation for the Gospel*.[15] On the other hand, the absence of actual quotations from, or references to, classical philosophers does not itself necessarily indicate any lack of influence. Both in the formal character of his writings and in the assumed, if unexpressed, premises on which they rest, the influence of Greek philosophy, above all that of Plato, is everywhere evident.[16] It would be a mistake, however, to regard him as a mere uncritical copier of the past, a sort of philosophical magpie.

His knowledge, however, was not accompanied by a conscious effort to create a system of his own. Some of his writings appear to lack the sort of self consistency we normally demand of a professional philosopher (even if we do not always find it). His usage of the 'philosophical' language of οὐσία, being, is slippery and, further, it needs to be remembered in this connexion that much of his writing was provoked by dogmatic threats, as he saw them, and not simply by a purely theological desire to explore the basis of the creed. Three of Gregory's basic theological and philosophical principles have a home in Plato: (1) Gregory believes, as does Plato, in the goodness of being and, more precisely, in the goodness of God. The coincidence of goodness and reality, of being and value, means that Plato and the members of his 'school' regard evil as in some sense 'unreal'; there is no 'idea of evil' to correspond with the 'idea of the good'. Evil in the Platonist framework, therefore, hardly exists at all and its shadowy existence is attributed to human freedom.[17] In the tenth book of his *Republic* he sums up his position as follows: 'The cause (sc. of evil) is the chooser; God is guiltless'. The desire to exonerate God from all responsibility for evil is a marked character of the whole Christian–Platonist tradition. For Origen, Gregory and Augustine God is good, just, wise and powerful, and evil is the effect of created human choices. For Plato and his later interpreter, Plotinus, evil exists somewhere between reality and unreality. This is clearly stated by Plotinus at *Ennead* 1.8.3[18] and any appearance of power and reality it may possess will disappear at the end when 'God will be all in all' [cf. I Cor. 15, 28]. (2) Side by side with this 'metaphysical optimism' both Plato, his great third-century AD interpreter, Plotinus, and Gregory also believed in the beauty of being and of God. This is very clearly brought out in his dialogue *On the Soul and Resurrection*, and by Plato in his two dialogues *The Banquet* and *The Phaedrus*, in both of which, unlike the *Republic*, beauty rather than goodness is treated as the dominant feature of the divine nature/ultimate reality. In all three writers this conception of the Ultimate imposes both a drive and an obligation on all derivative beings. The beauty of the Absolute in Plato is also the ultimate object of desire and can be attained by a life of self control and ascesis. In other words, the ascent of the hill of the Lord is not automatic, and needs to be harnessed – a point which some lazy admirers of Plato fail to notice. Like can only be known by like and it is only by our assimilation to the supremely lovely that we shall be able to attain unto 'the vision that maketh happy' (cf. Plotinus, *Ennead* 1.6.7.3). In a very similar vein Gregory writes as follows:

> For Beauty has in its own nature an attractiveness for everyone who looks at it. So, if the soul becomes clean of all evil, it will exist entirely in beauty. The divine is beautiful by its own nature. The soul will be joined to the divine through purity, adhering to that which is proper to it.[19]

For both writers the desire for the lovely which we all possess is not realized automatically, but depends upon our freedom for its actualization. (3) As a corollary to this ethico/mystical programme we also find in writers of the Platonic school a basic belief that the way upward is both demanding and, at the same time, a return to origins. At the end of the *Republic* Plato speaks of 'always keeping to the upward path' (621C). St Paul, too, at Philippians 3, 14, has this to say: 'I press onward to the goal for the prize of the upward call of God in Christ Jesus.' Gregory's own vision is a fusion of the two. His language, above all in his two great treatises on the spiritual life, the *On the Life of Moses* and *Commentary on the Song of Songs*, is peppered with a similar imagery of ascent 'anabasis'. But, whereas for St Paul this desired goal is new and can only be realized in Christ and with the help of grace, for Plato it is a return to a blessed beginning and there is no mention of the need for divine aid or even of a divinely inspired pattern. Gregory, while admitting the importance of Christ, says little of the importance of imitating him and prefers the more classical formula of 'imitating God', which owes much to a passage in Plato's *Theaetetus* 176, where that ideal is succinctly expressed. The Pauline stress on the centrality of grace and human fragility is less marked in Gregory.

The willingness and ability on the part of many Christian writers to 'colonize' Plato and the whole classical tradition, enabled the Church to speak with a more educated and certain voice to the increasingly large number of Christians whose background was gentile rather than Jewish. The appeal to pagans by use of their own authors and ideas had already found a place in the apologetics of St

Paul, in Acts 17, which provided both justification and a model for the Apologists of the second century, above all Justin Martyr in his two *Apologies*.

Towards the end of the second century, Clement of Alexandria and, in the third century, Origen (185–254), realised only too well the threat posed by the pseudo philosophy of Gnosticism. The former was thoroughly conversant with the literature of Greece, while Origen was more a philosopher and had studied under Ammonius Saccas, a noted Platonist in Alexandria (cf. Eusebius, *Ecclesiastical History* vi.19, 7–8).

This endeavour to use philosophy as an ally for exploring the message of the gospel was not everywhere regarded as desirable. Some Christians, who were really illiterate or who, like Tertullian, took up their cause, protested against this alliance. He and they saw in this cultural openness and friendship for philosophy a betrayal of the primal spirit of the New Testament, with its appeal to the uneducated and poor of this world. St Paul himself, despite his wider culture, had protested against any attempt to turn the gospel of Christ into any form of philosophy, and his words in I Corinthians 1, concerning the foolishness of God and the wisdom of this world, became a sort of text for the gospel of irrationalism preached by Tertullian. 'What', he asks in his *Apology* (chapter 46) 'have the philosopher and Christian in common, the disciple of Greece and the disciple of heaven?'.

But if the 'simple' Christian was opposed to marriage between faith and philosophy, marriage did not recommend itself either, to the 'cultured despisers of the Gospel' who resented the attempt made by the enemy to pillage the rich fields of pagan poetry, rhetoric and philosophy in the interests of a barbarian faith – a curious, but not altogether unknown, alliance between the cultured non-believer and the uncultivated believer.

This real, and at times highly articulate hostility, on the part of the pagan intelligentsia towards the 'vampire' activities of men such as Origen, had found early expression in the second century from Celsus in his *True Account* and, in the late third and early fourth century, from the arch critic, Porphyry, in his vast fifteen volume work *Against the Christians*, produced to give intellectual backing to the pagan reaction under Diocletian in the beginning of the fourth century. Hostility came to a head during the short reign of the last overtly pagan emperor, Julian, 'The Apostate' (361–363) – ironically the only fourth-century emperor to have been baptized in his youth.

His insistence that only professing pagans should be allowed to teach the classics of Greece was in conformity with earlier pagan objections to the cultural imperialism of Christians. The difference lay in the fact that Julian was able to impose his will and that his was the first attempt made to impose a religious test upon professors. Julian's attempt is also of interest because it offers to create out of Hellenism a religion and not simply a culture.

This move on the part of Julian had the effect of making thinking Christians seriously question the role the classics should take within a Christian context. Gregory's brother, Basil, moved to the defence of his position by compiling a collection of passages with Gregory of Nazianzus between 356/8, known as the *Philocalia*, drawn from Origen's works. This work was intended to display to the intelligent Christian, and perhaps also to the pagan, that even within the Church there had existed thoughtful writers and, further, that the profession of 'Christian' did not automatically involve a policy of intellectual isolation. The extracts were largely drawn from Origen's treatise *On First Principles* and offered to show the intelligent Christian approach to freedom and the interpretation of the Bible.

Basil also, perhaps for the benefit of his nephews, wrote a further work, *To Young Men on the Value of Classical Literature*.[20] He tries to vindicate the use of Homer by the young, on the ground that it has excellent moral lessons. Like Plato and Plutarch, the reading of Homer and the other poets was defended on moral, not aesthetic, grounds. The ultimate criterion, as Basil often indicates, is 'usefulness', by which is meant helping towards the realisation of good, moral attitudes in the reader. But it cannot in honesty be said that his attitude towards pagan learning and culture is particularly enthusiastic.

This defensive and rather cautious attitude to the riches of antiquity is, at the same time, both instructive and ironic. Instructive because it is a mixture both of awareness of the dangers inherent in an uncritical absorption of the spirit of Hellenism, with at the same time an evident affection for Hellenism. Ironic, for it means that despite Julian, and despite the coolness of men such as Chrysostom and Epiphanius, the culture and philosophy of the ancient world, with the demise of purely pagan faculties of philosophy in Athens and Alexandria in the fifth and sixth centuries, found its most enduring home within the austere if discriminating embrace of the Church.

Something of this reserve and the consequent need to 'rework' the inheritance is everywhere evident. A passage in part two of Gregory of Nyssa's *On the Life of Moses* lists several areas of agreement and disagreement between Christianity and Hellenism on the nature of God and of the nature and destiny of the human spirit. So in section 40 Gregory writes:

> Pagan philosophy says that the soul is immortal; this is a pious offspring. But it also says that souls pass from bodies to bodies and are changed from a rational to an irrational nature. This is a fleshly and alien foreskin. And there are many such examples. It says there is a god, but thinks of him as material. It acknowledges him as creator, but says he needed matter for creation.

A glance at a pagan 'catechism' written by Sallustius as a propaganda weapon for the emperor Julian in 362, illustrates well the sort of distinctions that Gregory makes between his cosmology and that of his cultivated non-Christian contemporaries. In *On Gods and the World* Sallustius insists, in the manner of Plato's *Timaeus*, upon the eternity of matter and of the physical universe (cf. section vii) and in section xx on the doctrine of transmigration of souls, of metempsychosis. The comparison between the two systems highlights the basic difference between them. For Gregory, God is above all and pre-eminently creator, in total control of the world both spiritual and material. For Sallustius, and indeed for the whole Platonist tradition, God is not creator. Souls are eternal and so is matter.

In answer to the question often asked, 'How Platonic was Gregory?', the answer must be always, 'It all depends on what is meant by Platonism'. The Christian doctrine of creation is indeed quite unplatonic, in all its forms. Yet the belief in the spirituality of the soul and the existence of a supreme, changeless spirit is one that Gregory shares with his Platonic inheritance.

BACKGROUND 2

Although Gregory of Nyssa, his brother, Basil, and their friend, Gregory of Nazianzus, the so-called Cappadocian Fathers, all came from a cultivated, wealthy and orthodox milieu, it is a mistake to suppose that they were typical of their fellow countrymen. Cappadocia not only had a reputation for being rather boorish – the Pseudo Lucian had once rather cruelly observed in his epigram 43 that it was as difficult to teach a tortoise to fly as to teach a Cappadocian to speak Greek.

Cappadocia had also produced several distinguished heretics. Among these were Ulphilas (c. 311–383), the apostle of the Goths and a convinced Arian. He was of Cappadocian ancestry, and had been ordained bishop in Constantinople by the Arian, Eusebius of Nicomedia, before setting out in c. 341/2 for missionary work among the Goths. But, of more immediate relevance for our present purposes, Eunomius, the extreme Arian and disciple of Aetius, also came from Cappadocia. Between them they had endeavoured to produce a version of Christianity which, under the guise of an extremely logical form, ended by reducing the Son to the status of a creature. It is true, of course, that they endeavoured to conceal their position by nearly qualifying it out of existence, but any reader of chapter 28 of Eunomius' *Apology* will see that some form of creatureliness is ascribed to the generate Son.

Both Aetius and Eunomius were men of great logical powers, skilled debaters who inspired such a mixture of reverence and terror in the eyes of their opponents that the empress Placilla herself was unwilling to expose her husband, Theodosius, to the subtle arguments of Eunomius. Both these writers assumed that the nature of God was capable of exact definition, in words that could be understood by all. They believed therefore in the availability of God and in his expressibility. They also offered a definition of God which, if accepted, would necessarily exclude the Son from the Deity. For them God was unbegotten or ingenerate. He was the absolute beginning of everything, including the Son. By excluding from the idea of God the notion of fatherhood, the Anomoeans (so-called from their insistence that the Son was unlike (= ἀνόμοιος in Greek) the supreme God) were easily able to exclude the Son from equality with the Father. What precisely lay at the root of their position is not quite clear.[21] Claiming to have an insight into the divine nature and of being able to define that insight exactly as absolute primary, underived being, had two distinct effects. To begin with, it did appear to bring their teaching into line with certain Old Testament passages, notably Exodus 3.14. But it also automatically excluded the Son from equality with God. Such a position could in no way be reconciled to the affirmation of Nicaea that the Son was 'very God from very God, begotten not made, and of one substance with the Father.'

The Cappadocian reply to this challenge, above all that which we find in Basil and Gregory of Nyssa, was disarmingly simple and in many ways effective. It amounted, in effect, to a strong assertion of the divine incomprehensibility and therefore of the impossibility of finding an adequate definition of his inner nature. In making such a claim the Cappadocians were not exactly breaking new ground. Plato, sometimes thought of as a prophet of rationalism, had also a mystic strain in his writings. In a passage from his dialogue, *Timaeus*,[22] which later became highly popular, he insisted that 'it was hard to know and difficult to declare to all the nature of god.' And, in an equally famous passage from book vi of the *Republic*, he insisted that the idea of the Good was beyond mind and being.

This tendency towards what came to be called apophaticism, received great impulse from the writings of the first century AD Jew, Philo, whose elaborate, allegorical commentary on Genesis insisted that God was incomprehensible.[23] Clement of Alexandria (c. 150–215 AD) continued this apophatic tradition, affirming the inadequacy of the human mind in the face of God. But until the time of which we speak, 'incomprehensibility' as a technical term had not entered significantly into theological debates. Ironically, it seems to have been a favoured term of the heretic, Arius. It occurs at the opening of his dogmatic poem, the *Thalia*. It was later dropped by his followers as being open to the objection that the affirmation of the divine incomprehensibility did not itself exclude the Son from the deity. If God is totally unknowable, then anything or nothing might be predicated of him.

Gregory of Nyssa, however, does not simply appeal to a long tradition in his rejection of the arguments of Aetius and Eunomius. He was too much of a rationalist for that type of traditionalism. He does offer an argument for the divine incomprehensibility, which depends on belief in the divine infinity. It is important to distinguish between these two notions. The former, weaker, claim that God cannot be known refers, above all, to the weakness of the human mind, faced with the divine majesty. The latter, stronger, claim insists rather on the intrinsic divine mysteriousness which, because it is the source of all and can be limited by none, is limitless. In making this assertion about the infinity of perfect being, Gregory is departing from the received wisdom both of Origen and Plato. Both these writers, while affirming the difficulty of knowing God, continued to regard absence of limit and form as a defect. For Plato, indeed, the absence of form or shape was something indicative of failure and evil, and matter which awaited the imposition of form from the divine architect.

Although it is true that Plotinus (205–270 AD) had, in all

13

probability, thought of the One as infinite,[24] he is in this, as in many other ways, scarcely typical of later Platonists and was regarded by some of them as a heretic. Moreover, it occurs in him from his own experience of ecstasy, in which the distinction between subject and object disappear. Gregory of Nyssa's assertion of the divine infinity, however, is more a result of controversy and perhaps of tradition, although in many ways, once accepted, it did in fact play a great role in his own account of the spiritual life. Important though this move was on his part in dispelling the exaggerated scholasticism of the Anomoeans, it was itself open to grave difficulties which his enemies were not slow to exploit, above all, to the charge of agnosticism, to which I now turn. It was only natural that critics of the Cappadocian response should seize upon agnosticism as the danger to which the stress on the divine infinity and incomprehensibility exposed Christian believers.

Both Basil in his *Letter* 234, and Gregory of Nyssa in *Contra Eunomium* 3.1.109, inform us that Eunomius quoted John 4.22 'You worship what you do not know', against their claim that God could not be known. To this charge Basil replies by elaborating a distinction which was to have a distinguished future. He argues that although the inner nature, or *ousia*, of God is inaccessible to us, we can know a good deal about his activities – '*energeiai*' is the name the Cappadocians gave to them – in so far as they affect us. Gregory offers a similar distinction in his attempt to wrestle with the seemingly intractable problem posed by Matthew 5.8: 'Blessed are the pure in heart, for they shall see God'. This he does in his Homily 6 *On the Beatitudes*.

A further mechanism developed by the Cappadocians for dealing with the Eunomian challenge was to claim that the ideas of 'Ingeneracy' and 'Sonship' did not apply to the divine nature as such, but only to the first and second persons of the Trinity respectively. The mysterious, incomprehensible, infinite and eternal nature of God was possessed equally by all three persons. In other words, in some sense the Father, Son and Spirit shared or participated in the nature of God. But did this move not lead to the unhappy conclusion that the divine nature was an abstract category in which all three persons had a part, and that therefore there were three Gods? In other words the question comes to be raised, 'How did the Cappadocians understand the "homoousios" of the creed of Nicaea?' Was 'God' for them the name of a person and therefore singular, or was 'god' the name of a class, to which three members belonged? In the first case, there was a danger of reducing the persons of the Trinity to predicates of one person, a heresy connected with the name of a second century Libyan writer, Sabellius; in the latter, the opposite danger of tritheism reared up before them.

Gregory of Nyssa was sharply aware of the second possibility, perhaps as an inference from some of his own writings. After all, had he not argued in *Contra Eunomium* i.227 that the three persons of the Trinity shared in the same λόγος τῆς οὐσίας even as did Peter, James and John in human nature? He was constrained to compose a treatise in order to refute the charge, entitled *To Ablabius, On Not Three Gods*. In this work Gregory argues that the word 'God' does not refer to the divine nature but only to its activities. These activities were seen as connected with differing etymologies given to the word '*theos*' in the ancient world: seeing, from the Greek word for 'see', 'theorein'; running from the Greek word for 'running', 'theein'; and ordering from the word for 'setting in place', 'tithenai'. They could not refer to the inner sanctuary of the divine existence, but served only to underline his mode of action. Gregory's other reply fails to supply a completely satisfactory answer to the problem of what status we should give to the word 'God'. But, on balance, it does seem to imply that Gregory was a pluralist in his account of the divine nature, that is, he seems to have given a generic sense to the word and idea underlying it. His attempts to evade the consequences of his own logic and of the examples he offers hardly satisfy, any more than does his idea of 'concrete universal', which he uses to suggest the more realist nature of the divine.

THE SYSTEM OF GREGORY

Some recent attempts have been made to impose a more uniform structure on Gregory's theology. This is a perilous proceeding for several reasons. Most of his writings are 'occasional', that is, written in response to particular challenges he and the Church felt themselves called on to face. This means in practice that we sometimes find him using quite inconsistent models in his desire to dispose of objections to his own particular understanding of the gospel.

A most instructive example of this facet of his approach occurs in his effort to dispose of the objections made to his and Basil's defence of the deity of the Son. As we shall see later, they can both be seen to be assimilating the idea of god to a general concept, to what Aristotle in his *Categories* vii calls 'second substance'. This means that Father, Son and Holy Ghost belong to the class 'God' in much the same way as Peter, Paul and John belong to the class 'Man'. The obvious drawback to this move was that it seemed to lead to tritheism. It is not altogether clear if Basil appreciated this difficulty. Gregory of Nyssa certainly did. He defended his position by composing a short and dense treatise called *To Ablabius, On Not Three Gods*. It is not wholly successful, partly because Gregory endeavours to operate with an idea of substance which belongs neither to Plato nor to Aristotle. Even so, despite its evident shortcomings, it is a bold attempt and he did face the question seriously.

It is also true to say that he was not a professional philosopher, in the sense in which such a term might be applied to either Plotinus (205–270) or to Proclus (412/3–485). But even they, for all their philosophical outlook, regarded themselves as primarily purveyors of Platonism. Even so, to call Gregory simply a 'sophist', that is, merely a fine writer with little or no interest in anything but expression, hardly does him full justice. Though not a technical philosopher, like Plotinus or Proclus, he was far more interested and considerable as a philosopher either than his brother, Basil, or than Athanasius (297(?)–373).

Two further considerations need to be weighed: (1) There is much in him that owes much to what is called *Toposforschung* and *Geistesgeschichte*, that is, to the particular genre in which he wrote and to the history of ideas. But his writing is more than a collection of ill-assorted plumes borrowed from foreign birds and not reworked into a coherence. There is a powerful mind behind all this which refuses to be dissolved into 'a picker up of learning's crumbs'. (2) He was also a man who, judging by his writings, modified his views with the progress of time. This last fact alone makes it difficult to extract the essence of his thought by a random selection of texts from his writings. Even so, the challenge presented by an effort to systematize Gregory's ideas is one faced by any serious attempt to come to grips with any ancient (or modern) author. If the so called 'diachronic' approach was the only one available, that is, an approach which is strictly chronological in its handling of the data, then it would be very hard, some would say impossible, to talk about, for example, 'The philosophy of Plato' or about 'The system of St Augustine'. The earlier so-called 'Socratic' dialogues of Plato, the *Laches* and the *Euthyphro* are, both in form and content, strikingly different from the *Laws*. Does this mean that it is impossible to create a systematic account of the teachings of Plato? Some, of course, would say quite firmly, 'Yes'. But not all. A discernible continuity remains.

St Augustine presents a similar challenge for the would-be systematizer, although for Augustine the situation is both harder and easier. It is harder because the amount of material to be digested is colossal; easier because we can trace his mental development with much greater sureness than we can that of most ancient thinkers, simply because we know in what order and when he wrote his various works because he tells us himself in his *Retractations* of c. 427 AD.

For the purposes of the ensuing sketch I assume that it is licit to view Gregory's writings and thought globally, without denying that with the progress of time the expression of his views, if not his actual views, *was* modified, partly under the pressure of outside challenges, partly through the different audiences he had in mind. It is also worth remarking that most of his writing, with the exception of *On Virginity*, belongs to the last fifteen years of his life. Great writers leave their 'footprints' in their works which are recognizable whatever the particular challenges they are facing.

Gregory's idea of God, with which we begin, represents in an original way the conflation of three quite distinct elements: the biblical, the philosophic and the doctrinal. He shares with the Bible certain primary ideas, some of which, although not all, find a parallel in the philosophical tradition in which he also stands. God for him is utterly real, 'really real', an idea which finds its most definite expression in the revelation made to Moses at the burning bush, 'I am who I am' [Exodus 3.14]. God is also morally perfect. 'One alone is good, your father in heaven' [Mark 10, 18].

However, the location of the Absolute in the realms 'beyond being' in *Republic* 509 and of the supreme position of 'that which is' in *Timaeus* 28, are not too far from the biblical expressions. Although it remains true that, for Plato, the Good is usually expressed in the neuter and therefore as apersonal, later Platonists, such as Alcinous, spoke of god as supreme and perfect. Again, Plato's whole concern to elevate the good as the supreme value, and his insistence both in the *Republic* and the *Laws* on the moral superiority of the god/the absolute, brings him into line with the biblical revelation. In other words, as was stated above, Gregory shares the Platonic conviction of the unity of being and value.

This fusion of ideas, taken from two open systems, is further

17

highlighted by the ease and the apparent indiscriminateness with which Gregory moves from personal to impersonal language, in his references to God and the divine nature. So, one of his favourite expressions for God is 'God who is above all', probably an echo of Romans 9, 5.[25] An equally favourite expression is the neuter 'τὸ θεῖον', 'the divine', perhaps in allusion to Acts 17, 29 but, more probably, to the Greek philosophical tradition beginning with Thales in the sixth century BC.[26] A further illustration of the apparent insouciance of Gregory to this sort of distinction can be seen in his indifference to the use of the masculine or the neuter in his reference to God as 'He who is' (more biblical) and 'That which is' (more Platonist).

To this fairly traditional compromise Gregory adds three further elements which elevate his theology well beyond the Origenism it otherwise embodies: (1) For Gregory, God is creator of all. This serves to distinguish him from the perceptions of Platonism and the Bible alike. The former knew only of information or emanation; the latter of a form of information, with a possible doctrine of creation from nothing; (2) The defence of Nicene orthodoxy and the consequent controversy with Eunomius forced the Church to rethink its inherited understanding of the divine nature in two distinct, though connected, ways. In order to offset the extravagant claims of Eunomius to grasp the divine nature in its entirety by means of a definition, Gregory (and his brother Basil before him) argued that, as the divine nature was infinite, it could never be adequately controlled by the human mind.[27] His argument was that God being the creator, he must be the inexhaustible source of all being and must, therefore, be infinite in the strict sense; (3) A further reason for making this important and relatively novel and unconventional claim lay in Gregory's argument that the divine goodness, unlike all created forms of goodness, had nothing to limit it and must, as a consequence, be infinite. For him, therefore, both the fact of God's being the source of reality and the object of all our moral striving, led to the important conclusion that God was infinite (cf. *Contra Eunomium*, 1.168; 274).

Whatever may be the judgment made upon the validity of these arguments, it still remains true that his insistence not only helped to mould the whole of his own spiritual theology around the catchword 'epektasis', a noun derived in part from Philippians 3.13, but it, more importantly, marks a break with traditional classical metaphysics. This point has been usefully made in a monograph by Professor

E. Muehlenberg.[28] This means, in effect, that although Plotinus and Gregory are united in raising the divine/absolute above limit, Gregory's God remains nevertheless more personal than the One ever is.[29]

This is a very clear example of the way in which Gregory uses, but at the same distances himself from, the metaphysical structures of his own day. For Plotinus, above all in *Enneads* 2.9. and 6.7, the supreme principle of the One is resolutely exalted above the second hypostasis of Mind/Spirit/Being. It is the source of existence and consciousness yet, at the same time, is quite distinct from and exalted above both. For Gregory, on the other hand, God is both infinite and utterly transcendent while, at the same time, remaining firmly in the class of 'being' and of 'mind'. Gregory's God, therefore, is always a conscious being as well as being the source of consciousness and being to others. This crossing of the barriers between the two hypostases of Plotinus need not be intentional on the part of Gregory. However, perhaps because of his doctrine of creation, it seems to have been important to him to insist that despite the immense gulf between the infinite, incomprehensible creator and the finite world that comes from him, it is possible even so to bridge the gap that separates the two by means of the doctrine of image. Philosophical purists see this feature of Gregory's whole approach as a good example of his ignorance or, worse, of his indifference to the claims of philosophical coherence.[30] It is perhaps fairer to see in Gregory an attempt to express the important truth, much insisted on later, that God is indeed like us or, better, we are like God, being made after 'his image and likeness'. Yet, even so, there exists between God and the world a vast chasm which no reality can traverse by itself, except the Son of God for our salvation. The whole debate surrounding the council of Nicaea (325) had been fought on precisely this issue – 'Were there any intermediates between God and the world?'. To this question had come the clear answer, 'None whatever'. Yet, despite the absence of intermediaries, it was clear that we can have some knowledge of God and are called to his imitation.

If the council of Nicaea had been responsible for Gregory's argument to the divine infinity, it was also responsible, as we have seen, for his attempt to provide a way of understanding the divine nature which will allow him to say that although there are three hypostases or persons in God there is still only one God. This attempt by Gregory to show how three into one can go is a second example of the way in which Christian doctrine encouraged him to rethink his understanding of divine unity.

In the treatise *To Ablabius, On Not Three Gods,* he argues that number does not apply within the divine realm.[31] So he can write:

> Only those things are enumerated by addition, which are seen to be individually circumscribed. This circumscription is noted by bodily appearance, by size, by place and by distinction of form and colour. What is observed to transcend these things, is beyond circumscription by means of these categories. What is not circumscribed cannot be numbered; and what is not numbered cannot be observed in quantities.
>
> (*GNO* 3.1.53.6–14)

Further, all three persons share in a concrete, not simply a logical, universal and because all three persons act as one they are therefore to be thought of as one. Clearly Gregory is wrestling with an intractable problem. But at the heart of it is the important conviction that in Christianity the absolute is not simply an undifferentiated monad, but is somehow three. The doctrine of the Trinity in other words upsets the philosophical position held from the time of Parmenides in the sixth century BC that singleness and simplicity is in all circumstances prior to, and preferable to, multiplicity. The Christian God is unique, but he is not absolutely simple.

THE SPIRITUAL TEACHING OF GREGORY, BETWEEN CIRCULARITY AND FREEDOM

The greatest spiritual geniuses of the western world, prior to the arrival of the gospel, had invested much in the idea that the life of the individual human being would in the end, after its purifying pilgrimage here on earth, once again return to its heavenly homeland. For writers such as Plato in his dialogue the *Phaedrus,* and for Plotinus in *Ennead* 6.9, the beginning of the process was the same as the end. Even if this circular vision appeared to cancel out any thought of progress in any absolute sense, neither writer was doing violence to the ancient disbelief in the possibility or desirability of progress. In a passage in *Ennead* 6.9.9.21 Plotinus, echoing Plato, writes as follows: 'This state [sc. of happiness] is the first and the final, because from God it comes, its good lies There, and once turned to God again it is what it was.' It is not absolutely clear what is the place of freedom in all this. It is not clear if the designs of an overreaching providence are such as to be cancelled out by the obstinacy of human resistance or whether, in the end, our return is assured *whatever* the action of the human mind. To judge from Plotinus' treatment of providence in *Ennead* 3.2, it would appear that 'all shall be well of necessity'.

How do Christian writers react with their stress on the seriousness of the morality and on the centrality of freedom? In Origen's case the need to insist on freedom was partially occasioned by the challenge offered by the determinism of the Gnostics. We find this tension, above all between freedom and necessity, in Origen. On one hand, it would be hard to find a writer in whom the claims of freedom are asserted more eloquently and frequently than him. Some modern writers see in him the philosopher/theologian of freedom *par excellence*. It is doubtless true that much of his libertarianism is occasioned by his determined resistance to the predestinationism of the Gnostics. However, it is impossible to dismiss his statements elsewhere as merely controversial. So he writes in his treatise *On Prayer* [29.15]: 'For God does not wish that good should belong to anyone by necessity but *willingly*' (my italics). Again Origen insists that freedom is the condition of the possibility of all virtue. 'Take away freedom', he writes in *Against Celsus* 4.3, 'and you take away virtue'.[32] On the other hand, Origen also exposes his understanding of the nature of human destiny within the context of an overtly cyclical apprehension of human destiny. For Origen, following St Paul's belief expressed at I Cor. 15, 24–28, God will in the end be all in all; the final state of the human race will simply replicate its initial condition. This circular vision is neatly encapsulated in his dogmatic treatise *On First Principles* 1.6.2, where he writes, 'Semper enim similis est finis initiis', 'The end is always like the beginnings'. There is clearly an unresolved tension here. The linear gospel of progress and freedom is hard to bring into harmony with a cyclical doctrine of return.

Much of Origen's patterning and puzzlement is taken over by Gregory. Indeed, for Gregory freedom is, if anything, more strongly emphasised than in his 'master'. For Gregory the image of God in man resides principally in his free will rather than in his intellectual abilities. In his *Address on Religious Education* (sometimes called the *Catechetical Oration*) he writes as follows (chapter 5) about:

> the most excellent and precious of blessings – I mean the gift of liberty and free will. For were human life governed by

21

necessity, the image would be falsified in that respect . . . .
What, therefore, in every respect is made similar to the divine
must certainly possess free will and liberty by nature.

But as in Origen, so here also, this strong libertarianism is modified
by a cyclical approach to spiritual destiny. Again we can sense the
marked influence both of classicism and of I Corinthians 15, 24–28.
Nowhere is the notion of a necessary return to beginnings for all
more constantly insisted on than in his writings. Germanus of
Constantinople (c. 640–c. 733) and others adopted the desperate
remedy of endeavouring to remove from his text evidence of his
universalism. But without success. Indeed, in at least one passage in
the *Address* he goes as far as to speak of the ultimate salvation even
of the devil: 'He freed man from evil and healed the very author of
evil himself' (chapter 26).

To this incongruous mixture of libertarianism and 'apokatastasis'
or 'universalism' Gregory adds a third element, 'epectasis'. This
word derives, in Gregory's vision, from the words of St Paul in
Philippians 3.13, where Paul writes of himself as 'stretching out
ahead'. For him, as for the Platonic tradition, the aim of life is the
imitation of God (cf. Plato, *Theaetetus* 176). As for Plato also this
idealism was primarily conceived on moral lines. But whereas for
Plato the proposed ideal was conceived in finite, attainable terms,
for Gregory, God being infinite, there could be no point of rest or
attainment. This rather exhausting approach to the problem of
Christian perfection is outlined in the prologue of Gregory's *On the
Life of Moses*:

> Since, then, those who know what is good by nature desire
> participation in it, and since this good has no limit, the partici-
> pant's desire itself necessarily has no stopping place but
> stretches out with the limitless.
>
> (section 7)

For Gregory there are no absolute ends in the spiritual life, either
here or hereafter, only new beginnings.

Gregory's modification of his inherited Origenism can be seen at
two significant and interconnected junctures: (1) Although he clearly
accepts the traditional and classical belief in the circularity of
human progress back to beginnings, Gregory rejects the Origenistic
belief in the preexistence of the human soul. On several occasions
in his dogmatic treatises he explicitly distinguishes his view from

22

that of an (unnamed) writer who had believed in the doctrine of the fall of souls. It is of course possible that some other writer is meant. But granted Gregory's habitual reverence for Origen and the fact that the latter is commonly accredited with such views, it is surely likely that he has Origen in mind;[33] (2) In his account of human advance in the life of the spirit Origen seems on the whole to believe that there is an ever present possibility of relapse into sin. For Gregory, however, as Danielou has argued, it is possible to arrive at a condition of spirit where upward mobility is the only option open to the created spirit, angelic or human. These contrasting perspectives are well illustrated by two passages from the authors in question. In Origen's 27th *Homily on Numbers* (section 12 in *CWS*, p. 263) Origen argues for the real necessity of temptations which, he says, 'are brought to it as a kind of protection and defence.' And again, 'For temptations are so mingled with virtues that no virtue seems to be seemly or possible without them' (p. 265).

Gregory's *On the Life of Moses* presents a different picture. From section 219 onwards, mainly in the discussion of eternal progress, the thought of a relapse into sin seems to be entirely missing. Brooks Otis (1958) draws attention to the difference between the two spiritualities when he writes that Origen's thought is governed 'by the ever present possibility of temptation and sin', while Gregory's is 'concerned almost exclusively with the sinless life of the saved and the blessed'.

How, if at all, is it possible to account for this difference of emphasis, where all else underlines similarities? The most plausible explanation is that for Origen, sin has its roots in the idea of a non-infinite God. This means that we can come to an end in our knowledge of God, to a point where there is no going beyond. Once arrived there, here or hereafter, we are vulnerable to both boredom and satiety[34] simply because there is nowhere further to advance. For Origen, therefore, sin is at root an intellectual failure, or rather the weariness which arises in the mind from absence of new worlds to conquer, and the created spirit, whether angelic or human, seeks satisfaction elsewhere, outside God.

Controversy with the Anomoeans, who believed in the possibility of a comprehensive definition of the divine nature, however, together with his own experience, led Gregory of Nyssa, as we have seen, to the conclusion that God is infinite and because infinite, beyond the reach of the human mind and only to be approached through the medium of faith.[35] Sin, therefore, for Gregory was less a matter of intellectual failure as it had been for the Platonic tradition. The cause of sin in us is never stated to be boredom. Rather Gregory argues in his attempt to deal with the intractable problem of the origin of sin, in chapter 6 of his *Catechetical Oration*, that sin derives (a) from the devil's jealousy of mankind and (b) 'from the devil's deceitfully mingling evil with man's free will and thus in some measure quenching and obscuring God's blessing.'

It is through our freedom that we are brought closest to God and through our freedom that we betray him. This perhaps helps to account for the extraordinary emphasis laid on virtue by Gregory in his account of spiritual progress. Likeness to God is presented to the reader at the opening of the *On the Life of Moses* as the aim of the Christian life, and this is seen as largely a matter of the informed will, ever striving to realise within itself that greater assimilation to God who, being by nature infinite, always permits of further efforts. The difficulty in this account is to discern at what point in its pilgrimage the created will, while always remaining mutable, is capable only of upward mobility. It is apparent from the end of this work that Moses does arrive at a stage, beyond which there is no possibility of sin. On the other hand, if that is the case, how are we to account for the fall of Satan, who fell through envy, yet was created as perfect as a spiritual creature can be? Why should the created spirit not fall into a similar fault, envying those in higher mansions than the one he inhabits?

What emerges, though, above all from this comparison, is that neither Origen nor Gregory shared a view of freedom of the type envisaged by St Augustine towards the end of his life, perhaps as a result of his controversy with Pelagius. He came to the sombre conclusion, that as human nature is constituted after the fall, we hardly possess freedom at all, only the shadow of it. Augustine supposes that we never lose the power of choice (= liberum arbitrium) but only the power to choose well (= libertas). But what we want can never be good until, that is, grace releases in us the power to do good. Then we acquire the ability not to sin. Only in heaven shall we be perfectly free, that is, incapable of sinning, and that by grace.[36]

In a sense Gregory occupies a mediant position between Origen and Augustine. For Origen, even in the life after death, there is always a possibility of change and of sin; for Gregory, mutability is the permanent condition of the created spirit; for Gregory after a period, upward mobility becomes the only possibility. For

24

Augustine, the will becomes capable under grace of never sinning at all, but only after death. Change in this life of time remains an ever present possibility.

A final issue ought to be addressed. What part in Gregory's scheme is played by the person of Christ? Something of Gregory's treatment of the relation of divine and human in Christ is discussed in chapter 2, but aside from his treatment of the interrelationship of God and man it must be admitted that we miss in Gregory the warm Christocentric piety that we find in St Paul and in later medieval spirituality.

The nearest approach we find to such an attitude occurs in Gregory's treatise *On Perfection*. There, an accurate knowledge of the titles of Christ becomes less a source of deeper knowledge, than a gateway to greater assimilation to him. Gregory takes us through largely Pauline expressions, 'unapproachable light' [1 Tim. 6, 16], 'high priest' [Heb. 4, 14], 'Passover' [1 Cor. 5, 7] and the rest, and goes on to show how they can be appropriated by the serious Christian. This is surely an early form of the imitation of Christ, though almost entirely independent of the Synoptic gospels. Gregory writes that the purpose of this knowledge is to enable us to refashion our lives in virtue after the pattern of the supremely virtuous Christ. The notion of μόρφωσις, that is, 'pattern' which also figures largely in classical authors, as Werner Jaeger has pointed out, is everywhere prominent. As ever in Gregory the accent on virtue, and on knowledge as the key to virtue, is everywhere dominant, rather than as a value to be pursued for itself, as it seems to be in Plotinus.

Of the divine side of Christ there is little talk and grace is not much mentioned, except as a useful aid to the practice of virtue. Neither do we hear much about the role the sacraments play in the process of growth in the account of Christian life in his ascetical works. Virtue and the sacraments are rarely brought into any close relationship with each other. What, however, is strangest is that while on one hand the three major theophanies in the *On the Life of Moses* occur in an incarnational context – the first at the burning bush is the most obvious – (*Life* ii.19 ff.) they seem unaccompanied by any strong or particular devotion to the divine person of Christ. Not unlike St Augustine in this respect, Gregory rarely, if ever, addresses himself to Christ, although unlike Augustine he is sparing in his address to God as well, but this may result from the more impersonal tone of his writing. Augustine's address to God is a feature primarily of the *Confessions*, but it also occurs at the end his great work, *On the Trinity*.

Gregory's reticence on this subject may spring from several causes. Partly it is due to a natural reserve, notable in most of the Greek fathers, to express his own personal experiences on religious matters. But it is also worth remarking that for the vast majority of the cultivated writers of the Christian East, the stress in spirituality lay rather on the search for God than on Christ. The sacred humanity, even in authors who defended the divinity of the Saviour, was treated more as a gateway to God than as an end in himself. This approach to spirituality stands in marked contrast to the personal devotion to Jesus, evident both in the East in the Jesus Prayer and in the West in the Christocentrism of such diverse writers as St Bernard, Julian of Norwich, St Francis of Assissi and St Ignatius Loyola.

2

DOCTRINAL ISSUES

1. AGAINST EUNOMIUS 1.156–182

Introduction

Although nowadays, largely through the prolific writings of J. Daniélou[1] and H. von Balthasar,[2] we think of Gregory primarily as a spiritual theologian, it is helpful and important to remember that this has not always been the case. Much of his popularity is due to the far greater accessibility of his writings, which until 1920 were largely available only in the *Patrologia Graeca* 44–45. It was in that year that a series of editions of his writings began to appear under the editorship of Werner Jaeger, who clearly regarded Gregory as a continuator of the classical tradition, to the study of which he had devoted his whole scholarly endeavours. The actual extent of Gregory's indebtedness to that tradition has been the subject of much controversy, as has already been suggested, and it would be fair to say that Jaeger tended to over-stress it. But whatever reserve one may feel about the extent of classical influence in Gregory, the value of the great edition piloted by Jaeger (and alas, still incomplete) is not open to question. Jaeger's opening contribution to the series was his own edition of the *Against Eunomius*, to which we now turn.

Eunomius was a fellow countryman of Gregory. It is hard for us to form a just estimate of him.[3] In most of our surviving sources, which come largely from the pens of those who 'won', he is uniformly vilified. Above all, this is true in the extensive preamble to his work that occupies the first 150 sections of Jaeger's edition. It is indeed mildly surprising to find a man of Gregory's calibre devoting so much time to assassinating Eunomius' character. One can only surmise that the animus he engendered in Gregory and Basil[4] arose from reasons other than purely theological. Whatever the justice of their complaints against the *system* of Eunomius, the slurs cast by Gregory on his character belong to a quite unseemly tradition of debate. According to him, Eunomius was a man of low birth and background, desperately eager, by whatever means his remarkable intelligence offered him, to rise up the social scale (cf. CE 1.49ff). In addition to this, it appears that Eunomius had evidence which, if true, would modify, even if it did not entirely destroy, the reputation of the great Basil himself. Basil seems to have behaved in a less than honest way at the Synod of Constantinople in 361. To these charges against his brother, Gregory felt himself called on to reply and did so (CE 1.76ff).

The exact chronology of events is hard to reconstruct. I shall assume, along with T. Kopecek,[5] that Eunomius' *Liber Apologeticus* appeared either at, or shortly after, the synod held in Constantinople in, or shortly after, 360. To this work Basil himself wrote, a few years later, perhaps in 364 or 365,[6] a three part reply, his *Contra Eunomium*. To this reply of Basil, Eunomius, for reasons not clear, produced his own defence in 378 entitled *Apologia Apologiae* (cf. Kopecek, p. 341). It is to this final surviving work of Eunomius that Gregory's own mammoth three volume reply is directed. Unfortunately this work of Eunomius does not survive independently and we are forced to reconstruct it from Gregory's reply, on the assumption that whatever may be thought of his methods of controversy, his actual reporting of the text of Eunomius is accurate. Richard Vaggione's edition of *The Extant Works of Eunomius* in the *Oxford Early Christian Texts* series provides both the Greek original, translation and invaluable commentary. Gregory's reply to the *Apologia Apologiae* must be dated to some time during his stay in Constantinople in 380 and 381, during which period he read a portion of his text to Jerome, (Jerome, *de viris illustribus*, 128 = PL 23.713).

Something of Gregory's intentions and method of reply may be gathered from the letter he wrote, either in 379 or early in 380, to his brother Peter, then or later bishop of Sebaste in Armenia, a cold and hostile place from which Gregory himself had but recently returned. The letter number 29 reminds us that although Eunomius' critique of Basil and his behaviour occupied two volumes, Gregory's reply was made to only one of them at that time. This reply to Eunomius occupies all his own *Contra Eunomium* 1 and 2, while his *Contra Eunomium* 3 is conceived as a reply to part 2 of Eunomius' own work.

Because Gregory's response to the Eunomian challenge is made piecemeal, it is not always easy to extract a clear picture of Eunomius' theology. But, whatever may be true (or untrue) about Eunomius' background and upward mobility, he certainly possessed a thirst for knowledge and was gifted with remarkable powers of reason. The very fact that on several occasions Gregory pours scorn on just this quality confirms the impression of that ability, as does the nervousness apparently experienced by the empress Flaccilla who evidently feared that a meeting between the heretic and her husband, Theodosius, might do the orthodox cause no good (cf. Sozomen, *Hist. Eccl.* 7.6.3). Further evidence of Eunomian competence may be derived from the fact that Basil, Gregory of Nyssa, Gregory of Nazianzus in his five *Theological Orations* and John Chrysostom in his five addresses *De Incomprehensibilitate Dei*, delivered in Antioch in September 386, found it necessary to combat the dangerous heresy of Neo-arianism.

It is relatively easy to provide a sketch of the Eunomian system, though less easy to be exact about the possible motives which led him to create it. The Eunomian *Confession of Faith*, appended to the manuscripts of the *Apology*, seems singularly innocuous and a mere expansion of the words of St Paul at I Cor. 8.6; 'There is one God, the Father, from whom are all things, and one Lord Jesus Christ, through whom are all things.' In some ways the whole system can be made to look like a vigorous defence of the uniqueness and primacy of God the Father, although Eunomius prefers the more philosophic term ἀγέννητος, Unbegotten, with which to designate God. This particular 'definition' serves a further and, from the orthodox point of view, a more sinister purpose. For, if the nature of God be so 'defined' it necessarily follows that the Son cannot be fully divine. The diminishing of the status of the Son therefore appears as a necessary corollary of the exaltation of the first God.

In the following passage from Gregory's work (= CE 156–182) we find him offering an extended critique of the highly philosophical τεχνολογία of Eunomius.[7] Immediately before the critique Gregory provides what purports to be the actual text of the Ἀπολογία Ἀπολογίας,[8] which he then proceeds to treat bit by bit. The first portion, with which the whole section from CE 1.156–183 deals, runs as follows:

The account of (sc. his) teachings consists of the highest and most real being (οὐσία), followed by a second being, superior to all other beings, while being after the first. Finally, there is a third being, ranked with neither of the others, but subordinate (ὑποταττομένης) to the first as to a cause, to the second as to an activity (ἐνέργεια).

To the criticism of this strictly subordinationist account of the Trinity, Gregory now turns.[9] (The numbering is by sections in the Jaeger edition.)

Translation

156. The first accusation to be made against this account is as follows. Although Eunomius promised to set forth the teaching of the Church, with the announced intention of improving on the word of Scripture, he fails in fact to use the language the Lord himself used when he expressed the mystery that perfects our faith. He makes no mention of Father, Son or Holy Spirit. Instead of 'Father' he speaks of the 'highest and most real being'; instead of 'Son' he speaks of 'one who comes after and derives his being from the highest being, while being himself superior to all other beings'. Finally, instead of 'The Holy Spirit', he speaks of one who 'is ranked with neither and is inferior to both.'

157. Now, had such a mode of speech been more appropriate, it is highly improbable that Truth itself would have failed to discover it. Nor, indeed, would those who subsequently received the preaching of the mystery, whether as initial hearers and servants of the Word, or those who subsequently filled the world with the preaching of the gospel have been so ignorant (sc. as not to be aware of the Eunomian usage).[10]

158. The same may be said of all those who at a later date, at particular junctures in common synods, came to decisions about disputed issues, whose written traditions are preserved in the churches to this day. Had it been permissible for them to employ this new language, and had piety allowed them, is it likely that they would have clung to the language of Father, Son and Holy Ghost and not, instead, transformed the language of faith into this novel jargon? Or could it be the case that these persons (sc. the Apostles and Fathers of Nicaea) were simple men and uninstructed in the mysteries and had never heard of natural names, of which he speaks, and consequently were unwilling to substitute their own private language in place of what has been handed down to us by the divine voice?

159. In any case the motive behind this novel nomenclature is obvious to anyone.[11] As soon as people hear the expressions 'Father' and 'Son', they at once automatically assume a natural and physical connection between the two on the basis of the names themselves. For natural relationship is at once suggested by these modes of address.

160. It was of set purpose to deter people from thinking in this way about the true Father and Only Begotten Son, that Eunomius steals from the hearers the natural sense of relationship suggested by the words and deserts inspired language by means of his own inventions. In this way he offers his own statement of doctrine in order to insult the truth.

161. Eunomius is quite correct in saying that it is only his own teachings that are so expressed, not those of the universal Church. Every intelligent man can immediately detect the irreligious intention of what he says. Even so, it is not out of place to examine one by one what he had in mind by assigning only to the Father the expression 'highest and most real' and by according neither title to the Son or the Spirit.

162. In my opinion the central aim of this manoeuvre is the denial of the real (? full) existence (= οὐσία) of the Only Begotten and the Spirit.[12] This is the covert intention of their verbal sophistry (= τεχνολογία),[13] the verbal admission of their existence and the actual denial of their reality. A brief acquaintance with his argument would easily confirm the truth of my interpretation.

163. Whoever believes in the independent existence (ἰδία ὑπόστασις) of the Only Begotten and the Holy Spirit should not be concerned with the quibbling discussion about the confession of names whereby he supposes he can exalt the 'God who is above all' [cf. Rom. 9, 5].[14] It would indeed be a sign of extreme stupidity to agree about the substance of belief and make a trivial fuss about words. Eunomius, however, by applying the expressions 'highest and most real' to the Father only, appears by his very silence to suggest the unreality of the others (sc. Son and Spirit).

164. For how could anyone suggest that something did indeed exist without at the same time applying to it the idea of 'real existence'?[15] And, on the contrary, where 'real existence' is not predicated, its opposite ought to be inferred. For what is not 'real' must be unreal, and the assertion of unreality amounts in effect to the

31

assertion of total non-existence. The innovative language employed by Eunomius in his dogmatic exposé seems to have some such purpose in view.

165. No one will claim that it was carelessness that led him into a thoughtless contrast between spatial 'up' and 'down', as though he were assigning to the Father a higher lookout post and to the Son one lower down the mountain.[16]

166. No one is childish enough to suppose that spatial distinctions have any part to play among intellectual and bodiless natures. Bodies, indeed, do have locations, but what is naturally intellectual and immaterial must exist without any local implication. What can he mean, therefore, by applying the term 'highest' to the Father's being (sc. οὐσία) only? To assume that anyone could arrive at such a conclusion simply as a result of stupidity is absurd, particularly when the man in question pretends to be wise and is indeed, as Scripture says, 'overwise' [Eccles. 7, 16].

167. But neither can he claim that this 'height' of being can refer to superiority of power or goodness either. Everybody knows, not only those with a reputation for wisdom, that the being (ὑπόστασις) of both the Only Begotten and the Holy Spirit is in no respects deficient as far as perfect goodness and power are concerned.

168. Every good thing, in so far as it has no element of the opposite in itself, has limitless good. The reason for this is that, in general, things may only be limited by their opposites – a truth verified in particular examples. Power is limited by the weakness that encompasses it, life by death, light by darkness and, in general, every good thing is restricted by its opposite.

169. If, therefore, he assumes that the nature (φύσις) of the Only Begotten and the Spirit can become worse, it is reasonable that he should predicate of them a reduced idea of goodness. If, however, the divine and changeless nature is incapable of deterioration – a fact our opponents grant – then clearly it will be unlimited in goodness.[17] For limitlessness (τὸ ἀόριστον) means the same as infinity (ἄπειρον). It is the height of stupidity to suppose that there can be any more or less, where it is a question of 'limitlessness' or 'infinity'. For how could the notion of infinity be preserved, if one were to postulate 'more' or 'less' in it?

170. Our understanding of 'more' is derived from comparison of limits. But where there *is* no limit, how might one suppose excess?

171. But it could perhaps be that it was not this type of superiority that was meant but some type of temporal priority in accordance with some greater age, and therefore that this is what he means by speaking of the Father's being (οὐσία) as 'highest'. Should this be so, let him inform us how he measured the 'more' of the life of the Father, seeing that no temporal moment can be conceived before the existence (ὑπόστασις) of the Only Begotten.

172. But let us suppose for the sake of argument that the Father is older than the Son. How is this temporal priority supposed to lead to an affirmation of the greater being of the Father such that it is 'upmost and real' and the Son's not so? For although in point of age the older is larger than the younger, this does not mean that the actual being of either is accordingly more or less.

173. This will become clearer through examples. In what way, for example, was David less than Abraham as far as 'being' (sc. *ousia*) goes, despite the fact that he was fourteen generations after him? Was the one more a man because he came before the other, and the other less so because he came after? Who is so stupid as to make such a claim?

174. The same definition of substance (sc. οὐσία) applies to both, unaffected by the passage of time. No one would say that the one was more a man because he had lived longer, or the other less so because he came to be at a later moment. Were this the case it would follow either that the nature (φύσις) had been exhausted in what went before or that time had spent its power in what was earlier.

175. On the contrary, it does not lie within the power of time to assign the measure of nature (φύσις) to each separate thing; instead, nature abides always the same and preserves itself through all that may happen to it. Time, however is carried along its own course, passing nature by and leaving it firm and unchanged within its own limits.

176. Therefore, even though it were to be granted that the Father *was* older than the Son, as their argument presupposes, it would by no means follow that the 'height' of being (οὐσία) belonged to the Father alone. But as *de facto* there *is* no temporal priority[18] (sc. on the part of the Father) – for how could there be any such thing in the case of a pre-temporal nature, such distinctions applying only beneath the divine nature (φύσις) – what possible argument is there left for those who endeavour to split up the eternal nature by distinctions of 'up' and 'down'?

177. In fact, the argument leaves no doubt at all that what he proposes is simply a repetition of Judaism. By insisting that only the being (οὐσία) of the Father exists, to which alone they attribute real existence (κυρίως εἶναι), the Son and the Spirit are classed among things non-existent.

178. For, whatever does not really exist is said to exist in word only and improperly, in much the same way as we may use the word 'man' improperly of an image in a likeness, as distinct from the real thing. The real thing is not the likeness of the man, but the reality upon which the likeness is based. The image is a man as far as the name goes and therefore does not possess fully what is attributed to him, because he is not in nature what he is called.

179. Therefore, if the Father's being only is said properly to exist, and the Son's and Spirit's not so, what is this but the clear denial of the message of salvation? Let them therefore leave the Church and return to the synagogues of the Jews for, in refusing to attribute real being to the Son, they are actually denying his existence. What is not fully real is in effect non-existent.[19]

180. But since he wishes to be wise in such matters and is contemptuous of those who attempt to write without logical expertise, let him inform our despised selves from what wisdom he learnt the 'more' and 'less' of being (οὐσία).

181. What argument ever established a distinction of the type that one being (οὐσία) is more real than another being? I am using the precise sense of οὐσία in saying this. He ought not to adduce, in defence of his claim, differences of quality or individuality, which are connected with being, but distinct from it.

182. It is not here a question of smell or colour or weight or power or differences of ways or of character, connected with either body or soul. I am here speaking of the basic substance το ὑποκείμενον, to which the name 'being' (= οὐσία) properly applies and I wish to see if its difference from another being can be described in terms of 'more being'. But so far I have not yet heard of two distinct beings described as 'more' or 'less' in this way. Both exist alike, as long as they do exist, with the exception, as I have said, of superiority of honour or duration.

183. If then he will not grant that the Only Begotten fully exists (ὅλως ἐν οὐσίᾳ) – and that is the secret drift of his argument – then let him not admit lesser existence for him, seeing he will not grant him full reality. If, however, he does admit that the Son is in some way a real power – a point we are as yet not debating – why does he take away what he has conceded, by proceeding to assert that he who was admitted to exist, does not really (κυρίως) do so, which is tantamount to saying that he doesn't exist at all (ὅλως)?

184. As it is impossible for someone to be a man, who does not possess all that is included in the notion of manhood, and where one of the distinguishing characteristics is missing, then the whole nature of the reality is altered, so also this is true in every other case, where being is predicated imperfectly or improperly. Partial predication of being offers no proof of reality. On the contrary, the assertion of imperfect being leads to a total denial of the reality in question.

185. If, then, he is of sound mind, let him change to a religious opinion. He should remove from his teaching any ideas of less or unreal from his understanding of the being of the Only Begotten and the Spirit.

186. But if, for some mysterious reason he has decided upon impiety, and wishes effectively to diminish his creator, God and benefactor, then he must himself forfeit the appearance of being a man of education. He has unintelligently tried to exalt being above being, calling the one higher and the one lower, in accordance with some mysterious logic. He assigns to the former reality, to the latter unreality. Even outside the faith we have never encountered anyone who argues in this lunatic way. For what he says has no resonance either in the inspired words of Scripture or in the common conceptions (κοίναι ἔννοιαι) of philosophy.[20]

2. AGAINST THE MACEDONIANS, ON THE HOLY SPIRIT 19–26

Introduction

Although the Council of Nicaea had, after a fashion, 'settled' the question of the deity of the Son by affirming him to be of one substance – homoousios – with the Father, it had relatively little to say about the person and status of the forgotten member of the Trinity, the Holy Spirit. All it asserted was 'and in the Holy Spirit'. As to whether the Holy Spirit was a power or a person, divine, semi-divine or created, on these vital issues the council remained silent.

There were several good reasons for this. First, and most importantly, Nicaea, aside from its canonical interest in dealing with the Melitian schism and various matters of canon law, had been convened by Constantine in order to define the precise relationship between the Son and the Father in such a way as both to unchurch Arius and to produce a document to which the other 220 assembled fathers could append their signatures. It appears that Arius had shown no great interest in the status of the third person of the divine Triad and, naturally, the council did not feel itself called on to add to their troubles by discussing matters that were not in question.

Again, despite the use of the Holy Spirit both in the baptismal formula (cf. Matt. 28, 19) and in the doxology which concluded the psalm, it does not appear that he had played any large part in the theology of the prenicene period. The role of 'go-between God' had been largely usurped by the *Logos*, to whom all the economic action of God in creation and redemption was assigned. Origen's treatment of the role of the third person in *On First Principles* 1.3. is typical of the tendency to restrict the spirit to the inspiration of prophecy, and even here there was a strong feeling that the more charismatic effects of the action of the Holy Spirit might be used by unscrupulous persons in order to undermine the established order and to diminish within the Church the importance of rational discourse. Although Origen never mentions by name Montanus, the second century author of a charismatic movement whose roots lay in Asia Minor, it is fairly clear that he has the Montanists in mind on at least two occasions when he censures the attempt made by some to hijack the Holy Spirit for their non-rational discourse. In *Contra Celsum* 7, 3–4 he insists that the Holy Spirit's action is one of enlightenment rather than of non-rational exaltation. He takes a similar position in *On First Principles* 3.3.4., where he writes that the effect of the action of the Spirit is *'sine ulla mentis obturbatione'*, 'without any mental disturbance'. This very restrained attitude to the Holy Spirit, which hardly distinguished him from the Word, led to a certain 'taming' of his power and forgetting of his presence and importance. In so far as his presence was acknowledged it tended to be in Scripture and in the sacraments.

The impulse to go beyond the restrained attitude of Origen and the cool minimalist statement of Nicaea came during the fourth century, through groups who were later judged to be doctrinally defective. All took a 'low' view of the Spirit, thinking of him as a power rather than a person – a consequence of the very word Spirit – and as either a creature or as a sort of divine outreach, not unlike the view of Professor Lampe in *God as Spirit*.

One such group flourished in Egypt. They were of seemingly unknown provenance[21] and were known as Tropici, from their habit of searching for tropological or allegorical exegesis of the Bible. We owe our knowledge of them largely to Athanasius who sometime

after 361 wrote four letters to Serapion, bishop of Thmuis in the
Nile Delta. To judge from these letters, the Tropici argued for the
created character of the Spirit on rather fragile grounds. Two texts
adduced by them in order to disprove the deity of the Holy Spirit
were Amos 4, 13 and 1 Tim. 5, 21. The former of these runs: 'Lo, one
who creates the wind'. As the Greek word for wind is the same as
that for spirit (πνεῦμα) the Tropici argued that the text proved the
created character of the Spirit. The second text reads: 'In the presence of God and of Christ Jesus and of the elect angels.' On the
basis of an *argumentum ex silentio* the Tropici argued that the silence
of the text on the Holy Spirit meant that he was not part of the
divine nature. To the demolition of these rather insubstantial arguments Athanasius devotes sections 3 to 14 of his first *Letter*, before
proceeding to a more satisfactory dogmatic treatment of the place
of the third person within the Trinity. The most powerful argument
comes in *Letter* 3, 5–6, where the inseparability of the Son and the
Spirit in prophecy and the Incarnation is adduced as the main reason
for affirming the deity of the latter. In this connection much use is
made of the account of the Annunciation in Luke 1, and of the
baptismal formula of Matt. 28, 19.

Although Gregory's treatment of the deity of the Holy Spirit
clearly owes a good deal to Athanasius,[22] the nature of the challenge
he was called on to meet had altered somewhat since the mid-350s.
Sometime during that period a group arose in Armenia connected
with the name of Eustathius of Sebaste.[23] It appears that some at
least of Basil's commitment to the ascetic life owed much to
his friendship with Eustathius, although it is highly improbable
that Basil was ever a member of the theological group over which
Eustathius presided, the Semi Arians or Homoeousians, that is,
those who advocated a position midway – so they thought –
between Arius and the strict followers of the teaching of Nicaea.
Now these same bishops also assigned an inferior position to the
Holy Spirit. Something of their position may be inferred from the
treatise Basil wrote in c. 375, *On the Holy Spirit*.

It appears that, on largely grammatical grounds, they insisted
upon the inferiority of the third person to the other two; and
although it is remarkable that the 'economy'[24] of Basil never allowed
him directly to affirm either the deity of the Spirit or his consub-
stantiality with Father and Son, even so he does insist that the Spirit
is divine (cf. *On the Holy Spirit* 23.54) and that he is not a creature and
is to be worshipped together with the Father and the Son (cf. *Letter*

159.2). Like Athanasius before him Basil laid a good deal of stress on the baptismal formula at the end of St Matthew's gospel.

Gregory's own contribution to the debate occurs mainly in the work under discussion, although the subject is addressed occasionally elsewhere.[25] It appears that he never produced a companion to Basil's *Against Eunomius* 3: his own extensive work with that title, which is divided into ten sizeable parts, deals exclusively with the Anomoean attack on the deity of the Son. The full title of this work is *On the Holy Spirit, Against the Macedonians, the Spirit Fighters*. The Greek text is preserved in only two, fairly late manuscripts of the twelfth and thirteenth centuries. It is printed in *MPG* 45, 1301–1333. The most recent edition is in *GNO* 111.1. by F. Mueller. It is traditionally assigned to some time shortly after the council of Constantinople in 381. Macedonius, the eponymous leader of the party, had been bishop of the capital in 340, and it is not entirely clear how his name came to be connected with a movement that sprang to prominence so much later. Their main contention, which Gregory is concerned to rebut, was that the Holy Spirit occupied a mediant position between creature and creator. In fact, their attitude to the status of the Spirit echoes that made for the Son by Arius, who had claimed that the Son was 'a perfect creature of God, but not as one of the creatures'. (*Letter of the Arians to Alexander of Alexandria*). Gregory's reply opens (= sections 1–5) with an argument not unlike the one we have already met in his critique of Eunomius, namely that within the divine nature there can be no question of ἐλάττωσις, of more or less. Part 2 of the reply (= sections 6–10) argues that because the Holy Spirit is in all respects perfect, possessing all the distinctive characteristics of the divine nature, he must himself be divine, 'proceeding from the Father and receiving from the Son' (97.12). Part 3 (= sections 11–14) argues for the total involvement of the Spirit both in the eternal life and external activity of the Father and the Son, above all in creation and redemption. Gregory stresses the close interconnection of all three persons: 'All activity begins from the Father, comes through the Son and is perfected in the Holy Spirit.' (100.9–11.)

This system of declension within the deity is highly characteristic of Cappadocian theology in general and may be paralleled in Basil's *On the Holy Spirit* 16.38, though the general outlines can be clearly seen in Athanasius, *Letters to Serapion* 1.9, where perfection (τελείωσις) is assigned to the action of the Holy Spirit. In part 4 again, the close association of the Son and Spirit is argued for as a ground for asserting his deity (sections 15–18). Both Christ's and our formation (μόρφωσις) and anointing (χρῖσμα) come to us through the action of the Holy Spirit. Part 5 (= sections 19–23) urges the inseparability of all three persons in baptism. This leads to a final short passage on the need to worship, while insisting at the same time on the close connection of all three persons (= sections 24–26). As to endeavour to think of the Father without also thinking of the Son is difficult, if not impossible, so too to form an idea of the Son, without involving the Spirit, is likewise barely possible (cf. 1 Cor. 12, 3).

Briefly, therefore, Gregory's argument is that the attributes of the Holy Spirit, his activity in the creation and redemption of the world and therefore his inseparable connection with the Father and the Son, fully justify his inclusion in the godhead. He is not, as Gregory's opponents had argued, a hybrid being, belonging in between creator and creature, (ἐν μεθορίωι τοῦ τε κτιστοῦ καὶ τοῦ ἀκτίστου). There *is* no in-between state. Such a suggestion is dealt with (and rejected) by Gregory in section 17. The following six sections in translation, 19 to 25, are primarily concerned with establishing the deity of the Holy Spirit by reference to his role in baptism.

Translation

Against the Macedonians 19–26 (= GNO III.1.105.19–110.23)

19. Let us now address ourselves to the next point. What is it that we achieve by holy baptism?[26] Is it not a share in the life that is no longer a prey to death? I hardly think that anyone who was in any sense a Christian would deny this. But is this life-giving power (ζωοποιὸς δύναμις) inherent in the water which we use for the sacrament? Surely it must be obvious to anyone that bodily ministration alone is ineffectual for our sanctification, when it has not been transformed[27] by sanctification. Further, what gives life to the baptized is the Spirit, as the Lord says of it, using his own words 'The Spirit gives life' [John 6, 63]. But it does not only give life when it is received through faith or the perfecting of grace, but also there must be faith in the Lord before this, and through this also life-giving grace is communicated to believers, as the Lord says 'He brings to life to whom he wills' [John 5, 21].[28] But, since the grace communicated by the Son is itself derived from the unbegotten spring, this must mean that belief in the Father, who gives life to all, must come first as the Apostle says [cf. I Tim. 6, 13]. From this source, as from a spring that bubbles forth life, comes the life-giving grace (ζωοποιὸς χάρις), through the Only Begotten Son, who is the true life and is then perfected in those who are deemed worthy by the action (ἐνεργείαι) of the Holy Ghost.

106.9. If, then, life comes through baptism, and baptism itself is perfected in the name of the Father, Son and Holy Spirit,[29] what do they say who account the provider of life as worth nothing? If the grace is small, let them say what is nobler than life itself. But if whatever is honourable is less noble than life itself – and by life I mean the high and noble life, in which irrational creation has no share – how do they have the audacity to reduce the grace, or rather the source of that grace to the level of their own conceptions [ὑπολήψεσιν] and so separate It from its divine and high nature and reduce It to the level of inferior reality. It may be, though, that they despise the gift of life, and therefore have no great reverence for the character of the One who bestows it. If so, they forget the conclusion of their argument which is that nothing great can be assumed of the Only Begotten and of the Father either, seeing that the very same life that is offered through them, is also ministered to us through the Spirit.

20 = 106.25. If then those who despise their very lives and are enemies of it and have, therefore, learnt how to dishonour the source of this grace, if these people, I say, suppose the gift to be small let them not imagine that their refusal of grace (ἀχαριστία) is limited to one person (πρόσωπον). In reality they extend their blasphemy through the Holy Spirit to the Holy Triad. For even as grace flows down uninterruptedly from the Father, through the Son and the Spirit to those who are worthy[30] so too blasphemy flows back in the opposite direction from the Spirit, through the Son to the God of all.[31]

107.2. For if we in effect despise the sender by making of no account the one he sends – and what a gap there is between the man and him who sends him – what punishment do we reserve for those who are so arrogant against the Spirit? It may be for this reason that an inexorable judgment has been passed against such a blasphemy by the lawgiver himself [cf. Matt. 12, 32] since through such a blasphemy the whole blessed and divine nature have been insulted at the whim of the blasphemer. He who makes an orthodox confession of the Spirit sees in the Spirit the glory of the Only Begotten and beholding the Son sees the image of the Infinite one.[32] In this way,

40

through the image the archetype is impressed on the mind. So, too, a contemptuous attitude, when it is insolently bold against the glory of the Spirit, by a natural consequence transfers the blasphemy upwards through the Son to the Father.

107.16. Wise men, therefore, should be on their guard against such brazen effrontery, the result of which is the total destruction of one who so dares. Our aim should be, as far as we may, to exalt the Spirit in word and even more in our thoughts. For it is impossible for expression (λόγος) to equal thought (διάνοια) in range. Once we have reached the height of human powers, as far, that is, as the human mind can go in height and greatness of thoughts, even then you must suppose that even that is well below the fitting honour. So it is said in the psalm, after 'Exalt the Lord our God', then comes 'Worship before the footstool of his feet' [Ps. 98, 5]. The source of this incomprehensible dignity is nothing else than his own dignity.

21 = 107.29. If, then, every exaltation within the reach of human power falls short of the grandeur of him who is worshipped (this is the hidden sense of the words 'footstool for his feet') what utter vanity it is on the part of those who have so high an opinion of their own ability, that they suppose it is their business to define the honour due to one who is beyond our power of honouring? Such is their arrogance that they even judge the Holy Spirit unworthy of some titles counted honourable; and they rate their own power so high that it exceeds that of the honour (ἀξία) due to the Spirit. What a pitiful and wretched lunacy!

They fail to see who they are who reason after this fashion, and what the Holy Spirit is, to whom they in their pride equate themselves. Someone should tell such persons that they are 'nothing but a breath, that goeth forth and returneth not', in the womb of a woman, erected like a house in the beginning through a filthy conception and dissolved again into the filthy earth. Their life was like that of the grass that withers; they flowered a little through the deceits of this life and then were dried up again. Their flower faded and disappeared. They were nothing before their birth and they were without sure knowledge of what their end would be. For the soul does not know its own place as long as it remains in the flesh. That is what human beings are [Job 34, 15; Ps. 89, 5–6; Isa. 51.12].

22 = 108.18. But the Holy Spirit, belonging as he does to that class of beings that are by nature holy, is the same as the Father and Only Begotten, both being by nature holy. So too is the Holy Spirit.

41

He is also life-giving [ζωοποιός] and incorruptible, changeless and everlasting, just, wise, straight, leading, good and powerful, the source of all good things and, above all, of life itself. The Spirit is everywhere and present to each thing, filling the earth and remaining in the heavens, poured out among the super terrestrial powers, filling all things according to the worth of each, and yet losing nothing of his own fullness [cf. Sap. Sol. 1, 7][33]. It is with all them that are worthy, yet not separated from the Holy Triad. It always 'searches the depths of God' [cf. I Cor. 2, 10], always 'receives from the Son' [cf. John 16,14] is sent forth yet not separated, is itself glorified, yet itself bestows glory [cf. John 16, 14]. For that which gives glory to another is clearly understood to be in surpassing glory itself. How indeed could that which is itself bereft of glory itself bestow glory? Unless something be itself light, how can it demonstrate the grace of light?

108.33. So also that which is not itself glory and honour and greatness and distinction will hardly be capable of demonstrating the power of glory. The Spirit, then, gives glory to both Father and Son. But he who said, 'I will glorify those who glorify me' [I Kgs. 2, 30] is incapable of deceit. The Lord says to the Father, 'I have glorified you' and again, 'Glorify me with the glory I had with thee from the beginning before the world was' [John 17, 4–5]. The divine voice answers, 'I have glorified and will glorify again' [John 12, 28]. You observe the circular course traced by glory, always going through things that are like. The Son is glorified by the Spirit; again the Son has glory from the Father and the Only Begotten becomes the glory of the Spirit. For by what else will the Father be glorified save by the true glory of the Only Begotten? Again, in what else shall the Son be glorified, save in the greatness of the Spirit? And so again the argument goes round in a circle, glorifying the Son through the Spirit and the Father through the Son.

23 = 109.16. If such be the greatness of the Spirit, and if whatever is lovely and good originates in God, comes through the Son and is perfected through the Spirit, who 'acts everywhere and in all things' [I Cor. 12, 6], why do they destroy themselves by means of their own life? Why do they distance themselves from the hope of those that are saved? Why do they cut themselves off from closeness to God [cf. I Cor. 6, 16]? For how shall anyone be closely connected to the Lord, if the Spirit does not effect this connection for us?[34] Why do they pick an argument with us about worship and adoration? Why do they conceal their thoughts against the divine and all powerful nature, by employing the language of worship, as though they were not benefiting themselves in their prayers for salvation, but rather conferring honour upon God? Do they really wish to be saved?

109.28. Prayer is to your advantage when you ask, not the honour of him who provides. Why do you approach your benefactor as though you were the one who was doing him a favour? Why, you do not even deign to address him as benefactor, who is the provider of all that is good? You yearn for life, while dishonouring the life giver; you search for holiness, while at the same time condemning the distributor of the grace of holiness, and, though you never deny that he can give good things, even so you deem his power unworthy of being asked. You seem not to realise that the giving of anything good is superior to the being asked for it.

110.4. The greatness of the request does not in every respect correspond to the one who has been asked. For it is possible that even he who does not possess (sc. something) could be asked for it. That (sc. asking) lies with the choice of him who asks. But he who has provided an unambiguous good, has made a display of the power that is his. Why, then, do you admit that he can do the greater – I mean that he has the power of providing whatever is lovely – yet insist on robbing him of being asked for anything at all, as though *that* were something great?

110.11. This happens frequently, as we have said, and even in the case of matters of no importance, through the deceit of the devil. For the slaves of vanity ask for things they want even from idols. But, their requests do not therefore add any honour to those idols. And they [sc. the idols] in the hope of having some share in the object of their hopes [sc. honour], never cease deceitfully providing what they are asked for. And do you, persuaded though you are of the character and dimension of the things the Spirit offers, even so fail to make any requests to Him. Instead you appeal to the law that lays it down, 'Worship the Lord your God and serve him only' [Deut. 6, 13], Tell me, how do you worship him only, if you separate him from his connection with the Only Begotten and the Holy Spirit? That, surely, is Jewish worship.[35]

110.24. But you will say that the thought of the Father naturally entails thought of the Son. But, tell me, once you have the thought of the Son in your mind do you not automatically think also of the Holy Spirit?[36] You would have no answer to give. For how could you confess the Son save in the Holy Spirit? [cf. I Cor. 12, 3] For when *is*

the Spirit separated from the Son in such a way that the Father may
be worshipped without also entailing the worship of the Son and the
Spirit? And what sort of worship can they suppose it to be, when
they are happy to offer it distinctly to the God who is above all[37] and
are even prepared to extend this honour to the Only Begotten, while
depriving the Spirit of like honour?

111.2. Human custom calls that worship, which involves a bending down of subjects to the earth, as a way of happily doing reverence to those who are more powerful than they. This is how the
patriarch Jacob behaved in his desire to avoid the anger of his
brother, and when he went to meet him displayed his inferiority in
this lowly fashion by adopting this posture [Gen. 33, 3]. Scripture
says, 'He bowed low to the ground three times'. Joseph's brethren
likewise, so long as they knew not who he was, and so long as he
affected not to know them, because of the distinction of his position, honoured his power by a prostration [Gen. 42, 6]. The great
Abraham, too, bowed low before the Hittites [Gen. 23, 7], he the
sojourner, before them, the people of the land showing, I think, by
what he did, that the natives of the land are more powerful than the
visitors.

111.14. It would be quite possible to cite many similar accounts,
both from narratives of bygone days and from current examples.
But is that what they (sc. the Macedonians) really supposed to be
worship? If so, is it not utterly absurd of them to think that the Holy
Spirit is unworthy of the worship, which the patriarch was prepared
to offer to the Canaanites? Or do they suppose there is another
form of worship, quite distinct from this, which is offered to men
which they suppose is fitting for the preeminent nature [sc. of
God]? How then can they completely outlaw worship offered to the
Spirit, and not even allow him a share in that worship, which they are
happy to offer to men?

111.25. But, what *is* the form of worship, which they suppose is
set aside for God? Is it a matter of words or of bending the body?
In that case, divine and human worship would be the same. In the
case of men, words are spoken and the body is bent low. What, then,
is distinctive about what is offered to God? It must be quite plain to
anyone, who is in any way intelligent, that human nature is unable to
find a gift worthy of God. He who made us, has no need of the
goods he gave us. But we men make displays of the honour and love
we have for each other, one in a more, the other in a less, lofty
manner, by our acknowledgement of the excellence of those near

us; and these we transfer to the worship of a higher nature offering him who is beyond all honour, our most honourable service. And it is for this reason that, when men approach kings or rulers and wish to ask some favour from them, they do not present a simple request, but endeavour to induce in their rulers a sense of pity and kindness, by humble expressions, by bending of the body, touching the knees and falling to the ground. So they endeavour by their laments to engage a further advocate in their pleas, and so hope to induce pity in them that listen.

112.13. For this reason, those recognize the one who possesses that true power, through which the whole world is ordered, address him in a similar fashion. Some approach with humble spirits for things in this world they are serious about. Others, with a noble spirit, are eager about eternal and mysterious hopes. But, because they do not know how to ask, and because human nature is incapable of showing honour adequate to the majesty of the glory of God, they have transferred the reverence, which we display towards our fellow human beings, to the honour of the divine. This is the worship with prayer and humility, which is the desire for things that are dear to our hearts.

112.23. Therefore, Daniel bends his knees to the Lord, as he asks for kindness for his captive people [Dan. 9, 3]. And again, he who bore our weaknesses, and prayed for us through the human nature that he had assumed, is said by the gospel [Matt. 26, 39] at the time of prayer to have fallen on his face, and to have made his prayer in this posture. It is my opinion that he did this in order to teach us not to be arrogant in time of prayer, but in every way to conform ourselves to a pitiable condition, since 'God resists the proud, and gives grace to the humble', [Jac. 4, 6] and, 'Whoever exalts himself, shall be humbled' [Luke 14, 11].

113.4. If worship, therefore, is a form of supplication, which acts as a sort of prelude, that is helpful before the actual asking, and if the act of asking itself is made to the Lord, who distributes all things, what possible meaning can be attached to their novel legislation ($\nu o\mu o\theta\varepsilon\sigma ia$)? I cannot begin to understand why we are not to ask from him who gives, not to bow down before him who rules, not to serve him who has power, and not to worship our supreme governor.

113.10. No one is such an enemy of himself and of the Spirit, as to deny that all these titles are applicable to the Holy Spirit. That which is by nature a leader, leads, 'that which acts everywhere in all things' [1 Cor. 12, 6] is indeed all powerful, that which according to his power 'distributes charismata as he wishes', is really Lord [1 Cor. 12, 11]. That which graciously bestows life, does good; the ransomer pities; what brings near to God, divinizes us; what offers us the kingdom, makes us like Christ and also sons of God. It (sc. the Holy Spirit) raises the corpse to life, lifts up the fallen, leads back the wanderer to the straight path, gives stability to him that stands, and brings him that has died to resurrection. Are all these things insignificant and worthy of no grace? Let them think of something higher, in which the Spirit has no share and allege that as a ground for refusing him honour.[38]

3. THE APOLINARIAN CONTROVERSY: AGAINST APOLIN(N)ARIUS 16–22

Introduction

The question of the interrelation of divine and human in Christ only began seriously to emerge once the full deity of the Word had been defined and accepted. *The Creed of Nicaea* had indeed implied, as Cyril was to point out at a later date in his *Second Letter to Nestorius* of 430, that the divine Word was at the centre of the person and activity of Jesus Christ, but no serious or controversial attention had been given to the harmony of the two elements. Some of the credit for raising this issue is due to the brilliant and subtle mind of Apolinarius of Laodicea in Syria. He and his father had come to the aid of a beleaguered Church shortly after the School Law promulgated by the emperor Julian in June 362. The effect of this law was to inhibit committed Christians from acting as teachers in school, because they could not conscientiously teach a culture whose principles they in practice rejected. It is the first historical example of confessional tests for teachers. The two Apolinarii tried to remedy the cultural vacuum for Christians created by this step by rewriting large parts of the Bible in classical style. So the four gospels emerged as Platonic dialogues; the historical books of the Bible in the style of Thucydides. The interests of the younger Apolinarius did not stop short at translation of the Bible. He seems to have influenced Basil in the direction of a more strongly unitary understanding of the Trinity.[39] But his main dogmatic importance is the result of his attempts to understand the person of Christ. On one hand, he was a firm supporter of strict Nicene orthodoxy. On the other hand, his view of

the human nature of Christ was, by the standards of later orthodoxy, decidedly defective. There seems to be no doubt that he
denied the existence of Christ's human soul and, in consequence,
had a defective view of his human nature. It appears that for him the
sinless saviour could not have a human soul, as that would of necessity involve him in sin, the mind of man being necessarily sinful.

At the council of Constantinople of 381 Canon 1 condemned the
followers of Apolinarius together with a large number of right and
left wing Trinitarian heresies, but without giving any content to this
censure. Canon 7 offers reception back into communion to any of
those, Apolinarians included, who renounced their errors, provided,
that is, that 'they handed over their libelli (presumably their heretical
manuals) and anathematized all heresy'. But here again the content
of their heresy is left unspecified. So successful was this condemna-
tion that the actual views of Apolinarius have to be reconstructed
from the writings of his critics, among them the two Gregories.

The response of Gregory of Nazianzus is contained in his two
Letters to Cledonius (= 101 and 102) and in *Letter* 202 to Nectarius, his
successor in the see of Constantinople. The first two were composed c. 382/3 and came to be regarded as the classical exposition
of the true faith, both in their style and their content. Indeed, it is to
him that we owe the celebrated formula 'What has not been
assumed has not been healed', '*to aproslepton atherapeuton*' (*Letter* 101,
32).

Gregory of Nyssa's two principal writings on Christology never
acquired quite this distinction. This is partly because his style is
more elaborate and less perspicuous than that of his namesake. It
also owes something to the method of composition, which treats
the statements of Apolinarius one by one instead of offering his
own counter vision. Finally, it must also be admitted, as his com-
mentators are not slow to point out, that there is a certain basic
incoherence in their general bearing. Gregory of Nyssa has been
variously designated a (crypto)-Monophysite and a (crypto)-
Nestorian.[40] Charles Raven says that he (sc. Gregory) has 'little
power of synthetic thought' and that it 'is difficult to discover what
his own views were'.[41] While J. H. Srawley, a more sympathetic critic,
admits that his Christology was 'crude and tentative'.[42]

Our principal sources for evaluating the justice of these rather
harsh judgments are two treatises, one written to Theophilus, patriarch of Alexandria from 385 to 412, the uncle of Cyril. The tone of
the letter from the very beginning indicates that Theophilus had

already become patriarch, therefore we must assume that Gregory's treatise entitled *Kata Apolinariston*, '*Against the Apolinarians*', was written some time after 385. It is not so easy to date Gregory's major treatise, entitled *A Refutation, Against the Writings of Apolinarius*. It begins absolutely and no particular addressee is mentioned. Lietzmann seems to favour a date slightly later than that at which the other work appeared. In addition to the works dealing expressly with the views of Apolinarius, there are less complete treatments of the views of Apolinarius at *Contra Eunomium* III.3. Also, chapters 9, 10 and 27 of the *Catechetical Oration* also contain statements of Gregory's views.

Gregory's own position in its general outlines bears a family resemblance to that of his 'master', Origen. Both writers assume that the close union of divine and human in Christ was worked out gradually and in stages. For Gregory as for Origen before him, the human nature of Christ progressed from a divisive to a unitary model. So, in *On First Principles* 2.6.3ff., Origen taught that the human soul of Christ, which is, as it were, the 'go-between' between the body and the deity, gradually by virtue becomes more and more attached to the deity until it is fused with it as is iron in the fire – a metaphor drawn from Stoic physics. Gregory likewise uses on several occasions the disappearance of the drop of vinegar in the sea with which to indicate the closeness of the union of divine and human in Christ but after the resurrection, not before.[43] It is for this reason that critics find it difficult to decide whether Gregory is to be classed as assertor or denier of the human nature of Christ. We also need to remember that Gregory lived before the great Christological debates at Ephesus and Chalcedon had taken place.

To three important truths Gregory is a witness: (1) The deity in Christ was real without the possibility of change or alteration and therefore incapable of suffering; (2) The human nature which he assumed was a real and sinful human nature. This is made abundantly clear from a forceful expression he uses in his *Reply to Apolinarius* 26,[44] 'He assumed and purified our filth [rupos]'; (3) Yet Christ was not two persons but one. Apparently, Eunomius had suggested that Gregory's defence of the deity of the Son must lead to the conclusion that Christ was both a fully human and a fully divine person. It is against this particular misunderstanding of his own position (of the irreducible duality of Christ) that a large part of *Contra Eunomium* III.3 is directed. So he writes (*Contra Eunomium* III.3.44):

The right hand of God [cf. Acts 2, 33] that is his creative power, the Lord, through whom all things were made [cf. John 1, 3] and without whom nothing was made, took up the man that had been united with him to his own high state. By means of mixture [anakrasis] with the humanity, he raised him to his own state and made him into what he himself was by nature.

This passage suggests a transformation,[45] μεταποίησις, at some stage either of Christ's own humanity or (though less probably) of common humanity into divinity, in the interests of unity. Perhaps the moment referred to is the resurrection, which would fit better with the context of Acts. 2, 33ff. Gregory makes no clear attempt to harmonize these three truths.

Although it is very doubtful that at any period Apolinarius ever taught that Christ was a 'heavenly man', '*epouranios anthropos*' [cf. John 3, 13; 1 Cor. 15, 47] in the sense that Christ came down to this earth already fully attired as a man in a human body, it can certainly be stated of him[46] that he rejected (1) the notion of two sons; (2) the idea that Christ was an inspired man, an '*anthropos entheos*'; (3) that Christ was a free and changeable being. He possessed, on the contrary, an unchangeable mind, '*atreptos nous*' (cf. *GNO* III.1.195.19) and it was this that rendered him immune to sin.

Despite the evident fact that it appears to suppress the human side of Christ, there is no denying that the system as it stands is neat and compelling. Hardly surprisingly, Apolinarius has been described as the most brilliant theologian of the fourth century. By comparison, as has already been hinted, Gregory's reply disappoints.

Gregory's reply, his *Antirrheticus adversus Apolinarium*, is composed of fifty nine chapters, and columns 1124 to 1169, in *MPG* 45 and in *GNO* III.1.131 to 233. It can conveniently be subdivided into seven sections with a conclusion:[47]

1 Chapters 1–12 (= 133.1–147.11), attacks the view that in any way shape or form God died in Jesus, a view that would upset any thought of the divine apatheia or superiority to feeling. Gregory's view is that divine and human coexist in Christ.
2 Chapters 13–21 (= 147.12–162.15) attacks the idea of a heavenly man and of the possession by Christ of a heavenly body.
3 Chapters 22–34 (= 162.6–184.30) attacks the view of Apolinarius that the humanity of Christ lacked a human mind.
4 Chapters 35–39 (= 184.31–194.27) attacks the view that Christ is simply an en-minded (= God possessed) body/flesh.

49

5 Chapters 40–41 (= 194.28–199.11) Gregory insists against the implications of Apolinarius' argument, that virtue presupposes both intelligence and freedom (cf. for a particularly Gregorian (and Origenistic) view, see page 198.1, 'virtue is a creation of choice (*prohairesis*)'.[48]

6 Chapters 42–45 (= 199.12–208.27) insist against Apolinarius that although Christ is as man perfectly free, even so there are not two οὐσίαι in Christ. Again, as in section v, free submission to the divine will is essential for true humanity.

7 Chapters 46–57 (= 208.28–230.30) deals with the claim that the tripartite division of man at 1 Thess. 5, 21 into body, soul and spirit implies the deity of the spiritual. In other words, in Christ the spirit equals the divinity. Against this Gregory insists on the impassibility of the divine, 'the nature that is beyond suffering cannot suffer' (223.14).

8 Chapters 58–59 (= 230.31–233.18) concludes the argument and repeats much that has been said.

The main points made by Gregory are clear enough. He insists on the full deity being present in Christ, without losing its superiority to change and pain, through connection with the human nature of Jesus. Again for Gregory the integrity of Christ's human nature is vigorously asserted, partly to preserve the divine changelessness, partly to ensure the reality of Christ's human nature. What is less clear is how Gregory proposes to meet the criticism of the apparently dualist position made by Apolinarius. Towards the end of section 54 (cf. especially 224.13ff) he does indeed use the language of unity and mixture with which to define his position and appeals, as had Origen before him, to the words of 1 Cor. 6, 17[49] about being one spirit with the Lord, with which to express his opinion, but this hardly solves the problem of duality.

Translation

Against Apolinarius 16–22

16 = 151.21. But I think we must pass by his mistaken understanding of each of the scriptural passages he adduces. The sense of each is easily available and it would protract the argument to examine them all in detail. In proof of his contention that he (sc. the Word) always had flesh and blood he produced a saying of the Apostle (sc. St Paul, Eph. 1, 7), which speaks of us having received redemption through his blood, the forgiveness of sins through his flesh. In one sense, I hardly think that any intelligent person would deny the truth of this. Who does not know the divine mystery, that the author of our salvation [cf. Heb. 2, 10], went after 'the lost sheep like a shepherd' [Luke 15, 4/Matt. 18, 12]?[50]

We human beings are that sheep, who through sin strayed from the rational hundred. He takes the whole sheep on his own shoulders. The sheep did not only stray partially, but the whole strayed and the whole is brought back again. It is not as though the outside skin were carried and the inward part neglected, as Apolinarius supposes. But it was the whole that was on the shoulders of the shepherd and which through being assumed became one with him in the godhead of the Lord. Therefore, when he wished to search out and save that which was lost, he took upon himself what he had found. The sheep was unable to be moved by its own feet, which had once gone astray, but was carried by the godhead. The sheep, that is the man, was what appeared, 'his footsteps' as it is written, 'were not marked' [Ps. 76, 20 [LXX]].

For he who carried the sheep upon himself displayed no trace of sin or straying in his human life. Rather, in the journey of this life clear signs of his deity appeared, such as were his teaching, his healing, his raising from the dead and his other miracles. Therefore by taking this sheep upon himself the shepherd became one with him. It is for this reason that he addresses the other sheep with the voice of a sheep, for how else could human frailty have endured the sound of the divine voice? Instead he addresses us in human, or one might perhaps say, in sheep-like terms, when he says 'My sheep hear my voice' [John 10, 27]. So, the shepherd who took upon himself the sheep and addressed us through it is both sheep and shepherd, sheep in what was assumed, shepherd in that which assumed the sheep.

17 = 152.30. Since then 'the good shepherd must lay down his life for his sheep' [John 10, 11] that by his own death he might destroy death, the 'author of our salvation' [Heb. 2, 10] becomes to our human nature both priest and lamb. He unmanned death in assuming a body capable of experiencing communion in suffering. Seeing that death is nothing else than the separation of soul and body, he who united himself to both, I mean to the soul and to the body, is separated from neither ('The gifts of God are irrevocable' as the

Apostle says [Rom. 11, 29]. By dividing himself between body and soul, through his soul he opens paradise to the thief [Luke 23, 43], through his body he stays the power of corruption [Rom. 8, 21]. This is the destruction of death, the rendering ineffectual of corruption by its disappearance in the life-giving nature. For what happened in their case was at the same time our own nature's blessing and also grace.

153.14. So, he (sc. the Son), who exists in both, unites again through his resurrection all that had once been separated (sc. body and soul).[51] Previously he had surrendered his body 'to the heart of the earth', as it is written [Matt. 12, 40] and, of his own accord, had surrendered his soul to his Father, when he says 'Into your hands I commend my spirit' [Luke 23, 46] and to the thief, 'Today you will be with me' [Luke 23, 43]. In both of these he spoke truly. Nowhere else are we to believe that the divine dwelling we call paradise is to be found, than in the spacious hand of the Father. So the prophet speaking for the Lord refers to the heavenly Jerusalem, when he says, 'Behold I have graven your walls on the palms of my hands; you are before me always' [Is. 59, 16].

153.26. So it is that he was in death, yet not mastered by death. The compositum is divided, the uncompounded not so. His uncompounded nature (sc. his deity) remains though the composite is split up; and although body and soul are separated from each other, neither is separated from the deity. Proof of this is the power which, as has been said, on the one hand gives to the body incorruption and to the soul a place in paradise. By the separation (sc. of soul and body) far from the simple, uncompounded nature (sc. of God) being split up, precisely the opposite occurs, for it makes them one. By his own inner indivisibility, he brings what has been divided into unity (ἕνωσιν).

154.7. This is made clear from the words, 'God raised him from the dead' [Col. 2, 12; I Thess. 1, 10]. For he was not restored to life by another power, as was the case with Lazarus and any others who came back to life [John 11, 43]. So must we not think of the resurrection of the Lord. On the contrary, the Only Begotten God raised up the man that had been mingled with him.[52] He separated his soul from his body and again united the two. In this way did the common salvation of our nature take place. Hence he is termed the 'Lord of life' [Acts. 3, 15]. In him who died and rose from the dead the Only Begotten God 'united the world to himself' [2 Cor. 5, 19]. By means of his own blood, which was the same as ours, he brought us back, like captives who had been taken in war, and who shared the same flesh and blood as he did. This is the meaning of the apostolic saying which says, 'In him we have redemption through his blood' [Eph. 1, 7]; the forgiveness of sins through his flesh.

154.21. This is our position, based on the words of the Apostle, unlike that of Apolinarius. Let everyone who judges assess with great care which of us is the more religious. Is it we who say that the glory dwells in our land in the Incarnation or is it as he says, that flesh was not *acquired* by the godhead, but was of one substance with it and came to be along with it.[53]

18 = 154.28. Whether or not Zachariah the prophet [cf. Zach. 13, 7] inclines in his mysterious language to one or other position hardly requires careful examination. It is not worth discussing whether the words refer to the Lord or to someone else. Zachariah says, 'Awake, O sword, against my shepherd and against my fellow tribesman'. We think the threat is uttered by Scripture against those who act unjustly towards their fellow men. Apolinarius, however, supposes the sword to be stirred up against the Lord because of the use of the singular 'shepherd', in the text. What he fails to appreciate is that it is often the usage of Scripture to apply terms like shepherd to those in authority.[54]

155.9. Again, his way of dragging the letter to the Hebrews, into his argument, for the same purpose, displays his ineptitude in his argument. Anyone can see this with only a modicum of intelligence. He interprets the words, 'In many and various ways God spoke of old to our fathers in the prophets; but now in these last days, he spoke to us in a son', [Heb. 1, 1] to mean that the humanity of the God who appeared to us was itself eternal. For he writes in this way, interpreting the Apostle according to the text. It is clear from the text, that the man who spoke to us the words of the Father is indeed god, the creator of the ages, 'the reflection of the glory of god, the very stamp of his nature', [cf. Heb. 1, 2/3]. This same was God in virtue of his own spirit and did not simply possess God within himself as someone distinct from himself. He through himself, that is, through his own flesh, purified the world of sins. This is what Apolinarius says on the text and, what he says, has in no way been distorted by us.[55]

155.27. If it was indeed a man who spoke these words, then he is also the maker of the ages, as our word spinner supposes, and his flesh is the reflection of God, while the form of a slave gives shape to the divine hypostasis. Should this be the case, it seems to me pointless to contest what has been said. The only appropriate response is to bewail this novel manner of talking for its lack of perception.

156.1. He who spoke to us after a human fashion using our language, who spat with his mouth and made clay with his hand, who put his fingers into the ears of the deaf and touched the sick and the dead, who relieved his weariness by sitting down and by sleep, who wept, was afraid, grieved and was hungry, had feelings, desired nourishment and asked for water, was a man. Is this very same, in his very flesh and humanity, really to be thought of as responsible for the ordering of all things, and is the nature of flesh, which is composite, hard and resistant, really God?

156.11. Let the ears of the pious be stopped and let not the divine and pure teachings be insulted and defiled with fleshly passions by those who reduce the Divine to human level.[56] For who is ignorant of the fact that the god who appeared to us in the flesh was on the one hand, in accordance with our pious tradition, immaterial, invisible and without parts and, further, always unlimited and without circumscription, everywhere present and penetrating the whole of creation;[57] on the other hand, in his appearance among us, he was seen in human shape? It is necessary that every body be encompassed by a surface and the surface of the body that is enclosed by it is its limit. And, whatever is circumscribed by a limit, is constricted by a definite size. Further, what is limited cannot at the same time be infinite. The prophet, however, says, 'There is no limit to his greatness' [Ps. 144, 3]. If, therefore, as our logician informs us, the divine nature is flesh; and if flesh is, of necessity, enclosed by the limit of its surface, how can the divine greatness, in accordance with the prophet, be infinite? Or how can the infinite be conceived by the finite, the unlimited through the limited?[58]

156.28. Or more importantly, as we have already said in what goes before, how may the strong come out of death? If, as he supposes, the man that spoke is the creator of the ages, then he did all things through himself, that is, through the flesh, according to Apolinarius. If, therefore, the divine voice is to be accepted when it says 'the flesh is weak' [cf. Matt. 26, 41] it follows that, if Apolinarius is to be trusted, that (all things coming from the flesh and the flesh being weak) weakness is the source of whatever is powerful and mighty and strong and of all noble and divine ideas.

19 = 157.10. Even that is not so bad, for as the argument progresses, in an examination of its logical sequence, it touches on blasphemy against the Father. He claims that the man is the radiance of God and that in a fleshly God which he, in his utterly foolish reasoning, has made into an idol, the very hypostasis of God is shaped. The ray has a family relationship to the sun, and the light which is reflected from the lamp, has a relationship to the original light, and the character of a particular man reflects human nature. It logically follows, therefore, that if what appeared among us is indeed, a 'reflection of the glory of the Father', and if the 'very stamp of that nature' is flesh [cf. Heb. 1, 3], the Father's nature must itself be fleshly. For he would never say that what is without body, could be expressed by a body, or again that what is unseen could shine forth from what cannot be seen. Instead, as is the glory, so too is the radiance, and as is the impression (character), so too is the reality. The consequence is that if one of the two is a body, the other cannot be without one.

157.27. At this point he has recourse to the teaching of Nicaea in which the synod of the fathers with one voice pronounced the 'consubstantial' (*homousios*). No one would claim that this meant 'of a different kind' (*heterogenes*). But, on the contrary, where there is one and the same nature, there the expression 'consubstantial' is completely applicable.[59] If, then, the Son is a fleshly God, being by nature what he is from all eternity, that is, flesh, and if, further, he is consubstantial with the Father – a fact not contested by our long-winded writer – and therefore they are consequently consubstantial with each other, being embraced under the same definition, then Apolinarius is forced to assume, that the nature of the Father is both human and fleshly. He must do this if he is to preserve the definition of consubstantial in both cases. He has only two possibilities before him. He must either admit that the Father is without a body, while the Son's deity is fleshly, in which case he must conclude that they are of different natures or, confessing the deity and nature of Father and Son to be the same, endow the divine nature, even of the Father, with flesh.

158.9. But, as if to correct this absurdity in the foregoing, he offers the following exegesis of the words of Zechariah [cf. Zech. 13, 7]. He argues that their natural reference is to the Father and to the Son and therefore that the expression 'of the same tribe' (*symphylos*) means 'of the same nature and consubstantial' (*homousios*). Whether or not he is correct in this assumption would require another argument, but what he proposes is as follows: 'The word of the prophet means by these expressions, not that he (sc. the Son) is

55

consubstantial with the God according to the flesh, but according to the Spirit, which is united to the flesh'.

158.17. But how is his fleshly god united to the flesh before the foundation of the world when the ages did not exist nor, indeed, anything else that is a part of creation? The flesh, however, is something very complex, and the last of the things that came to be in the created order. With what manner of flesh, therefore, was he united, seeing that human nature had not as yet sprung to existence? But perhaps he had some other form of flesh, quite distinct from that of a man's. And how can he say, that the very man, who spoke to us the things of the Father, is the same that made the ages? Who will explain to us the strangeness of these new riddles? [He writes of] a man existing before men came to exist, of flesh more ancient than its own manufacture; he speaks of that which came to exist only in these latter as being more ancient than the ages and of many other things which he discusses in this confused manner.

20 = 158.31. But our word-spinner, should he so wish, can lose himself in his obscure reasonings. We, however, using the same texts of the Apostle as he did,[60] in order to refute his impious assumptions, will carry on with the argument. He (sc. Paul) says 'He was in the form of God', not having a form like God's which would be said of one who was in the likeness of God, but 'being in the very form of God'. For everything that is in the Father is in the Son. This means that, in order that in every respect the form of the Father's character may be preserved in the Son, the Son must be eternal, without size, material and bodiless. In all these respects he must be the equal of God.

159.9. But how can such equality admit the idea of any difference or discrepancy? How can the idea of equality be applied to beings who are of different natures? If the one is fleshly, while the other is quite free of the flesh, how could anyone possibly claim that one thing was in any sense like something quite different?

159.14. Paul continues 'He emptied himself, taking the form of a servant', [Phil. 2, 7]. What is the form of a servant? Surely the body. We never heard from any of the fathers that it was something other than that. When, therefore, Paul said that he took the form of a slave, and the form is the flesh, he meant by this that he was one thing according to his divine nature and then assumed the form of a slave, which possessed a quite different nature. In fact, the use of the word 'emptied' clearly implies that he was not always what he appeared to us to be, but rather that he was in the fullness of his deity, equal to God, unapproachable, distant and, above all, incapable of being enclosed within the narrow confines (βραχύτητι) of human nothingness.

159.24. But once he had emptied himself, in the words of the Apostle, and become confined within the frail nature of flesh, he reduced the unspeakable glory of the godhead to the narrow limits of our humanity, with the result that, while remaining on one hand great, perfect and incomprehensible, what he assumed was of equal dimension to the limits of our own nature. For the words, 'being in the likeness and appearance of a man' [Phil. 2, 7] make it perfectly clear that he was not surrounded with this nature in the beginning, nor was he shaped after a bodily fashion. For how should a shape be impressed upon that which is without a body? Only then did he acquire an outward shape, when he fashioned a form for himself and so circumscribed himself. In other words, he took a body for himself.

21 = 160.3. 'Being found as a man' [Phil. 2, 7] – he was indeed truly a man, even if not so in every respect – but 'as a man' because of the mystery of the virginity (sc. of Mary), and this in order to make it perfectly clear that he was not subject to the laws of human nature in everything. Instead, it was in a divine manner that he came as a dweller among us and had no need of the cooperation that comes from marriage for the construction of his own body. He was found, therefore, 'as a man', because he was not in every respect like a normal man, simply because of the unusual mode of his formation.[61]

160.11. So 'he humbled himself' [Phil. 2, 8] and without himself changing, became a man. If he had been such from the beginning, of what did his self-abasement consist? But as it is, the most high humbled himself, for the sake of union with the lowly state of our nature. Once he had been united with the form of the slave which he assumed, and so become one with it, he made his own the passions of the slave. As it happens in our case, because of the cohesion of the limbs of the body, if something falls even on the tip of a nail, everything suffers with the suffering part and the awareness spreads to the whole body so, too, he who is united to our nature makes his own our sufferings, even as Isaiah says, 'He took our weaknesses and bore our diseases' [Is. 53, 5], enduring the blow for our sake in order that, by his stripe, we might be healed. Not, of course, that the godhead itself was bruised.[62]

160.26. All this took place that the road of death might be undone, in exactly the same way as it had taken place. For as it was through disobedience that the death of the first man occurred, for that reason it was through the obedience of the second man that death was exiled. Therefore did he become obedient unto death in order that through his obedience he might remedy the disorder that had entered through disobedience and, by rising from the dead, might annihilate the death which entered through disobedience. For the resurrection of man from death spells the destruction of death.

161.5. 'Therefore', it says, 'God exalted him' [Phil. 2, 9]. This is, as it were, the seal of the previous conception. It is quite clear that the most high is in no need of further exaltation; on the contrary, it is the lowly that is exalted, becoming now what it was not previously. For human nature, being united with the Lord, is raised up along with the deity and that which is exalted is the same as that which had been lowly. It was the form of a slave, that was lowly and which subsequently became Christ and Lord through its exaltation.

161.13. Now the human side of Christ, in accordance with normal human custom, was named by a particular name which he had received through the revelation (μυσταγωγία) made by Gabriel to the maiden, and the name of his humanity, as has been said, was Jesus. His divine nature, however, cannot be expressed by a name but the two [sc. the divine and human natures] became one through their co-mingling (*anakrasis*). For that reason God receives his name from his humanity.[63]

161.19. 'For at the name of Jesus every knee shall bow', [Phil. 2, 10] and a man becomes 'above every name'. This is a distinctive feature of the deity which cannot be expressed by means of a particular designation. The aim is that what is lofty came to be lowly, so what is lowly should put on lofty titles (ἰδιώματα).[64] As the deity is named through the man, so that which has been raised up to the deity from its lowly state, acquires a 'name which is above every name'. In a like fashion, the dishonour attaching to the form of a slave rises to a higher plane where it is made equal to the deity, mingled with the slave. And, as the honour offered to the deity by the whole of creation is now accorded to the one who is united to the deity so, too, 'In the name of Jesus Christ, every knee shall bow, of things in heaven, on earth and under the earth, and every tongue shall confess Jesus Christ is Lord to the glory of God the Father' [Phil. 2, 10].

3

GREGORY AND PHILOSOPHY

1. CONTRA FATUM

Introduction

Something has already been said about Gregory's indebtedness to philosophy and about the difficulty of isolating both the areas and extent of this indebtedness. Most of his surviving work has a specifically Christian audience in view and the themes he treats would have held little interest for a pagan readership. Therefore, it is in the area of underlying and general principle rather than in the arena of overtly philosophical concern that his colonization of a dependence on the Platonic tradition is to be found.

A word must be said about this tradition. It was by no means dead by the second third of the fourth century. Three great names enhanced its reputation in the third and fourth centuries AD. Plotinus, sometimes regarded by more modern writers as something of a heretic in his own school, was the last truly great philosopher of Greece. Born in Alexandria in 205, he studied there under, among others, Ammonius Saccas, who had also taught Plotinus' older contemporary, Origen (185–254). The tradition of reverent criticism and reconstruction of traditional Platonism, begun by Plotinus, was continued by his own admiring disciple and biographer, Porphyry 230–c. 306/7 AD. He it was that organized the writings of the master into the six *Enneads* we now possess, although doubts have been raised about the extent of his understanding of, or adhesion to, the great lines of Plotinian metaphysics.

It is hard for us to realize what a truly great and revolutionary thinker Plotinus really was. His interest in the inner world and the mystical experience that marks it has been found so attractive by such very different people that his untypicality for later Platonism hardly strikes us. Porphyry reminds us of his austere attitude in *Life of Plotinus* (10). His pupil, Amelius, is said to have urged him to celebrate with him 'the day of the moon and other holy days'. To this invitation Amelius received from the Master the famous and chilling rebuff, 'It is for those beings to come to me, not I to them'. Hardly surprisingly such an attitude failed to endear him to later Platonists; he is rarely cited by them. Had not the divine Plato himself and his master, Socrates, sacrificed to the gods, as witnessed by the opening words of the *Republic* and the closing words of the *Phaedo*? Even Aristotle, generally regarded as areligious was, perhaps maliciously, reported to have ordered the erection of statues to Zeus and Hera in his will.

Iamblichus was a very different figure. He was 'born in Chalcis in the region of Coele Syria'[1] sometime during the second half of the third century AD. The only credible element in his life is that he began as a pupil of Anatolius and later studied under Porphyry. He is credited with having rerouted Platonism into a more recognizably religious and ritualistic path. Despite or, more likely, because of this, he became the favoured philosopher of the emperor Julian (ob. 363) and is always termed 'the divine', an epithet regularly applied by Gregory of Nyssa to the Apostle Paul. His principal surviving work, *De Mysteriis (On the Mysteries)*, was written sometime before 325 AD in defence of the practice of theurgy, which was apparently attacked by his master Porphyry in his *Letter to Anebo*. Professor Dodds in *The Greeks and the Irrational* (p. 287) describes *De Mysteriis* as 'a manifesto of irrationalism' – 'an assertion that the road to salvation is found not in reason but in ritual'. It is only fair to note that although it is true that he has much to say about the importance of theurgy as uniting us to the divine, Iamblichus also makes it clear that he is not rejecting the teaching of others, presumably Porphyry, and not rejecting it outright.[2]

Julian never lived to implement fully the pagan renaissance. It led him to inhibit Christians from teaching by means of his *School Law*,[3] and to embark upon a programme of teaching and beneficence, both 'copied' from the Christians. On the educational front he saw to the writing of a sort of pagan 'catechism' by one of his functionaries, Saturninus Salu(s)tius Secundus. On his arrival in Constantinople on 11 December 361, Julian made Salustius Praefectus Orientis and induced him to write his *De Dis et Mundo (On the Gods and the World)*. This short treatise occupies only twenty one chapters and attempts to bring together cult and philosophy, oriental mysticism and traditional religiosity.[4] The themes treated include the nature of god and of the gods, of the world and of human nature, of fate, or virtue and vice, the origin and nature of evil, punishment, (essentially remedial) and the transmigration of souls. Even such a brief account of the contents shows both its traditionally classical character and its similarity with but, more importantly, its difference from, Christian treatments of basic teaching. We hear nothing of the Trinity or the Incarnation or the sacraments, although, to be fair, the inner nature of God, his eternity, existence, power and moral goodness are themes shared in common by Origen, Gregory of Nyssa and Salustius. A few of the topics addressed are 'pagan' in tone, but not aggressively so. For example, chapter 16 entitled *On Sacrifices* and chapter 20, *On Reincarnation*, despite their evident Hellenistic feel, might be at home in a Christian treatise on the Mass or the after life. To judge by the paucity of surviving manuscripts it was never widely used – a fate it shared in common with the *Meditations* of Marcus Aurelius.

It is impossible to say, as was hinted earlier, how much pagan philosophy Gregory was acquainted with. The *Praeparatio Evangelica* of Eusebius of Caesarea had saved Christian writers from the necessity of individual research by providing them ready made, as it were, with a collection of passages from the main Hellenic sources which might be thought to shed some light on the gospel. It is still true that on some issues, despite their Christian dress, the problem addressed was essentially philosophical or could be re-expressed in philosophical language without doing injustice to the basic problem. So, for example, Gregory believed both that there would be universal salvation for all, even for the devil, in other words the restoration of all things[5] by a sort of universal law or principle, *and* that we all possess indestructible freedom, the primal image of God, which makes us godlike and remains with us even after the initial fall. How is one to reconcile necessity and freedom? This problem is not particularly Christian and had occupied the best minds in antiquity, above all when they tried to come to terms with the idea of fate and that of pattern, order and freedom in the world.

Since Homer wrote his poems, if not before, the problem of the interrelationship between fate and the gods, between human freedom and an overarching determinism or pattern, had not been far away. Even in the Homeric poems we can trace a shift from the powerlessness of the divine before fate in *Iliad* xvi.434 to a greater measure of divine control at *Odyssey* xix.592. Plato also wrestled with the problem in the last book of the *Republic*, and Aristotle was commonly, though erroneously, supposed to have limited the realm of providence to the superlunary sphere. It is with Carneades (214–129 BC), surnamed 'dux academiae novae', a sceptic of the Platonic school, that we find some of the most complex answers to the problems posed by astral determinism and genethliology. His arguments were taken up, often without acknowledgement, by all writers, whether Hellenistic or Christian.

This whole topic has been fruitfully explored by Dom Amand in his copious study.[6] Among the pagans who owed a debt to Carneades were Cicero and Alexander: Cicero in *De Divinatione*; Alexander of Aphrodisias (flourished 200 AD), a follower and acute commentator of Aristotle, in *De Fato*. Three *Enneads* of Plotinus, ii.3 *Are the Stars Causes?*, iii.1 *On Fate* and iii.2 and 3 *Two Treatises on Providence*, address this issue and show dependence on Alexander.

Christian writers also wrestled with the problem. Donald Sykes, in his commentary *St Gregory of Nazianzus, Poemata Arcana*, p. 180 (Oxford: Clarendon Press, 1997), provides a useful survey of the Patristic evidence and modern discussions. He cites, *inter alia*, Tatian, *Oration against the Greeks* 8. Origen's anti-Gnostic polemic made him a vigorous champion of human freedom, as is clear from *On First Principles*, iii.3, 2–3 and *Against Celsus* iv.3. In the former of these passages Origen argues that the evil powers of this world may foresee on occasion what is to happen, but are unable to influence affairs. Plotinus, Origen's younger contemporary, held a similar view, 'the stars may indicate, without causing, the future' (*Ennead* 2.3.7).

Among the Cappadocians the issue had been discussed by Basil in his *Homilies on the Hexameron*,[7] itself the genesis of Dom Amand's study. As Sykes notes (op. cit., page 183), speaking of Gregory of Nazianzus, 'There can be no doubt that in addressing himself to astrology, Gregory was attacking a contemporary problem.'

In the West the influence of Carneades is also perceptible in Augustine's treatment of the problem of fate in his *On Christian Teaching* 2.xxii.32. Gregory of Nyssa's own very thorough and fair minded treatment of the subject occurs in his treatise *Contra Fatum*. The treatise – according to Dom Amand – is 'entirely philosophic' (p. 430) and 'merits thorough attention by specialists in Hellenistic philosophy'. It is to the study of this illuminating work that we now turn.

As to the dating of *Contra Fatum*, it is impossible to be certain. A note on page 31 of the Leiden edition[8] suggests that the occasion may have been an encounter with a philosopher in the course of the council of Constantinople of 381. It is also suggested that the addressee of the work, written in the form of a letter, was his own brother, Peter, bishop of Sebaste in Armenia. This suggestion arises from the superscription in one of the older manuscripts, S, which reads 'To his brother Peter', but we have no further means of proving this suggestion.

The form of the letter is largely artificial. It begins, indeed, with an address, in the second person singular, '$Μεμνῆσαι$', 'you remember' but there is little attempt made to continue the illusion. Although the work is peppered with an uncharacteristically large number of $ἐγω$ $δέ$, these serve to preserve the marginally more probable fiction of an actual dialogue with a fatalist, rather than the less plausible one of a letter to a brother. This is not the only occasion when Gregory made it his business to use the letter form in which to enshrine his thoughts. We find the same in his *Life of Macrina*, although there Gregory himself discusses his use of the form in the prologue.[9]

The treatise itself divides into three unequal sections: (1) It opens with a short prologue providing the *mise en scene*. Apparently the addressee had asked Gregory to provide him with a transcript of a discussion held with a philosopher in 'the great city of Constantine' on the subject of fate (31, 3–32.9); (2) Section 2 is devoted to a full and fair account of the objections to freedom and defence of fate on the part of the unnamed disputant. Conversion, he argues, is a matter of determinism and we can do little or nothing about it. Stoic arguments and those derived from a form of astral power and movement are then expanded. The idea of God is either dismissed or identified with the force of fate itself (32.10–39.13); (3) Section 3, by far the longest, contains an elaborate critique of the whole determinist thesis and deploys many of the familiar tropes of Carneades, with which to defuse its case (39.14–63.11).

The treatise possesses considerable interest from several points of view. It illustrates the simple fact that astral determinism was a live issue at the time of writing. It shows Gregory's acquaintance with and dependence upon Hellenistic, anti-fatalist arguments. It also shows how important it was for Gregory to establish the reality of freedom, which played so large a role in his own thinking.

Translation

(1) Prologue

Doubtless you recall what happened to me on the occasion that, to use the language of the gospel, [cf. Matt. 17, 20] the great mountain of unbelief was transformed into faith at your house. This happened because Eusebius gave advice worthy of his grey hairs, that is if we are to assign responsibility to human agency and not rather to the divine assistance of one who disposes all human affairs for our good. I was filled with amazement at this extraordinary event, that one who had been once so lacking in belief had now, by the immensity of his faith, far exceeded the amount of his unbelief.

As our fellowship carried on, a discussion arose among us on the subject of fate and you charged me, my dear fellow, to provide you with an account by letter of the discussion between myself and a philosopher on the subject of fate that took place in Constantinople. Having a little leisure at my disposal I have reduced the discussion to size and lay it before you in a simple unartificial narrative, taking particular care not to exceed the limits imposed by a letter, by allowing the treatise to become a book.

(2) The objections to freedom

32.10. I produced for the benefit of the man who was trained in secular wisdom as I could guess at from what he said, the arguments of our faith and tried to persuade him by means of arguments derived from Hellenism to accept the truth of our teaching. He, however, spent some time endeavouring to establish that we do not possess the power to achieve what we want to do, and that human life is under the control of necessity, without which nothing would take place of the things that do take place. With the following argument he endeavoured to disprove my own by saying that if it were fated for him to become a Christian he would become one in any case, even if we did not want him to; and conversely that if he were prevented by the necessity of fate, it would be utterly impossible to discover a way of exercising compulsion on fate.

32.22. As he spoke, I naturally supposed that he was trying to avoid learning about the faith by means of his Hellenism and that in this way he was trying to upset the logic of my case. But he persisted in the same arguments and claimed that everything was bound by the necessity of fate, which was in charge of everything. All things yield to its wish and that includes length of life, differences of customs, choices of life, structures of bodies and differences of reputation. He who rises to authority does so in obedience to fate, and in the same way slavery, wealth and poverty attend upon fate. Strength and weakness of body, brevity and length of life depend on the same cause. (Brevity of life and longevity do not arise from our own drives, but depend entirely upon necessity.)

33.14. Further the manner of death, natural or forced, is allotted by necessity and, again, where it is a question of violent death, all the varied types are fated, whether they be accidental or by strangling, by judicial vote or by plot. To these he added more universal and all embracing sufferings, earthquakes, shipwrecks, floods and conflagrations and all that sort of evil attributing them all to the same cause. He insisted that it was not the reason of the chooser that was responsible for the varied activities of life, but whether they be philosophy, rhetoric, farming, sailing, living a married or unmarried life – all serve the iron hand of fate. Necessity is lord even of virtue and vice.

33.27. This means, he went on, that an unalterable fate assigns to one man the higher life (ζωή), in a life (βίος) that is without possessions and free from restraint, while another for the same reason becomes a graverobber or a pirate, leads a life of profligacy or becomes debauched among prostitutes. He went through all these and thought he had adequately demonstrated that our reason is not responsible for what we do, and that it does not rest with us to execute whatever we will, but that we must instead wait upon the power of fate. Once necessity provides the starting point for such an impulse, reason must follow, even unwillingly. But without it, however strongly we may will, we are rendered impotent.

34.11. While he was discoursing after this fashion I asked him if he supposed that he who had power over all things and was called by the name of fate, was some god, by whose will everything was ordered. Spying the foolishness of my question he said, 'You seem to know nothing of the heavens, otherwise you would have known the power of fate and the source and nature of the control it exercises over all things that happen in unalterable sequence.'

34.18. I was so perturbed by what he said and so eager to achieve greater clarity that I asked him whether he supposed that fate was some power of free and sovereign choice existing in an exalted empyreon or was something quite different from that. At this he once again rehearsed the same argument and said: 'Anyone who has considered the movement of the heavenly beings, the circle of the zodiac and its twelve divisions divided by equal intervals from each other by the circumscription of the separate animals; whoever has considered the power of each of the stars, both their individual strength and the combined effect of their mixture with each other, as occurs when the particular character of each is either close to or separated from another sign; whoever has considered the effect of the declension of the lower sign or the eclipse and restoration in its passage of the higher one, the varied configurations of the stars as they come together and separate, creating as they do so triangles, some of them irregular, others of another geometrical configuration; anyone,' he said, 'who understands these things will appreciate the meaning of fate. He will understand that under the name of fate is embraced whatever is achieved by the varying combinations of the stars joining things together in an unbroken chain.'

35.17. Since this dismayed me yet again (being untutored in this wisdom I grasped nothing of what was being said) I asked him to explain to me the meaning of fate through language I was capable of understanding. I told him I had heard also from others all about the circular movements of the stars and their varied relations to each other, their opposite motions as they are whirled round in an undeviating circle, as they revolve in the circle of the zodiac. As a result of this I had no doubt that the lights of the stars grew near to and separated from each other in accordance with the circular motion of each, that the lower went down and the upper was hidden from our eyes, should it happen to get behind the back of the descending star. All these things and others like them I was able to infer.

36.6. I also understood what pattern is created by them, when the circle leads the star that lies in it back to its original position by its own motion so that it either crosses straight over the passage of what lies above or turns aside from its course. The length of time could either be brief or more lengthy according to the size of the circles traced by each, which makes the turning round either faster or slower.

36.14. I asked him to say nothing on such matters as these and simply to reveal to me clearly the power of fate, and to tell me whether it was some god that bore the name of fate, who was endowed with power over all things and who ordered all things with authority in accordance with his design by the superiority of his great might.

Perhaps he supposed the power of fate was itself the slave of some higher power so that, in some sense, fate lay under the control of some higher cause. If, however, it is believed to have power over all things, the logic of the argument prevents us from assuming that anything is superior to it. But, if he argues that fate depends on the motion of the stars and then itself controls all else by force, it would be far safer to assign almighty power to what leads than to what merely follows. In that way the stars, or the unchanging circular motion, or the cycles that exist within them, or the ecliptic would be master of everything. If, for the sake of argument, it is said that they do not move at all either in endless cycles among each other or from each other, but that they always remain in the same position, this would not preserve (the concept of) fate. For if the motion of the stars gives birth to fate, then fate, which is subject to a superior cause is wrongly said to be in control of everything else, even if there be no motion at all.

37.12. At this the philosopher said, 'It is not the intention of our argument to suggest that fate is to be thought of as existing by itself in its own individuality (ὑπόστασις). Rather do we mean that there is one universal sympathy and a continuity which unites the all to itself and each individual object within the all (τὸ πᾶν) as is the case in one body. All the elements are in harmony with one another, the upper sphere (*lexis*)[10] is in control, while the things on earth are all in agreement with what leads them and look in their direction.

Things here of necessity move in accordance with the upper motion, the difference resulting from the respective power of the separate stars. In medicine, for example, if differing qualities of elements are mixed according to differing proportions they produce something quite distinct from the original items and from what each was before the mixture with each other. In a similar fashion, although the astral powers each possess an individuality all of their own, the interweaving (συμπλοκή) of their differing characteristics, as they approach to and depart from each other, produces varied differences in the lives of those so influenced. It is as though there is some great influence [sc. of the stars] coming down uninterruptedly from them to us. It is for this reason that the predictions of those who have carefully studied such matters never go astray.

38.12. So too, an experienced doctor can predict the outcome of mixing such diverse elements as the warm or the numbing with the salty or the astringent and can also foretell the particular character and effect of the mixture of opposites. He can also predict the extent of its (sc. the mixture's) powers and its potential for destruction and preservation. So, whoever devotes himself attentively to the things above and grasps the nature of each separate being, will know what the power from each separate conjunction will effect.

38.19. But the influence from each is not always in every respect self consistent. This same influence, because of its constant mobility, necessarily produces the movement of closely connected stars; it is itself ever undergoing change because it is so closely connected with the otherness that is produced by change. It is always intimately connected with the variousness of change, forever varying with the movement of the stars.[11] Each of us that enters life receives that portion of fate which is allotted to him at the exact moment of his birth and becomes whatever that particular moment designs and intends for him.

39.3. Even as, when a seal has been impressed upon wax, the shape of the image remains, the same holds good for the life of man. Whatever portion of the power that emanates from the motion of the stars falls to our lot, in accordance with that portion each one of us is fashioned and becomes whatever his particular fate has in store for him, immediately on his entry into life. Once he has been sealed with it in accordance with the power that derives from above, he is of necessity fashioned in accordance with it in his own particular life. Whatever he does or endures, he does in accordance with the principles and causes that emanate from the primary influence of the stars.'

39.14. As he carried on talking I said to him, 'Will you never stop this senseless chatter, maintaining as you do that an indivisible point is itself the cause of our sharing in all the things that flow down to us in a particular moment of time from above? You fail to tell us if this cause is alive and capable of making decisions. Nor, again, are you able to show us how it is that what is itself lifeless, insubstantial and without the power to act at all, is capable of governing things full of life. Instead, you establish as tyrant and master over all beings that are possessed of counsel, rational forethought, education, diligence and virtuous action, a reality that is itself devoid of life and choice. You elevate what is unstable, passing, indivisible and insubstantial above reason.

40.2. By making the setting up and preservation of all beings depend upon its (sc. fate's) power do you not realise the inconveniences your argument leads to? For if the fate which proceeds from the emanation possesses such power that it can determine the outcome of whatever comes to be from the first moment of its existence, it must follow that it exercises its power not consequentially but principally *"ouk apokoluthetikos all proegumenos"*.[12]

40.8. It will, therefore, precede the child that is being born and will not subserve the accident of birth. But it is quite unclear when two people are born at precisely the same moment of time, which of the two comes first. For a man, even before he comes from his mother's loins, is already somehow in motion, being moved through either diminution or growth (for this is a type of motion) while the star, even before man draws breath moves about, and is not stationary. The concurrence of two realities, both in motion, which happen to coincide with each other, renders impossible any judgment about their respective priority. *They* are moved in their cycles; *it* (sc. the unborn child) makes its way naturally. If their coincidence takes place in the same moment of time, in what way are they distinct from one another, so that one is more powerful than the other ? For if man exists because of the stars, his nature would entirely disappear, if there were not the slightest gap between them (sc. the stars) and the appearance of the man.[13] But if, on the other hand, there are many gaps among things that take place, this is proof positive that human birth does not depend on the motion of the stars. Stars are always in motion, the child is not always being born. Rather does the child proceed by its own natural sequence on its own and there is no necessity (ananké) which joins together things disparate in nature.[14]

41.5. But if your argument seeks to establish that the cause of all that happens to us in life is dependent on a particular moment of time, consider for a moment how many kings and tyrants have been disposed of in the course of one day and night. Each day is divided into small and indivisible portions of time, first of all into twenty four hours of day and night, then each hour is itself subdivided into sixty minutes, finally each of the minutes is itself subdivided into the same number of seconds. Those of your number who have investigated the subject with great precision argue that each of these small divisions can again be subdivided into an equal number of very small units. The sum total of these infinitesimal points, which are our gods, masters, tyrants – call them what you will – amounts to more than 210,000 units. If one hour contains so many tens of thousands, twenty four hours multiplied by the ratio of one produces tens of thousands of parts ($\mu o \hat{\iota} \rho a \iota$ = fates).

41.22. But your argument insists that each of these portions has an invincible power. Hence it follows that none of them is idle. For who would ever claim that ineffectiveness could be the particular characteristic of power? Rather, is it in activity (*energeia*) that we recognize power? So, also, are the outworkings (ἀποτελέσματα) of power. From this it follows that the number of temporal subdivisions should of necessity be reflected in the number of births that take place every hour. And if to each segment we ought to assign equal power, the equality of that power displays itself upon all rulers alike, the long lived, the powerful, the fortunate, the happy and whatever is of more honourable status (λῆξις).

42.7. Deficiency in any of these is a sure indication of imperfection of power. No one would attribute equal power to one who achieved both great and little effects. One man lives for over a hundred years in prosperous and happy old age, surrounded by his children, attended by his descendants, rejoicing in his many offspring, healthy, without pain, full of honour, without sorrow, with abundance of wealth, enjoying whatever is thought of as honourable, as this world sees it, pronounced blessed by all. Another is suffocated straightaway at birth, something that often happens to children born of fornication or adultery. Their mothers who bore them outside marriage strangle them with their own hands and by their death endeavour to remove the reproach that should be theirs.

42.19. Where is the power of fate in their case? How is it that the strength of destiny failed to preserve them for the same length of life? If your argument assigns power to fate, its power will appear evenly everywhere. It will not be powerful in some areas and not in others if it really is assumed to be powerful and its power is demonstrated in its achievements. Life should demonstrate no inequalities, if everything displays equally the highest degree of happiness, simply because on your argument all things lie under the control of fate and because you assert the universal equality of its power. If, therefore, fate has a universal and equal power, it will be in control in all situations.

43.5. In fact, however, many and various differences of life befall men in their distinction and prosperity, in their length of life, the constitution of their bodies and in everything else which makes a man happy or wretched. The inequality of what actually occurs clearly displays the feebleness of the fate or destiny they have constructed. For if length of life is a product of power, then most assuredly will brevity of life be the result of weakness. In such a case it will be necessary to postulate the weakness of some, and the power of other, fates. And as brevity of life is the very reverse of longevity, both of them must necessarily arise from opposites. No one would derive happiness and misery from the same cause.

43.17. If the one came to be through power, the other most certainly does not owe its existence to failure of power. Wretchedness cannot be understood in any other way than as the inability to become happy. But there are far more wretched people in life than the opposite, which displays the frailty of fate rather than its power. Where, then, is this invincible, all powerful irresistible necessity, upon whose mighty shoulders rests the control of whatever occurs in this world? Surely the logic of our argument has found it wanting in the majority of cases.

43.27. 'But', you will say, 'Fate designs one thing for this person and another thing for another, and in either case it can do what it wants'. You are therefore, I suppose, quite capable of producing a reason for the difference in choices. Let us take the case of two distinct men. You can see no difference of nature in either case. Neither the one nor the other has become noble or evil by a deliberate act of choice on his own part. One leapt from his mother's womb just a fraction of a moment before the other, such being the accidental working of nature, the other came after him, either at once or after a brief interval. And for that very reason (sc. on your argument) the pair of them have different lives assigned to them. The one is blessed or a king, perhaps, surrounded with gold and purple from his earliest days, while the other is a pauper or a slave, without even rags to be wrapped round with by his parents.

What wrong had the latter done, in being just a fraction of a moment before or after the other? For it was not as a consequence of his own decision, but of a movement of nature, that he received this dishonour as his lot in life. What sort of excuse will you find for your mistress on such a charge as this? Where is justice, where is piety, where is holiness? Or do you claim that fate has no interest in such matters, that she has no concern for virtue, and has no care for anything good?

44.19. But, if she cares for none of these matters, perhaps all her care is expended on the opposite. For aversion from the good naturally implies some familiarity with the opposite. But perhaps you have no mind to assign one or the other to her. Does that mean that you suppose her to be soulless, choiceless, unaware of the difference between good and evil if, that is, she has neither soul, nor choice, nor knowledge of the separate characters of good and evil? On your understanding of the issue, she is supposed to possess such power that she is in charge of and controls all beings with the power of choice, and though she is herself without any substantial existence, is able to control things which are real. Again, she (sc. fate) who is herself without life is mistress of things that live, and though herself soulless rules what things that are ensouled, she who is without the power of choice controls things that live with choice, what is without virtue is ruler of beings who pursue it, and in general, what does not exist, is lord of what does.

45.6. In what then does the reality (ὑπόστασις) of this much discussed name consist? It is not a living being, nor is it capable of definition, nor do we suppose it to be a god. For how could what has no interest in either virtue or justice be god?[15] What, then, is that which is none of these things? But it may be you fancy that fate is simply the perpetual existence of time. For time always accompanies every motion of the rivers, of stars and of men. It hardly matters whether one sits beside the water and measures the intervals of omnipresent time by the movement of the water, or of a ship carried along by the wind, or of men on a journey, or the motions of the stars. There is one measure of the movement of beings in motion that is the change from the position in which one is to that in which one is not.

45.19. But, if neither the motion of streams, nor the movement of ships, nor the journeyings of men, which indicate the passage of time, if none of these causes fate, how does it come about that you create out of the temporal divisions of the movements of the stars, the genesis of fate, and claim that this hour or this small division of an hour, that is signified by the sign of the movement of the stars causes fate? Why can we not say that the births of men are not influenced by every possible movement (sc. of water or stars)?[16]

46.3. I shall repeat, once more, the same argument. The source of the favourable or unfavourable state of a man is the same as the source of his existence in the first place. If the cause of someone's present condition is of a particular kind, so too will be the cause of his birth. On the contrary, if the birth does not owe its existence to those causes, neither will what follows the birth. But the reason for denying the influence of those causes (sc. fate) upon the birth, is quite clear. It is quite impossible for human births of children that are born, which take place at intervals of time, to depend upon the uninterrupted passage of time, after the fashion of a river. But, of the generation of those fates, which time works out as it flows by with the endless revolution of the stars, it is quite impossible to discover the slightest interval, either in imagination or thought.

46.15. No amount of careful argument has as yet been able to grasp the character of this fate. It is unclear if it be one power that is responsible for everything or many small powers, temporally distinct from each other. Do you say that the stars move? We advance the same claim for movement of rivers. But, say you, the stars are everywhere operative. We make the same claim for rivers. They, you say, are in time. So, too, are ours. But, in their case (sc. the stars) it is impossible to discover their temporal beginning. But in the case of rivers, where will you be able to find a beginning? But they (again, the stars) always move in exactly the same way. But no one would be able to discover a contrary motion on the part of water, which always flows from what is elevated to what is level. The consequence is that either you grant us that the movement of the rivers begets fates, or we will not grant to the movement of the stars any such power.'

(The rest of this treatise continues to explore the ways in which the imagined fatalist would reply to Gregory's strictures on his position and then offers its own analysis of the reply. So the argument is carried forward. It ends [62.15–63.11] by suggesting that the success of such false views is largely a result of demonic power, which in its turn owes its effectiveness to our failure to direct our attention to the 'all powerful authority of God'.)

2. ORATIO CATECHETICA 19–24

Introduction

Gregory's interest in the views of contemporary Neoplatonism was not restricted to refutations of their erroneous views (as he saw them) about the respective roles of fate and freedom in the created order. He was also aware of *their* criticism of Christian doctrine. Indeed, it is not too much to say that the vast majority of his *Oratio Catechetica* or *Address on Religious Education* (= *Or. Cat.*) is conceived of as a refutation of philosophical objections, twenty six in all, to Christianity.

In this respect, it is interesting to contrast Gregory's approach with that of his younger contemporary Augustine, who in a similar work, *De catechizandis rudibus*, written only twenty years later in c.405, presents a very different picture. Augustine seems not to allude at all to the pagan opposition, but contents himself with appeals to morality and the Old Testament. It would appear that a remarkable change had occurred in the climate of opinion in those years, even if account be taken of the differing audience and locality of the addressees. This is all the more remarkable if it be remembered that although Augustine on several occasions acknowledges his indebtedness to Platonism, as for example in his *Confessions*, for emancipating him from the heresy of the Manichees, on no occasion does Gregory confess any debt whatever to any non-Christian author.

The central accusation levelled against the Gospel, which Gregory is repeatedly challenged to refute, is that to accept the Gospel means a rejection of the noble ideas of the deity which all philosophers would accept. For his purposes, therefore, he must show that the God he preaches not only meets the highest demands of the critic, but is in every important respect superior to them. This means that it is up to Gregory to prove that the two crucial doctrines of Christianity, the Trinity and the Incarnation, far from upsetting the highest ideas of God current among the Platonists, actually reinforce them, by going beyond them.

Gregory's method and basic intention can be glimpsed both in the underlying structure of his work and in the vocabulary which he employs. As was mentioned above, the *Or. Cat.*, not unlike Athanasius' *On the Incarnation*, is primarily geared to defend the time and method of the Incarnation of the eternal Word. However, despite this similarity and certain other areas of possible dependence of Gregory upon Athanasius, Gregory gives the objections of the Hellenists a far more lengthy airing than does his less philosophically conscious predecessor.

So he addresses the following problems: How can God be One if he be accompanied by Son and Spirit? (= chapters 1–4). Then he turns to the central thrust of his treatise, the attempt to harmonize the Incarnation/Redemption with the idea of the divine fittingness or *Theoprepeia*. In his Index III 'Greek Words' in his edition of the *Catechetichal Oration* (Cambridge: CUP, 1903) Srawley lists over ten occurrences of this word and idea, and his list is by no means complete. Gregory leaves us in no doubt about the precise meaning of this term. In chapter 1 he insists that God to be God or, as he more frequently states, 'the divine *To Theion* to be divine' must instantiate the following characteristics, 'power, goodness, wisdom, immortality and eternity and any other fitting idea'. To this collection of attributes Gregory later adds justice, primarily in order to answer the objection that 'If God really *is* powerful why does He not save by a mighty act of power?' (cf. especially chapter 17).

But what for our purposes is important is that in his treatment of these issues the terms of the debate are dictated by an idea of the Deity, which owes as much to Plato and Origen's adaptation of Plato in, for example, his *Contra Celsum* 3.70, as it does to any specifically Jewish or Christian account of the Godhead. One has only to recall the notion of the divine justice as it appears in St Paul, above all in the *Letter to the Romans*, primarily in chapters 9 to 11, and especially 9.15; 16, and later in St Augustine's *Enchiridion* 32 and 98, to detect the difference. For neither of these writers is God, as it were, 'hampered' by the consideration of human justice. For them the thought of philosophically conceived justice as outlined, for instance, in book 5 of the *Nicomachean Ethics* of Aristotle, seems not to affect their perception of the idea of the divine justice and election. For Gregory, on the other hand, what we naturally understand by the word is determinative also for God.

The following passage from Gregory's *Or. Cat.* will help to illustrate the way in which he relates the specifically Christian doctrine of the Incarnation to the traditional philosophical understanding of the Divine as powerful, wise, just and good. Chapters 19 to 22 are envisaged as a defence of the delay in the redemption of the world and, further, as an answer to the pressing question, also treated by Athanasius in *De Incarnatione* 44, and by Gregory in chapters 15 and 17, about the manner of the redemption. 'Why', runs the objection, 'was the work not effected by a simple "fiat" (*horme thelematos, thelemati mono*) on the part of God, without any need for an Incarnation and Cross?' In other words, if God is truly all powerful, could he not have simply annulled the power of evil and rescued the human race from the effects of sin, without resorting to the costly and unnecessary expedient of becoming man? To this charge Gregory begins by replying that we should not question the divine methods of pedagogy (chapter 17). Again, the effects of the Incarnation, above all in the shape of the disappearance of idolatry, attest the reality of Christ's work (chapter 18). At this point, Gregory seems to admit that his answers so far may have failed to satisfy either Jews or Greeks and to their difficulties he now turns.

Translation

Chapters 19–24

19. But since what we have produced fails to persuade either the Greeks or the leaders of Jewish thought (δογματων) of the divine presence, it would be an excellent notion to discuss the charges against us individually, and so to try and explain why it is that the divine nature mingles with ours in order to save the human race through itself, rather than achieving its purposes by a simple command. What might then be the beginning that would conduct our argument by a proper chain of reasoning *akolouthos* to the conclusion we have set before us? Could there be any other than going through orthodox conceptions about God, one by one?

20. Everyone agrees that we must confess the divine (τὸ θεῖον) to be not only powerful, but also just, good and wise, and whatever leads the mind upwards to some nobler idea. It follows, therefore, that in the case of the present dispensation (= the Incarnation) (ἡ πάρουσα οἰκονομία), it is not reasonable that one or another of the divine attributes should tend to be manifested in history, while another is absent. For speaking generally, it is not right that one of the lofty titles existing by itself in isolation from the others should be accounted a virtue. The good is not truly good, when it exists unaccompanied by justice, wisdom and power. For what is unjust or foolish or weak is not good. Nor again is power, separated from justice and wisdom, to be considered a virtue. (Power of such a kind is both bestial and tyrannical.)

The same principle applies everywhere. Wisdom must be accompanied by justice, and justice by power and goodness, otherwise one might more properly label them vices (κακίαι). For how should that which lacks what is better be accounted as good? But if it is correct that all should be present in one's conception of God, let us see if the Incarnation[17] is deprived of any of the god-fitting conceptions.

We are searching for signs of goodness in God. And what would be a clearer evidence of goodness than making his own what had once deserted him and further that the divine nature which is unchangeably good, should be untouched by the changeable will of man? For he would never have come to save us, as David says, unless his goodness made such a proposal, neither would his good intention have been any use, unless wisdom had made that love of humanity operative.

76

When people are feeble, although many may wish the sufferer freedom from his pain, it is only those who have the technical skill that can make their choice effectual and cure the patient. This means, in effect, that wisdom must always be closely allied to goodness. How then, in what has occurred, may wisdom be contemplated together with goodness? For it is not possible to discern in the abstract that which is good in intention. And how could that intention itself be recognized, unless it were displayed by what actually happened? The events themselves [sc. of the Incarnation] proceeding in orderly sequence[18] exhibit the wisdom and competence of the divine economy.

But, as has been said above, wisdom becomes virtue only on condition of its being joined to justice and if it be separated, by itself it is not good, it would be excellent in our account of the Incarnation (the Economy) to consider the two together, I mean wisdom and justice.

21. What then *is* justice? We recall entirely the distinctions we made in an orderly fashion in the beginning of our treatment of the subject. Man was initially made as a reflection of the divine nature. Together with all other goods and above all in his freedom of will[19] he kept the divine likeness, but he was necessarily subject to change. For it was not possible for one who owed his very existence to change to be exempt from the process of change. The progress from non-being to being is a change, when what is unsubstantial becomes substantial through the divine power.

Since man is an imitation of the divine nature, that which does the imitating, unless it be reproduced in some other material, would be in every respect identical with what he imitated. It is precisely at this point that the difference between the archetype and the copy is evident, the former is naturally immutable the other not so but comes to exist through change, as we have already noted, and therefore does not always remain in the same state.

(Change, you must know, is a movement which never ceases, from the condition one is in to another. There are two types of movement. There is one in the direction of the good, which is always taking place, where progress is endless, because there is no boundary to that which is explored. The other is in the opposite direction, whose very reality (hypostasis) consists in having no reality. When we contrast the opposite of good with good, as we said in what goes before, we mean much the same as when we say that the existent is

77

logically opposed to the non-existent[20] and subsistence to non-subsistence).

But seeing that our nature cannot remain unchanged by itself, simply because it possesses an indestructible urge towards movement, its free choice is always moving towards something, as the desire for the beautiful is ever drawing it naturally towards movement.

Now beauty itself can be either really beautiful or can be decked out with the semblance of beauty. The power to distinguish between the two is the mind that resides within us. Here, too, two possibilities present themselves. Either we can arrive at real beauty or we can turn through the deception of appearance and decline in the opposite direction. The heathen fable well illustrates this point when it speaks of the bitch (τὴν κύνα) looking in the water at the shadow and letting go its real food, as she opens her mouth to swallow the shadow of food and so remains hungry. In a similar fashion, the mind, being cheated of its desire for that which is really good, was carried away to what is unreal (τὸ μὴ ὄν) through the deception of the counsellor and inventor of evil (sc. the devil),[21] by having been persuaded that that truly is beautiful, which is the opposite of beautiful. For his guile would have been quite ineffectual, had not the semblance of good been spread upon the hook of evil like a bait.

Man then was freely (ἑκουσίως) involved in this disaster; he had yoked himself to the enemy of life through (sc. his choice of) pleasure. Therefore, in the same respect, you can find all that fits the divine attributes, that is goodness, wisdom, justice, power, incorruptibility and whatever else is of superior meaning. Therefore in his goodness he takes pity on our fallenness; in his wisdom he knows the method of our recall. It is also a part of wisdom to be a judge of justice, for true justice should never be an adjunct of foolishness.

22. Where in all this was justice to be found?[22] In God's refusal to use tyrannical power against him who held us in his grasp, and by his superior mastery to release us from the control of our master and so leave him, who had enslaved us through pleasure, the grounds for a just plea in his own defence. Even as those who have sold their own liberty for a price are justly slaves of those that bought them, and it is not right for them or for anybody else to claim liberty on their behalf. This is, indeed, even the case with well-born persons who have so surrendered themselves. If anyone in his concern for such persons should use force against those who purchased them, he will seem to be unjust in tyrannically wresting such lawfully possessed captives from the grip of their just captors.

On the other hand, if he should try to buy back such a one, no law will stand in his way. In the same way, once we had sold ourselves freely, the one who was out of his goodness to lead us back again into freedom must think up a method of recall which was not tyrannical but just, and therefore must be one which allowed the captor to select any ransom he might choose in return for his captive.[23]

23. What, then, was the more likely price for the captor to select (sc. in exchange for his captive)? We can make a reasonable guess about the nature of his desire, once the evidence of the sort of things he seeks becomes clear to us. According to the account we offered in the beginning of this work (cf. chapter 6), it was out of jealousy (*phthonos*),[24] for the happy state of man that the devil blinded himself towards the good, and gave birth within himself to the darkness of vice. This became in him the beginning of his downward course, and in his sickness gave birth to a thirst for power, which became the source and mother of the rest of his evil deeds. For what, therefore, would he exchange the one he held in his power except, clearly, for something higher and greater? In no other way could he more effectively nourish within himself the desire for vanity than by seizing the greater in exchange for the less.

But, among all the events related from of old, he never saw anything to compare with what occurred then, in connection with him who appeared then, the virginal conception, the virginal birth, the virgin giving suck, and the voices from the unseen world, witnessing to the surpassing worth (sc. of him who was so born). Then, too, there was his simple and natural power to heal the sicknesses of our nature, by a mere word, or a motion of the will. Then, also, there was his power to recall the dead to life, the fear he engendered in the demons, his power over diseases in the air and his own ability to walk upon the waters. In his case, unlike that of the miracle of Moses, where the waters parted to right and to left [cf. Exodus 14, 19–29], the surface of the waters offered a solid base for his steps and supported them by a kind of safe resistance.

The devil also perceived his own contempt for food for as long as he wished, and also his bountiful provision of food in the wilderness for the many thousands that fed there. They were filled, neither with the manna rained down from heaven, nor with the bread that the earth produces in its natural course, but rather by the munificence (φιλοτιμία) that springs from the inexhaustible, heavenly treasuries of divine power. The bread was multiplied in the very fact of distribution at the hands of those who administered it, and became increased the more they were filled. Further, the banquet of fish they enjoyed came to them, not through the provision of the sea, but of him who provided the sea with fish in the first place. How should anyone give a detailed list of each of the gospel miracles?[25]

The enemy, then, perceived this power in him, realised that by the exchange he would acquire more by possessing him than he already had. Therefore, he selected him, (sc. Christ) to become the ransom (λύτρον) for those who were constrained in the prison of death.[26]

But it was impossible for him (sc. the devil) to gaze upon the unveiled appearance of God without seeing in him some portion of that flesh (sarx) over which, through sin, he had already gained the mastery. Therefore was the deity clothed in flesh, so that, looking at what was well known and familiar, he would not be alarmed at the approach of exceeding power and, perceiving the might that shone out quietly, but increasingly, from the miracles, he would suppose that that which appeared was more to be desired than feared.

You see now how the good and the just are closely linked together, and that wisdom is separated from neither of them. We can see how, through the covering of the flesh, the divine power is made accessible to us, and his saving action (oikonomia) on our behalf, was not hindered by fear of the divine epiphany. And all of this was a demonstration of the goodness, power and justice of God. That he chose to save us is proof of his goodness; that he made the ransom of him who was held captive a matter of exchange demonstrates his justice, and that he made his incomprehensible nature capable of being mastered through a device is an indication of heavenly wisdom.

24. But it would be quite in order for anyone who has followed the argument thus far to ask where is the power of the deity, where, in what has been said, is the incorruption of the divine power visible? In order that this too may become clear, let us explore the rest of the mystery, above all that area, where the power is mingled with love for humanity.

To begin with, the ability of the all powerful nature to condescend to the lowliness of our condition is a surer instance of his power than his working of great and wonderful miracles. That something great and high should have been achieved by the divine power is perfectly natural and in accord with God. It would not surprise anyone to learn, for example, that the whole visible and invisible order of the universe owes its existence to the divine power, once the divine will had so decided. But the descent (sc. of God) to a lowly state, is a surpassing display of power which is not limited, save by elements foreign to its nature. So, for example, it is a distinctive character of the nature of fire to be born upwards; nor would anyone count it a wonderful thing for fire to behave in accordance with its natural character. But, should anybody see the flame going down, in the manner of heavy bodies, such indeed would be accounted a marvel, namely that fire, while retaining the character of fire, in its manner of motion, behaves in an unfiery fashion and moves downwards. In like manner, the condescension (*synkatabasis*)[27] of the Word to the frailty of our nature displays the divine and excellent power of God more effectively than does the size of the heavens, the light of the stars, the ordering of everything and the omnipresent administration of all that exists. In a wonderful way, in the Incarnate Lord, what is lofty appears in what is lowly and appears there without sacrificing its loftiness. Again, how wonderfully the deity is mingled with human nature, becoming one with it and being it.

We said above (sc. in chapter 23) that the opposing power was incapable of coming into direct contact with the pure presence of God and of enduring his brightness; therefore, in order that the exchange might be more easily effected, the divine was concealed by the covering of our nature in order that, after the manner of greedy fish, the hook of the deity might be swallowed down along with the bait of the humanity. In this way, once life had made its home with death and light had shone upon darkness, whatever was opposed to light and life might vanish away.[28] For, in the presence of light, darkness has not the power to remain, nor has death any power where life is active.

Therefore, in a brief summary we shall resume the inner logic of the mystery and so make an effective defence of the divine economy, against those who attack it, and show why it was that the deity brought about our salvation, on its own, without using any means inferior to itself. The divine must in all things possess its fitting attributes and not be such that one attribute is very evident with him, while another characteristic of the proper dignity of God is sacrificed. Instead, every high and fitting conception must be in every respect believed of the divine and each must be duly connected with the other. The good, the wise, the just, the powerful, the exemption from corruption, all these have been shown by our argument to be exemplified in the Incarnation.

The goodness has been seen in the free decision to save what had been lost; wisdom and justice are evident in the mode in which our salvation took place; power in his appearance among us in the form and likeness of man, on the one hand in the lowliness of our nature, and in the hope entertained, engendered by his likeness to us, that he could be mastered by death. Yet, on the other hand, once he had come, he acted in entire accordance with his nature.

It is the peculiarity of fire to destroy darkness and of light to destroy death. Having been taken away from the straight path in the beginning, we turned away from life and were carried along with death. That being so, what is there we learn from the mystery, which is inappropriate? Purity lays hold of those stained by sin; life, of those who were dead, and guidance of those who had been led astray, so that the defilement may be cleansed, the wandering cured and the dead might return to life.

Conclusion

Despite the fact that Gregory was aware of and, as we shall see, made considerable use of ideas drawn from the philosophic amalgam of his time, it is worth noting and perhaps surprising, that on no occasion does he refer by name to any of his contemporary or near contemporary philosophers except, as we have seen, in his *De fato*, although even there he fails to mention the actual name of his opponents. By contrast, Gregory of Nazianzus is more forthcoming. His first theological oration mentions a large number of errant philosophers by name in section 10 and in his third oration (section 2) he makes mention of one 'who philosophized among the Greeks', perhaps Plato, as Mason suggests, perhaps a Neoplatonic philosopher. However, he does not agree with him. Even so, Gregory of Nyssa is by contrast reticent, especially since he is thought of, rightly, as more deeply imbued with philosophy than his namesake. He may at times use ideas derived from philosophy but he does not attribute these ideas to their sources.

Our difficulty in discovering his sources is further aggravated by the obvious fact that we simply do no know the composition of his library. His literary education, he attributes to his brother Basil in *Letter* 13. Are we to assume that his philosophical studies were also in his brother's hands? If so, it is clearly the case that he greatly exceeded his brother in the range and profundity of his interests.

Gregory's indebtedness to, and distancing himself from, 'philosophy', above all Platonic philosophy, has been the subject of numerous monographs. Some, like H. F. Cherniss who wrote 'The Platonism of Gregory of Nyssa' in 1930, see Gregory as little more than a Platonic wolf in the clothing of a Christian sheep. Other writers, like Heinrich Doerrie, see Gregory as fundamentally antiphilosophic, using the language of philosophy indeed, but in a distinctly aphilosophic fashion. His position could be caricatured as that of a Christian wolf in the clothing of a Platonic sheep. Others, again, like Professor Stead, think of Gregory as a flawed philosopher, using indeed the language of philosophy, but with inconsistency and incoherence.

Perhaps it is better to use the language of *Umdeutung* to describe Gregory's method. This means that he took the language of philosophy and then subtly reworked it for his own Christian purposes. Gregory's actual attitude can be inferred from three distinct considerations: (A) His *Catechetical Oration*; (B) His discussion of the doctrines of the Trinity and Christology; and (C) His *De fato*.

(A) The main thrust of this work is the defence of Christian doctrine, above all the Incarnation, but also the Trinity, against the voiced criticism of (Neo)platonist philosophers. Gregory's whole aim is to prove that the doctrine of the Trinity is not a rejection of the unity and unicity of God, and that the doctrine of the Incarnation and redemption does not require the critic to deny either the changelessness or the moral perfection of God. This means that the agreed premises upon which the work rests are ideas which would have met with the approval of his (unnamed) critics. In the prologue of the work he lists, for the first time, the four basic characteristics, which God must, as it were, display in all his dealings.

Gregory's insistence on the inseparability of the power, wisdom, goodness, justice and fullness of being of God, which I have illustrated, mean in effect that for Gregory, as for Plato and Plotinus, value and being are inseparable. It may be that in his striving to establish the reasonableness of the divine action, we hear remarkably little in the *Or. Cat.* of the divine infinity and consequent, ultimate inaccessibility to the human mind. But this is hardly surprising once the largely apologetic nature of the work is admitted. What is remarkable is that nowhere does Gregory appeal to the sovereign power of God in his account of the redemption of the world.

Gregory's God must always work within the rules established by the harmony of the four attributes, that is, by his known and inferable nature. This, together with his insistence on the organic, ordered character of the divine action expressed by the terms *heirmos* and *akolouthia* make his whole approach highly rationalist in tone.

(B) In his theological understanding of the Trinity and Incarnation Gregory uses models imported from philosophy. When dealing with the unity and threefoldness of God he will, at times, use the Aristotelian language of 'second substance' which appeared to some of his critics to lead to straight to tritheism, as can be seen, for example at *Contra Eunomium* 1.227. Gregory wrestles with this problem on several occasions, as has already been noticed. He clearly wished to insist on the unity of the divine *ousia* or *physis* (words, it should be noted, that he appears to use as synonyms for each other), while admitting the distinctness of the three hypostases. At *Contra Eunomium* 1.503, commenting on John 10.30 he speaks of 'the distinct individuality of the separate hypostases', combined with a unity of being/nature. Further, in his short treatise *To Eustathius, On the Holy Trinity*, previously assigned to St Basil as his *Letter* 189, he argues from unity of *energeia* or activity of all three persons to unity of nature. Gregory is, arguably, dealing less here with an Aristotelian abstract idea than with a Platonic universal. In other words, Gregory can use ideas drawn from a wide spectrum of philosophies and does not regard himself as committed only to one in order to illustrate and defend his faith.

What is true of his theology proper, that is, of the Trinity, is also valid for his treatment of the relationship of divinity and humanity in Christ. In this case, however, it is less to Plato and Aristotle that he 'appeals' than to a form of Stoicism, as had Origen before him. This means that he uses the idea of mixture, *anakrasis*, to explore the nature of the unity. If it be urged that this movement back and forth displays a certain philosophical insouciance, the charge must be admitted, but it must be insisted that he does use the language and models of some philosophy to achieve an avowedly Christian and dogmatic end.

It may also be worth noting that the Hellenistic philosophies of his period and earlier were by no means slavish followers of the great fourth-century BC Athenian philosophers. As Professor Dodds has pointed out, Plotinus, although professedly a follower of Plato, produced a version of his master's teaching which diverges in important respects from the views of Plato himself, notably in his importing a dynamic notion into the world of the spirit, which contrasts markedly with the static perfection of the world of forms.

(C) As we have seen, Gregory was concerned in *De fato* to rebut certain false ideas, as he saw them, about the nature of the world. In that treatise it is of particular interest that Gregory shows a precise familiarity with the case of the fatalists and, at the same time, a considerable acquaintance with the replies to fatalism issued by Carneades, Alexander of Aphrodisias and others. In this respect he adopts the same sort of approach to pagan positions as Origen in the *Contra Celsum* – a point well brought out by Henry Chadwick in *Early Christian Thought and the Classical Tradition* (Oxford, 1966), especially pages 104–108.

It is also worth noting that both in general theme and in language and ideas, several of Gregory's other more philosophical writings betray substantial Platonic influence. This is true, above all, of the *De anima et resurrectione*, which looks to Plato's *Phaedo* for its pattern. Both works are deathbed scenes, Plato's of his mentor, Socrates, Gregory's of his sister and mentor, Macrina. Both are also discussions of the nature of the soul and, above all, of its survival after death. It is true that the thought of resurrection of the body modifies considerably the notion of immortality, but the same problems of the simplicity of the soul and of the place and value within it of the passions trace the same ground.

Again, although less obviously, the treatise of Gregory *De hominis opificio* owes something to Plato's *Timaeus* and even to the *Symposium*, especially to the picture of the primal creation of the human being as discussed in Aristophanes' speech at *Symposium* 189Cff. and by Gregory in chapter 16 of his work. In both cases, the primal condition is asexual. Sexual differentiation is introduced as a consequence of actual sin in the case of Plato and, in the case of Gregory, of the foreseen misconduct of the first human beings.

Finally, the Platonic theorem that the upward march of the created spirit to the knowledge and enjoyment of God is a process that is occasioned by the loveliness of God and demands moral perfection as well as mental abstraction, is at the centre of all Gregory's strictly spiritual, as distinct from his more controversial writings. The driving force of ἔρως lies at the heart of both the *On the Life of Moses* and the *Commentary on the Song of Songs*. The pattern, shown most notably in the *Symposium* of Plato in the speech of Diotima (= 208C to 212C) and, in his wake, by Plotinus in *Ennead*

1.6, is the literary model that underpins the progress outlined in these two writings and also, perhaps more obviously, in the *De virginitate.*

4

GREGORY AND SPIRITUALITY

1. AGAINST EUNOMIUS 2.84–96

Introduction

So far Gregory's contribution to dogmatic debates about the deity of the Son and the Spirit and the person of Christ, and his attitude to and use of philosophy, have been discussed and illustrated. But it would be quite misleading to offer a version of his teaching which ignores his influence in the area of spirituality. For many people, scholars included, Gregory's sole importance is his spiritual teaching, above all his 'doctrine' of the divine infinity and his corresponding defence of both non-verbal prayer and of the everlasting progress or stretching out [cf. Phil. 3, 13] – επεκταsιs – of the created spirit, angelic or human, in search of God.

How innovative this was has been much disputed as we have already seen, partly because the doctrine of perpetual progress can be paralleled in both Origen and Augustine (for the latter especially at the opening of his sixty-third *Tractate on John*).

A further point calls for mention. To what extent is it fair to label Gregory a mystic at all, and what relationship does his teaching bear to that of Origen? Both these issues have been fruitfully explored by Jean Daniélou and Henri Crouzel.[1] I think that Daniélou rather overstates his position in his enthusiastic effort to assimilate Gregory's teaching on the cloud, in the *On the Life of Moses* 2.162ff., to the later teaching of Denis the Areopagite and his spiritual descendants, above all, John of the Cross.

But was Gregory a mystic at all? In the sense that mysticism advocates a direct, unmediated *awareness* of God, beyond all images and concepts, it may be doubted that he was so. His spiritual teaching is more a form of sublime moralism, supported by increasing knowledge of God, than an invitation to direct union with God or the absolute, ending in the ecstasy, described by Plotinus at the end of his *Enneads*.

Gregory's first datable essay on the spiritual life appeared in c.372 in the shape of an elegant treatise, *On Virginity*, probably designed as a rational account of the monastic ideals of his brother, Basil. Although, as its title suggests, it begins as a defence of virginity, it becomes clear as it progresses that it is not primarily concerned with physical virginity, but rather with that virginity of the soul which is available to all Christians, married or otherwise. Towards the middle, in chapter 10, it becomes more definitely Platonic in tone, with a discussion of 'what ought truly to be desired'. In the ensuing chapter it becomes clear that the ultimate object of desire is the truly beautiful. It soon becomes even clearer that God is being so defined, even as St Augustine had defined him in *Confessions* x, xxvii 38. The rest of the Christian's efforts are directed to the enjoyment of this wonderful reality. The final chapter interprets the sixth beatitude in the light of the vision of the beautiful. It is not hard to see that this pattern owes much to the *Symposium* of Plato, which had already been so influential on pagan and Christian writers alike, above all, on Origen and Plotinus.

But in 372 Gregory seems not yet to have discovered, or made his own, that teaching on the divine infinity which distinguishes his more mature spiritual writing. In *On Virginity* Gregory seems not to find any problem in the idea of 'seeing the beautiful'. He writes in chapter 23 (= *GNO* VIII.I.3/4) of the vision of God without the sort of difficulties which harass him in his homily on Matt. 5, 8.

This brings us at once to one of the distinctive features of Gregory's spiritual teaching – the firm anchoring in doctrinal considerations, some of which appear to arise from his controversy with Eunomius. The first passage we look at is indeed derived from his *Against Eunomius* 2.84–96. One of its distinctive features is its marked preference for the language of *pistis* (faith) over that of *gnosis* (knowledge).

The exact motive for this upsetting of the pattern, which, arguably, appears for the first time in the sixth book of Plato's *Republic* 511D, is not at all clear. Dissatisfaction with an over-rationalist approach to religion which, he assumed, lay at the root of Eunomius' heretical speculations, may be partly responsible. If so, it is mirrored in later, non-Christian writers, like Proclus.[2] Their dependence on Gregory is disputed, but they may reflect a growing distrust in the aggressive pretensions of reason as, at least in the West, the late Roman empire staggered to its close.

Translation

84. How wretched are they in their acuteness, how unhappy and destructive is their precise and exact philosophy. Who goes so eagerly to the pit as do they who have dug for themselves, by their toil and eagerness, the pit of blasphemy? What a distance separates them from the hope of Christians. By what a chasm are they walled off from the faith that saves? How exiled they are from the faith of the bosom of our father Abraham?

85. If we may, in accordance with the noble nature of the Apostle [cf. Rom. 4, 11ff. and Gal. 4, 24ff.], interpret language allegorically and without, at the same time, denying its historical truth, give to history a deeper meaning [*nous*], Abraham left his own country and his own people. In so doing he set out upon an exodus, fitting for a prophet who was striving to arrive at the knowledge of God.

86. It is not to some spatial transposition that the spiritual understanding of truths refers. On the contrary, Abraham came out of himself and his own country, that is his lowly and earthly thoughts, and raised his understanding as best he could above the common bounds of nature. He forsook his soul's fellowship with his senses. Disturbed no longer by sensory appearances and obscured no longer in his apprehension of things unseen, with his hearing not upsetting his mind and his eyes not misleading his intelligence by the world of sense, he walked, as the Apostle says, 'through faith and not by sight' [2 Cor. 5, 7] He (that is, Abraham) was so uplifted by the greatness of his knowledge, that he supposed himself to have arrived at the limit of human perfection. He grasped as much of God as it was possible for our limited and frail power at its most exalted to comprehend.

87. For this reason, the Lord of all creation becoming, as it were, the discovery of the patriarch, is especially called the God of Abraham. Even so, what does Scripture say of him? 'He came out, not knowing where he was going' [Heb. 11, 8], incapable of grasping the name of the one he loved, yet not for that reason vexed at his ignorance, nor ashamed of it.

88. This indeed was his safest path for the discovery of what he sought. He was not guided in his thoughts about God by any immediately available consideration, nor was his mind so absorbed by what he had grasped, that he made no progress further in the journey to what lies beyond things already known.

89. He surpassed, as it were, by reasoning, the wisdom of his own country. I mean the philosophy of the Chaldeans which stretches only as far as appearances. He became superior to things known through sense, and was eager to contemplate the primal beauty from the beauty of the things he had already beheld and from the harmonious order of the heavenly wonders. In the same way, all other things that in his reasoning he had been able to master, power, goodness, the being without beginning or end, in short any other consideration about the divine nature, all these he treated as provisions and stepping stone for the upward journey.[3] He always depended on what he had found and was ever 'stretching forward to what lay ahead' [Phil. 3,13]. He always treasured, as the prophet says, 'beautiful ascents in his heart' [Ps. 83, 6]. He always considered what he had achieved by his own power as smaller than what he still looked for. In his conceptions about God he went beyond every thought which might be derived from considering his name; he purified his reasoning of all such ideas and so embraced a faith, unmixed and free of every such conception (*ennoia*). This he laid down as an infallible and clear sign that we know God – the conviction that God is superior to, and higher than, every semantic marker.

90. For this reason, after the ecstasy that had fallen upon him, he looked down once again from the high ideas he had to his human frailty and said, 'But I am dust and ashes' [Gen. 18, 27], by which he meant that he had neither voice nor strength with which to express the good he had perceived.

91. To my mind it seems that dust and ash signify what is, at the same time, both lifeless and sterile. As a result, the law of faith becomes his rule of life. By means of his own story he instructs those who would approach God that there is no other way of drawing close to God except through the medium of faith, that of itself knits together into one the searching mind and the incomprehensible nature.

92. Abraham left behind him the vain search for knowledge. As Scripture says, 'Abraham believed God and it was reckoned to him as righteousness'. The Apostle continues, 'This was not written for his sake, but for ours' [Rom. 4, 23]. It is faith not knowledge that God accounts as righteousness for men.

93. For knowledge implies some sort of direct experience which in some way accords with what is known. But Christian faith is not like that. 'For it is the substance of things hoped for' [Heb. 11, 1], not of things known, and what we have in our possession we do not hope for. For he (sc. the Apostle Paul) says, 'Why should we hope for what we possess?' [Rom. 8, 24]. Faith makes our own that which exceeds the grasp of our minds, through its own secureness, providing a guarantee for what is not seen. So the apostle says of the man of faith, 'He persevered, as though he saw him who is invisible.' [Heb. 11, 27]. He, therefore, is a vain fellow who says that it is possible to know the divine nature by means of 'knowledge that is vainly puffed up' [cf. 1 Cor. 8, 1].[4]

94. No man is so mighty as to put his power of comprehension on a level with the Lord. ('For', as David says, 'who in the clouds shall be like the Lord?' [Ps. 88, 7]). Nor, on the other hand, is the object of search so insignificant as to be comprehended by our restricted powers of reasoning. Hear the words of Ecclesiastes advising us to say nothing in the presence of God, because he says, 'God is in the heavens above and you are in the earth below.' [Eccl. 5, 1].

95. He shows, I believe, through this conjunction or, rather, disjunction of elements with and from each other, how much higher is the divine nature than the over-cleverness of human reasoning.

The superiority of the stars to the grasp of our fingers is nothing in comparison with that of the nature which exceeds every mind to our earthly reasoning.

96. The higher the exalted character of that nature, the more we ought to remain peaceably within our own limits. It is safer and more reverent to believe that the majesty of God far exceeds what we already know, than by restricting his glory within our conceptions to suppose there is nothing superior to them.

2. HOMILY 6: ON THE BEATITUDES
(= *PG*44; 1264B; *GNO* VII.I.136–148)

'Blessed are the pure of heart, for they shall see God.' [Matt. 5, 8].

What people normally experience when they look down from some lofty promontory upon some mighty sea, that is the experience of my mind as I peer down from the height of the Lord's voice, as from some mountain peak, upon the inexhaustible depth of my thoughts. In seaside districts one not infrequently comes across a mountain split down the centre. The part that faces the sea has been worn away to smoothness from top to bottom. In the upper part, however there is a sharp projection, gazing towards the deep. Anyone looking down from such a high promontory into the sea beneath would be quite dizzy. In the same way, my soul also is dizzy (*ilingia*), as it is caught up in this mighty word of the Lord: 'Blessed are the pure of heart for they shall see God.' God lies before us as a vision for those who have been made pure of heart,[5] the same God, as the great John declares, 'God, whom no one has ever seen' [John 1,18]. The lofty Paul is in agreement with this when he says 'God no man can see' [I Tim. 6, 15]. This is the smooth sheer rock which provides no foothold for itself in our thoughts. In the same way, Moses, in his own teaching on the subject, insisted that it was in no way possible for the human mind to come close to God, seeing that all power of grasping had been worn away through abstraction, 'For' he says, 'it is not possible for anyone to see God and live' [Exod. 33, 20].

'But', you urge, 'eternal life is seeing God'. Yet the impossibility of this is urged upon us by the pillars of our faith, John, Paul and Moses. Do you not perceive the dizziness with which the soul is drawn to the depth of what it has contemplated? If God is life, he who sees him fails to see life itself. Yet the inspired prophets and apostles are agreed that God cannot be seen. If so, what role does hope perform for human beings? Even so, the Lord supports our wavering hope, even as he did in the case of Peter who was in danger of drowning, by setting him safe on the firm and solid surface of the water [cf. Matt. 14, 28–31]. If the hand of the Word comes to us and supports us upon some firm idea in the whirl of our speculations, we shall be freed from fear, as we take a firm hold on the Word that takes us by the hand. For he says, 'Blessed are the pure of heart for they shall see God' [Matt. 5, 8].

The promise is so great that it vastly exceeds the highest bound of blessedness. What could anyone possibly desire after such a good as that, since he already has everything possible in what he has seen? In scriptural usage, seeing means the same as possessing. So it is that when Scripture says, 'May you see the goods of Jerusalem' [Ps. 127, 6] it means the same as 'May you find'. Similarly, when it (sc. Scripture) says, 'Let the wicked be removed so as not to see the glory of the Lord' [Isa. 26, 10] the prophet means by 'not seeing' the same as 'not sharing in'. Therefore, whoever has seen God has possession through that sight of whatever is contained in the list of good things, that is, life without end, everlasting freedom from corruption, immortal happiness, a kingdom that knows no end, unceasing joy, true light, the spiritual and sweet voice, unapproachable glory, perpetual rejoicing, the complete good.

Seeing, however, that the manner of rejoicing has been shown to depend upon purity of heart, once again my mind finds itself in a state of dizziness, (ἰλιγγιᾶι), in case purity of heart turns out to be something impossible and wholly beyond our reach. For if that is the way forward to see God, and Moses did not see him and Paul laid it down that neither he nor anybody else could see him, it would appear that there is something impossible lying before us in this beatitude. For what profit is there in knowing how God is seen if we lack the power to implement this promise?

It is rather like saying, 'It is a blessed thing to be in heaven, because there we shall see things that are not visible in the world beneath'. If there were some method of transportation to heaven described by Scripture, it would be of some advantage to those who were told to learn that it was a wonderful thing to be there. But as long as the upward journey is an impossibility, what possible advantage does this knowledge of heavenly happiness convey? It merely saddens those who have learnt of it to discover what they are deprived of through the impossibility of the upward journey.

Does, then, the Lord exhort us to something beyond our nature? Has he exceeded the bounds imposed on human capacity by the immenseness of his command? Not so. He does not bid wingless creatures fly, nor those to live under the water whose allotted realm is the dry land. If then in every other case the law is adapted to those who receive the ordinances, and enjoins nothing above nature, we are surely at liberty to conclude that the prescription of the beatitude is not without hope of fulfilment.

How then could John and Paul and Moses and any like them have fallen short of the lofty beatitude, whose essence consists in the vision of God, neither Paul who says, 'A crown of righteousness is laid up for me, which the just judge will give me' [2 Tim. 4, 8], nor he who lay on the breast of Jesus [cf. John 13, 25; 21, 20], nor he who heard from the divine voice, 'I have known thee above all' [Exod. 33, 17]. If, then, we cannot doubt that they are blessed 'who are proclaimed to have possessed a superhuman knowledge of God, and blessedness depends on seeing God and seeing God on being pure of heart, purity of heart, through which our blessedness is assured, cannot be an impossibility.

How then can we say that those speak the truth who with Paul

93

claim that the knowledge of God is beyond our power? Should we not say that the voice of the Lord himself contradicts them in promising the vision of God to those who are pure of heart?

It seems to me that it would be an excellent idea to discuss the matter briefly to ensure that our investigation of the subject in hand proceeds in an orderly manner. The divine nature in and of itself, whatever its essential character, lies beyond our human apprehension. It is unapproachable and inaccessible to human conjectures. There has never been found among men anyone to grasp the ungraspable with the human intelligence, nor has there ever been found a method of comprehending the incomprehensible. For this reason, the great apostle calls his ways 'unsearchable' [Rom. 11, 33]. He means by that that the road which leads to the knowledge of the divine essence cannot be trodden by human reasoning, for as yet none of those who have gone before us on the road have provided us with a trace of how He may be grasped by a knowledge which is above all knowledge. He who by nature is above every nature, He who is both beyond the senses and beyond the mind, is seen and grasped by some other method.

There are many methods of such understanding. So, for example, it is possible by means of the wisdom that can be seen in all things [cf. Ps. 103, 24] to have some sort of perception of him who made all things in wisdom. In much the same way in human constructions, some perception of the artist may be inferred from looking at his creations, on the assumption that his work displays his art. But it is not the actual nature of the artist that is so revealed, but only the artistry that he has displayed in his work.

In a similar way we may look at the order of creation and so receive an impression of the wisdom not of the nature of him who ordered all things in wisdom [Rom. 1, 20]. Again, if we consider the cause of our own life, and remember that God made us not out of necessity, but out of a good choice [cf. Plato, *Timaeus* 48A 1–2; Plotinus *Enn.* iii.ii.2.33–36], in this way too we can speak of seeing God, becoming aware of his goodness, not of his essence. In a similar way, whatever else raises the mind to a better and nobler conception, each and every one of these we can call knowledge of God, each of these noble ideas bringing God before our eyes. Power, purity, immutability and freedom from the opposite, imprints upon our souls the image of a divine and noble idea.

What has been said displays after a fashion the truth of the Lord, who promised the vision of God to the pure of heart. Nor, again, is

Paul a liar when he displays in his own words that he has not seen God nor can see him [cf. Eph. 1, 19; 3, 7; Phil. 3, 21]. For God who is by nature beyond our sight is visible in his activities (*energeiai*), being perceived in the characteristics (*idiomata*) that surround him.[6]

But the ability to infer something of the nature of the agent from his activity is not the sole purpose of the beatitude. Some perception of the supreme wisdom and power of God might perhaps be available to the wise men of this world by inspecting the harmonious order of the universe to the children of this world. The nobility of the beatitude seems to indicate something further for those capable of receiving this advice. The idea that occurs to me will be clarified by examples. In human life bodily health is a good. But the blessing derives not simply from knowing the nature of health but actually from being healthy. For if someone discoursed on the excellence of health while living on a sickly and unwholesome diet, what advantages did he derive from his praises of health, if his own life is worn out by illnesses? So, too, ought we to understand the text that lies before us, namely that the Lord is insistent that blessedness consists not so much in knowing God as in having God within.

'Blessed are pure of heart, for they shall see God' [Matt. 5, 8]. It does not appear that God is offering a face to face vision of Himself to those who have purified the 'eye of the soul'.[7] Instead the nobility of the saying perhaps means, what is elsewhere stated with greater clarity, that 'the kingdom of God is within us' [Luke 17, 21]. By this we are to learn that whoever has cleansed his heart from every passionate disposition, perceives in his own inner beauty the image of the divine nature.

By means of the few words he spoke, the divine Word seems to contain the following advice,

> Men, whichever of you longs to have sight of absolute goodness, do not lose hope of ever beholding the object of your desire, when you hear that the divine splendour is raised above the heavens, that its glory cannot be told, that its beauty is past telling and its nature cannot be grasped. For what you are able to grasp is the measure within you of the knowledge of God, for he who made you formed you in the beginning, at the same time adorned you with such goodness.
>
> When you were first created God imprinted upon you reflections of his own nature not unlike someone impressing the form of a seal upon wax. Vice, however, poured round this

95

godlike character, has made the good in you of no value, hidden as it is by base coverings. If you, however, by a careful manner of life, were to wash away the filth that has become coated over the soul, your own godlike beauty will shine out. The same sort of thing happens with iron. Once it has been freed of rust by the whetstone, what was previously black now shines out with its own rays to the sun and affords great brilliance.

Your inner man, which the Lord calls the heart, is like that. Once it has scraped off the rust like incrustations that grow on the soul like a sort of evil mould, it will recover its likeness to its archetype and will be good. For good is in all respects like the good. Therefore, whoever sees himself sees within himself the object of this longing and so the pure of heart becomes blessed, for by contemplating his own purity he sees the archetype in the image. In a similar way, those who contemplate the sun in a mirror, even though they do not look straight at the sun, see the sun no less in the ray in the mirror than do those who look directly at the circle of the sun. So too you, even though you be inadequate for the contemplation of the unapproachable light, if you return to the grace of the image which was planted in you at the beginning, you will find what you look for within you.

What is the deity but purity, freedom from passion and separation from every kind of evil? If these things be in you, then assuredly God himself is within you. As soon as the power of reasoning within you is unmixed with any kind of vice, free from passion and separated from all manner of defilement, then you will be blessed by great sharpness of sight, because in your purified condition you will know what, to those who have not been so purified, remains unseen. Once the material mist has been stripped away from the eyes of the soul, you will see in the pure clarity of your heart the 'blessed vision'[8] brightly. What then is it? Purity, holiness, simplicity, all the lightful rays of the divine nature, through whom God is seen.

That these things are so from what has been said no one will dispute, yet the initial difficulty seems nowhere nearer to a solution. As he who is in heaven has a share in the heavenly wonders, whereas inability to ascend thus high means that we gain no profit from what we profess, in the same way no one will doubt that purity of heart is a passport to happiness, yet the mode of being freed from such defilement is not unlike the ascent to heaven.

What ladder of Jacob, what fiery chariot of Elijah lifting him to the heavens will be found, whereby our heart may be raised heavenward and shake off its earthly burden? If anyone thinks of the soul's necessary passions, he will at once admit how difficult and hard it is to be freed from the evils that surround us. Our very birth is the fruit of passion, growth takes place by its means, our life terminates in it. Evil has been intermingled with our nature from the outset, because of those who received passion into themselves at the beginning by disobeying and so giving the disease a home in themselves. And, as in every species of living being, the same nature persists as one follows the other, so that as far as nature itself is concerned, what comes into existence is identical with that whence it came, so it is that man comes from man, the passionate from the passionate, the sinner from the sinner. In some sense, therefore, sin comes to exist along with things that come to be. It is born with it, grows alongside it and ceases only when life is ended.

Virtue, on the other hand, is hard to come by and demands much sweat and labour, and is achieved only with much seriousness and struggle. This is the lesson we have often learnt from the divine Scripture when we hear 'that the road that leads to the kingdom is narrow and hard' [Matt. 7, 13; 14]. On the other hand, the road that destroys life is broad, downward and easy to walk on. Scripture never defines the higher life as totally beyond us, especially as it lays before us in the holy books the wonders of so many men.

There are two distinct ideas contained in the promise of seeing God. The first is actually knowing the nature of him who is totally above us; the second is being mingled with him through the purity of our lives. As to the first manner of knowing, the voice of the saints lays it down as being an impossibility for us. The second the Lord promises to human nature through his present teaching, when he says; 'Blessed are the pure of heart for they shall see God' [Matt. 5, 8].

But how this purity may be achieved you can discover by examining nearly all the teaching of the gospel. By examining its exhortations one by one, you will find a clear account of the meaning of purity of heart. There he (sc. Christ) distinguishes two types of vice in words and in deeds. The former, that is the evil manifested in action, is castigated in the old law. But now he has laid down the law

97

about another type of sin. He does not punish the evil action so much, but tries instead to ensure that the evil shall not occur in the first place. He does this by removing vice from the will and in this way distancing life itself even further from evil deeds.

Vice is many sided and has many faces, and to each of the forbidden things, he has offered a remedy through his own exhortations. Because each of us suffers from the weakness of anger throughout the whole of our lives, he begins his healing from a higher ground, by laying down absence of anger[9] as an ideal at the outset. He says [cf. Matt. 5, 21–22], 'You have been taught by the old law, you shall not kill, now you must learn to distance your soul from anger against your brothers.' He does not absolutely inhibit anger – sometimes we can use such a spiritual impulse for a good purpose – but what he does forbid absolutely is an angry disposition towards one's own brother for no good purpose. He says, 'Whoever is angry with his brother without good reason' (though this is not in the text of Matthew, or in the *apparatus criticus*). The addition of the qualification, *eikhi*, shows that often enough the use of anger can be quite appropriate, when our passion is aroused for the correction of sin. This type of anger Scripture ascribed to Phinees when by his slaughter of the lawless he propitiated the anger of God against the people [Num. 25, 6–11].

He moves on thence to the healing of sins committed through pleasure and by his command removes the improper desire for fornication from the heart [Matt. 5, 27–32]. So you will find the Lord correcting the rest, one by one, in order, by his precepts emending every species of evil. By forbidding us even the right to self defence he prevents the unjust use of our hands. He exiles the passion of greed by commanding us to give even what is left over to him who would take something from us [Matt. 5, 39–40]. He cures our cowardice by bidding us despise death [Matt. 10, 28]. So, in general, you will find through each of the commandments the dissecting Word [cf. Heb. 4, 12][10] acting like a plough, rooting out the evil roots of sin from the depths of the heart and, in this way, securing purification from the crop of thorns.

In both these ways, therefore, does he benefit our nature; he promises us what is good and offers us teaching to help us on our way thither. If the zeal needed for good things seems to you burdensome, throw in your lot with the opposite life and you will discover that vice is even more demanding, that is, if you attend not to the immediate present but to what follows. The very sound of hell will serve to separate a man from his sinful pleasures without any labour or zeal. Fear by itself, once it has taken root in his thoughts, will of itself be sufficient to do away with his passions.

One might increase one's desire even further simply by considering what is implied, rather than stated, by the beatitude. If the pure of heart are blessed, those whose minds are filthy are surely much to be pitied, simply because they contemplate the face of the adversary. If the divine character is imposed upon us by a virtuous life, it is quite clear that a vicious life takes upon itself the form and features of the adversary (sc. the devil). God is variously named by each of the many good things we predicate of him; light, life, immortality and other things of the sort. In like fashion the inventor of evil[11] will be named from the opposite qualities; darkness, death, corruption and whatever else shares the same nature as these.

Once we have discovered in what ways vice and virtue are formed, seeing that we possess freedom of choice in both directions, let us fly from the form of the devil and take upon ourselves the likeness of God. Let us become pure of heart that we may be blessed, as the divine image is formed in us through the purity of our lives, in Christ Jesus our Lord, to whom be glory for ever and ever Amen.

3. ON THE LIFE OF MOSES

This important and influential work of spiritual theology was composed at some period probably late in Gregory's life. On the slender basis of a reference to 'grey hair' at i.2 it has been inferred that the *Life* is a product of Gregory's old age, but such a conclusion is a lot to base on such frail premises, especially once it is realised that such a description is applied to Gregory by himself, when he was only 40.[12]

The full title of the work is *On the Life of Moses* or *On Perfection in Virtue*. But what does the treatise understand by the term 'virtue'? Does it mean what it appears to mean, simply moral virtue, or does it have a wider meaning? As the treatise is commonly viewed as an exercise in 'mystical theology' it would be inconvenient, to say the least, if it turns out to have been composed with the principal or sole purpose of encouraging the reader in the practice of the cardinal virtues. It seems better to assume that the word 'virtue', as used in the work, has a wider meaning than moral excellence. The sixth *Homily on the Beatitudes* translated above, seems in places to

99

identify the knowledge of God with moral excellence, as if the vision of God meant exactly the same as possessing him and possessing the same as living a life of virtue. Certainly that homily brings the two fruitfully together and prevents one from falling into the illusion that mystical experience can be had without living a morally upright life.

The close connection of these two elements of life and vision is asserted by Gregory in *Life* ii.166. 'Religious virtue' is divided into two parts, that which concerns God and that which concerns right conduct. This refusal to divorce right conduct from correct belief, sets Gregory apart from pagan religion, on the one side, which seems to have practised a form of amoral worship, and from those Christian writers on the other, who seem to have thought that a stage could be arrived at after which virtue ceased to matter or to be demanded, simply because it was already firmly possessed. Such appears to be the teaching of Evagrius in his treatise *On Prayer*. It is also the legacy of those who divorce morality from mystical experience on the plea that the two are independent of each other. With such a convenient divorce Gregory will have nothing to do.

The treatise is traditionally divided into two unequal sections called respectively 'History' and 'Contemplation'. The earlier, shorter part is simply an expanded paraphrase of the story of Moses as it is contained in the book of Exodus. The longer portion, Θεωρία, is basically an allegorical interpretation of the passage just expounded. Gregory follows the fortunes of Moses from his birth [ii.1] to the final discovery [ii. 305] derived largely from the vision of God in the rock of Exodus 33.23, that perfection consists in endless progress, that being the only way in which the finite spirit can come close to the infinite God. In other words, the second part makes it clear that for Gregory perfection has two elements, the gnostic and the virtuous, and neither can manage alone.

Gregory has often been credited with the discovery of mystical theology, or rather with the perception that darkness is an appropriate symbol under which God may be discussed. There is much truth in this. He was not the first to give to Exodus 33.23, 'My face thou shalt not see', an apophatic sense. Philo had arrived at the same conclusion in his treatise, *On the Posterity and Exile of Cain* 15/16; 169. But Gregory seems to have been the first Christian writer to have made this all important point, partly under the pressure of the Eunomian controversy.

Origen does indeed discuss the passage from Exodus in the

course of his twelfth homily on Exodus but, instead of treating it as a proof of the divine inaccessibility, as did both Philo and Gregory, Origen sees in it evidence of future promise. He connects it with 2 Cor. 3, 16/17, with the promise of the removal of the veil with the coming of Our Lord. The *posteriora*, or back parts of God, are interpreted to mean 'the things that are done in latter days, as distinct from those done in the days of Moses'. Interestingly, Origen offers no exegesis whatever of Exod. 20, 21, which refers to the 'darkness where God was'. It is differences of emphasis of precisely this type that have led some writers to see in Gregory a significant departure from the so-called 'gnostic' theology of Origen.

In several important respects Gregory can be seen as the anticipator of Denis the Areopagite, above all in his treatise, *The Mystical Theology*. Certainly in chapter 1 Denis clearly refers to passages in Gregory's *On the Life of Moses*, which touch on the theme of darkness. But, in three respects, Denis goes well beyond his 'master', and shows himself to be a disciple rather of Proclus, the Neoplatonist. (1) For Denis, God is frequently stated to be 'beyond all being'. In the opening of the work *On the Divine Names*, he writes of 'that hidden divinity which transcends being'. With such an understanding Gregory's frequent insistence on God as 'He who' or 'That which is', (cf. Exod. 3, 14) does not easily accord. (2) For Gregory the sharp distinction between creator and creature is everywhere insisted upon. For Denis, with his teaching of outflow and return of all reality to its divine source and especially with his use of James 1, 17 in *The Celestial Hierarchy* 1.1 and with his remarks at *On the Divine Names* 4, 14, the cardinal distinction between creator and creature is blurred almost to the point of pantheism. (3) Denis structures the spiritual life in a quite unGregorian fashion, as the progessive return of the outflow to its source by the purgative, illuminative and unitive way of which he seems to be the first clear exponent. The scheme occurs in *The Mystical Theology* 1, 3., 'When every purification is complete . . . Moses sees the many lights. . . . Then he breaks free from them, and renouncing all the mind may conceive, is united, by a completely unknowing activity of all knowledge, and knows beyond the mind by knowing nothing.' The idea of union is peculiar to Denis, though foreign to Gregory.

Translation 1: (i) i.46

Moses, then, once he has been liberated from the burden of the timidity of the people and is by himself, makes a bold attempt upon the darkness and comes inside the realm of things unseen, being himself no longer visible to those that see. Having entered within the sanctuary of the divine mystagogy, he was there present to the unseen, himself being invisible. He taught us, I think, by what he did, that whoever would have fellowship with God must go beyond all that is seen and like someone standing on the peak of a mountain, stretch his intelligence (*dianoia*) to what can be neither seen nor grasped and believe that the divine (*to theion*)[13] is there where the understanding does not come.

Introduction

Moses' ascent of the mountain of the Lord in part 2 of the *Life* is structured around three principal theophanies, a translation of which follows. The first of these centres around the account of Moses' encounter with the burning bush (Exod. 3.1–14) with its climax at verse 14 with the revelation of God as 'I am who I am', or in the Septuagint version Gregory would have used 'I am He who is' which amounts in practice to a confession of God as 'The really real', and enables Gregory to identify Him with the ultimate reality of traditional Platonism.

The second theophany is taken from Moses' experience of darkness on the mountain, and especially at Exod. 20, 21, 'Then the people stood at a distance, while Moses drew near to the thick darkness (γνόφος) where God was'. This appearance is discussed at *Life* 2.162–166 and leads to the important conclusion that God is beyond the reach of the human mind.

The third and final theophany is discussed at *Life* 2.219–235 and is largely an exegesis of Moses' request to behold the face of God and of the divine reply at Exod. 33.23, 'My back parts you will see, but my face you will not see.' The consequence of this particular revelation is that God is infinite in his own nature, not simply incomprehensible to our feeble intelligences (section 236), and is also the object of infinite desire, that is, of a desire that can never be stilled (section 233).

Translation 2: (ii) 2.19–30

19. As soon as we are established in this peaceable non-combative condition, the truth will shine upon us, bringing light to the eyes of the soul[14] with its own rays. The truth that then shone on Moses through that wonderful illumination was God.

20. And if the light which enlightens the soul of the prophet comes from a thorn bush, that too is not without its value for our search. For if the truth is God and the truth is also light – and the gospel attributes both these high and divine titles to the God who appeared in the flesh – it follows that a virtuous life brings us to the knowledge of that light which descends as human nature. This light comes to us not from one of the bright lights around the stars, in case anyone should suppose that the ray emanated from some underlying material. It comes instead from an earthly bush, yet exceeds the lights of heaven with its brilliance.[15]

21. The vision also teaches something about the mystery of the Virgin, from whom the light of the Deity shone onto our human life through the birth (sc. of the Word). As the flame failed to destroy the burning bush, so too the flower of virginity was not corrupted by the birth.[16]

22. The light instructs us what we must do if we wish to remain within the rays of the true light. If we wish to ascend to so great a height, where the light of truth is seen, we must take off our shoes. This means that the dead and earthly covering of skins must be removed from the feet of the soul; a covering we acquired in the beginning, once we had been denuded through our disobedience to the divine will. Once we have done this, the knowledge of the truth will follow us, manifesting herself to us. For knowledge of that which is (or He who is) purifies us of any unreal opinion.

23. In my opinion the definition of truth is 'being free from error about the nature of reality'.[17] A lie is an illusion in the soul about what is unreal, which suggests that what does not exist in fact exists. Truth, on the other hand, is a firm perception of what really does exist. So anybody who has thought at leisure about such high matters will gradually perceive what 'being' really is, which has being of its own nature, and what non-being is, which enjoys only apparent reality, without any substantial nature of its own.

24. It seems to me that what the great Moses learnt in the theophany is simply this, that neither those things grasped by sense, nor those that the mind can understand, have a real existence. The only reality that truly exists is the one that is above all of them, the cause of all from which everything depends.

25. Whatever else the intelligence finds in existence, in none of these does it discover that complete independence of all else, which enables it to exist without participation[18] in The Really Real. Always to exist in the same way, never to become greater and never to be diminished, to be totally beyond all change whether it be for the better or the worse, means that the Divine is doubly incapable either of deterioration or of improvement. To be totally independent of all else and, at the same time, to be the sole object of desire; to be participated in by all, yet to be in no way thereby diminished, that is to be The Really Real (*to ontos on*) and knowledge thereof is the knowledge of the truth.

26. Once Moses then, and now those who follow in his footsteps, rid themselves of earthly encumbrances and see the light from the bush – that is the light that shines on us through the thorn bush of the flesh which is, as the gospel says, 'the true light' and 'the truth' [cf. John 1.9; 14, 6] – once, that is, they had arrived there, then they were in a position to be of service to others. They were able to destroy the evil tyranny that controlled them and to lead out into freedom all that were under the domination of an evil slavery. The alteration of the right hand and the transformation of the stick into a snake were the first of the miracles [cf. Exod. 4, 1–9].

27. By this it seems to me that the mystery of the appearance of the godhead of the Lord through the flesh was displayed, whereby both the destruction of the tyrant and the freedom of those under his control were indicated.

28. I am led to this conclusion by the combined witness of prophets and gospel alike. The Prophet speaks of the 'alteration of the hand of the most high' [Ps. 77 [LXX 76]11]. It is as if the divine nature remained unaltered, yet was changed to our shape and form by reason of its condescension[19] to the feebleness of human nature.

29. For there, the hand of the lawgiver being put outside his own breast, took upon itself an unnatural colour. Once, however, it had been restored to its original place, it returned once again to its own natural grace. And 'the Only Begotten God, who is in the bosom of the Father' [John 1, 18], he is the right hand of the Most High.

30. When he came forth from the bosom of the Father he was changed to become as we are. But, once he had erased our weaknesses, he restored the hand that had been among us and been coloured as we are to his own bosom – the Father being the bosom of the right hand. Then (sc. at the end) it was not the impassibility of his nature that he changed into something that suffers but, on the contrary, he transformed[20] our changeable and passible nature into impassibility, by means of its fellowship with what cannot change.[21]

Translation 3: (iii) 2.162–166

162. What is the meaning of Moses 'being within the cloud and seeing God there' [cf. Exod. 20, 21]? What is now recorded seems to be in some way the very opposite of the first theophany [sc. at Exod. 3.14]. Then the Deity (*to Theion*)[22] was seen in the light, now is it seen in the cloud (*gnophos*). We should not, however, suppose that this is out of harmony with the sequence (*eirmos*) of ideas so far considered.[23] The sacred text teaches us that religious knowledge is a light quite distinct from the one we first encountered. In fact what is thought the opposite of piety is indeed darkness while the turning away from darkness takes place by sharing in the light.

However, the further the mind advances and the greater and more perfect its attention to, and knowledge of, the realm of reality becomes, the nearer, in fact, that it draws close to contemplation (*theoria*), so much the more is it aware of the unavailability of the divine nature to human knowledge.

163. The mind leaves behind all that appears, not only what the senses grasp, but also whatever the intelligence (*dianoia*) seems to behold and ever seeks to move further inward, until it penetrates by reason of the activity of the intelligence to what is unseen and incomprehensible and there sees God. For it is precisely in this that true knowledge of what is sought consists, and precisely in this that seeing consists, that is in not seeing, because we seek what lies beyond all knowledge, shrouded by incomprehensibility in all directions, as it were by some cloud.[24] Hence the mystical John says, the same who penetrated into the shining cloud, that, 'No one has ever seen God' [John 1, 18]. By this denial he insists that the knowledge of the divine nature is unavailable not only to men, but also to all rational creatures.[25]

164. It is only when Moses has increased in knowledge that he confesses that he beholds God in the cloud, that is, that he knows that the Divine is by nature something above all knowledge and comprehension. For Scripture says, 'Moses entered the darkness where God was' [Exod. 20, 21]. Who is God? 'He who', as David says, 'made the darkness his hiding place' [Ps. 18 [LXX.17] 12]. For David also had been initiated into the secret mysteries in that very same shrine.[26]

165. Once arrived there he is once again taught by reason what he had already learnt through the cloud. The reason for this is, I think, that our conviction on this matter might be more firmly grounded once it had been assured by the divine voice. What the divine word above all inhibits is the assimilation by men of the divine to anything that we know. Every thought and every defining conception which aims to encompass and grasp the divine nature is only forming an idol of God, without declaring him as he truly is.

166. Religious virtue may be distinguished in the following way. Part deals with the divine; part deals with moral behaviour, for part of religion is purity of life. To begin with we must know how we are to think of God, and that knowledge entails entertaining none of the ideas which are derived from human understanding. The second part of virtue is taught by learning by what practices the life of virtue is realised.[27]

Translation 4: (iv) 2.231–244

231. When the soul is moved towards what is naturally lovely, it seems to me that this is the sort of passionate desire with which it is moved. Beginning with the loveliness it sees, it is drawn upwards to what is transcendent. The soul is forever inflaming its desire for what is hidden, by means of what it has already grasped. For this reason, the ardent lover of beauty understands what is seen as an image of what he desires, and yearns to be filled with the actual substance ($\chi\alpha\rho\alpha\kappa\tau\acute{\eta}\rho$) of the archetype.[28]

232. This is what underlies the bold and excessive desire of him who desires to see no longer 'through mirrors and reflections, but instead to enjoy beauty face to face' [cf. I Cor. 13, 12]. The divine voice concedes what is demanded by actually refusing it, and in a few words displays the immeasurable depths of its ideas. On the one hand, the divine generosity grants the fulfilment of his desire; on the other hand, it promises no end to desire nor satiety of it.[29]

233. In fact, he would never have shown himself to His servant if what was seen were enough to still the desire of the beholder. For, he declares 'My face you shall not see; for no one shall see my face and live' [Exod. 33, 20].

234. Scripture makes it plain that it is not the vision [sc. of God] that is the cause of death. For how should the face of life be the cause of death to those who draw near it? But since the divine is naturally life giving and, further, that it is the special character of the divine nature to lie above all definition, whoever supposes that God is one of the things he knows, is himself without life (n.b. $\zeta\omega\acute{\eta}$)

having turned aside from The Really Real to what is supposed to be grasped by a concept.

235. For The Really Real (τὸ ὄντως ὄν) is the true life and is inaccessible to our understanding. If, then, the life giving lies beyond our knowledge, what we have grasped cannot be the life. And what is itself not life is powerless of itself to communicate it. Moses' desire, therefore, is satisfied precisely in so far as his desire remains unsatisfied.

236. Moses is instructed through what has been said, that the Divine is of itself infinite (ἀόριστον), circumscribed by no limit. For if the Divine could be thought of as in some way limited, it would be absolutely necessary to consider what comes after it along with it. Whatever has a limit has a boundary, even as air is a limit for winged creatures and water for what lives in the water. And even as fish are surrounded in all their parts by water, so, too, are birds by the air; so, too, the limit of the water for the fish, and of the air for the birds, is the extreme surface of either which serves as a boundary for the fish of the sea or the birds of the sky, respectively. The same operates in the case of the Divine. If it were thought to have a boundary, this would imply the existence of a limit distinct in character from itself. And our argument has shown that whatever limits is greater than that which it encloses.

237. Every one admits that the Divine is by nature beautiful. But what is by nature distinct from the beautiful is something quite opposed to it; and what is outside the beautiful is assumed to be of the nature of evil. We have already shown that the container is greater than that which it contains. It necessarily follows from this that those who suppose the Divine has a limit must also admit that it is bounded by vice.

238. And as that which is bounded is always less than the nature which bounds, it would follow that the superiority of what does the bounding would have to be conceded. Whoever, therefore, circumscribes the Divine with a limit is in fact preparing for the control of the beautiful by its opposite. On the other hand, there is nothing that can be supposed to embrace the infinite nature. And all the desire for the beautiful which is drawn towards the upward ascent never ceases in its incessant pursuit of the lovely.

239. And the true vision of God consists in this, in never reaching satiety of the desire. We ought always to look through the things that we can see and still be on fire with the desire to see more. So let there be no limit to curtail our growth in our journey upwards to

God. This is because no limit to the beautiful has been found nor can any satiety cut short the progress of the soul in its desire for the beautiful.

240. What is the place referred to by God? What is the rock? And again what is the space within the rock? What is the hand of God, which covers the mouth of the hollow in the rock? What is the passage of God? What is the back part of God, which God promised to give Moses who had asked him for a face to face vision of himself?

241. It should be the case that each of these things is great and worthy of the munificence of the giver. Once his great servant had received this wonderful revelation, what followed must be believed to be both grander and more lofty still. How might anyone grasp the nature of this loftiness from what has been said? For it is there that after all his previous ascents Moses himself desires to ascend, as does He who 'works in all things for good to those who love God' [cf. Rom 8, 28] and so through his leadership facilitates each ascent. For, 'behold', he says, 'there is a place beside me.'[30]

242. This idea is in close agreement with our previous discoveries. For when it speaks of place it does not mean by that something circumscribed by quantity (for where there is no size there can be no measure either), but by using the image of a measured surface it conducts the listener to what is unlimited and infinite. The sense of the utterance seems to be something like this. Your desire is always strained forwards and your forward motion knows no weariness; further, you know no limit to the good and your desire is always intent on something more. This all means that the 'place' is ever near you, so that whoever runs therein never comes to an end of his running.

243. Yet from another point of view this running is also a standing still for, he says, 'I will station you upon the rock' [Exod. 33, 22]. And this is the greatest paradox of all, that the same thing is both stationary and on the move. For normally he who ascends never stays still, while he who stands still does not ascend. Yet, in this case, it is precisely through being still that the ascent occurs. The meaning of this is that the more firm and immoveable a person is in the good, so much the more does he accomplish the race of virtue. For whoever is uncertain and unstable in his convictions, has an unsure grasp on the noble (*kalon*); he is 'storm-tossed and carried around', as the Apostle says, and in doubt and shaken in one's conceptions about reality and, as a result, incapable of ascending to the height of virtue.

244. It is like people who endeavour to make their way upward through sand, who despite their taking great strides, labour fruitlessly. Their footing always slips on the sand as they go down with the result that, despite their perpetual motion, they fail to make any advance. But if anyone, in the words of the psalmist, says [Psalm 40.2 = 39.3 [LXX]] 'extracts his feet from the miry bog' and sets them instead firmly on the rock, that is, on Christ [1 Cor. 10, 5], who is perfect virtue, he will be firm and immoveable in virtue. So the aspostle exhorts us [1 Cor. 15.58] so much the more speedily will he accomplish his course. He uses his stability as a sort of wing and makes his way upward, his heart winged as it were by his firmness in the good. In showing Moses the place God encourages him in his course, and by promising him stability on the rock, he shows him how he is to run this divine course.[31]

Commentary on the Song of Songs 15 on Song 6.1–9

Prologue

The Apostle[32] Philip came, we are told, from the same town as Andrew and Peter. Indeed, it seems to me that it was by way of praising Philip that we are informed that he was a fellow citizen of the two brothers whose praise is in the gospel through their history. Andrew, on the Baptist indicating to him who was 'the Lamb of God that takes away the sin of the world' [John 1, 29], acknowledged the mystery and followed after the one who had been indicated. He found out where he dwelt and told his own brother that the one who had been foretold by the prophecy was actually present.

431.10. He (that is Peter) began to believe almost before he had heard and attached himself with his whole soul to the Lamb. Through the change of his name by the Lord he was named and became Peter instead of Simon [John 1, 37–42] and so was transformed into something more divine.

In a quite different way, only after many a theophany much later, the Lord shared a blessing with Abraham and Sarah, which derives from their names, appointing the one as father and the other [sc. Sarah] as leader by changing their names [Gen. 17, 5; 15]. Similarly Jacob, only after his all night wrestling, was thought fit to be called Israel and receive his power [Gen. 32, 29]. The mighty Peter did not advance to this grace by gradual increase but the moment he heard his brother he believed in the Lamb, was perfected through faith and became Peter through his closeness to the rock.

432.5. This same Philip, therefore, was thought worthy to be a fellow citizen of such remarkable men, once the Lord had discovered him, even as the gospel says, 'Jesus' [John 1, 43] 'found Philip'. Afterwards, he was appointed when the voice of the Word said, 'Follow me'. He drew close to the true light and, like a torch, drew to himself fellowship with the light and himself shone upon Nathaniel handing on to him the mystery of religion through his words, 'We have found him of whom Moses and the prophets spoke, Jesus from Galilee in Nazareth'.

432.14. Nathaniel received the good news with intelligence; he had been instructed by prophecy about the mystery of the Lord, whence he learnt, first, that the first appearance of the Lord in the flesh would take place at Bethlehem and, second, that he would be called a Nazarene because of the time he spent in Nazareth [cf. John 1, 46]. He attended to both these (sc. prophecies) and reflected that because of the economy of the Incarnation, the mystery of cave, the swaddling cloths and manger must take place in David's Bethlehem. Galilee, on the other hand, will be named (Galilee is the place of the nations) because of the preference the Word displayed for the nations. For this reason he agreed with him who had shown him the light of knowledge and said 'Something good *can* come out of Nazareth'.[33]

433.13. At this Philip became his guide to grace saying, 'Come and see' [John 1, 47]. Nathaniel left the fig tree of the law, whose shade inhibits fellowship with the light, and by this he means anyone who, because of absence of good works, dries the leaves of the fig tree. Therefore he is attested by the Word as a true and not a false Israelite because of the straightforwardness of his choice.[34] He manifests in himself the pure character of the patriarch. 'Behold', says the divine Word, 'a true Israelite, in whom there is no guile' [John 1, 47].

434.5. The point of this elaborate prologue is quite clear to my better instructed hearers simply by reading the ensuing extract of the *Song of Songs*. Andrew was directed by the voice of John to the Lamb; Nathaniel was enlightened by Philip and delivered from the constricting shadow of the law, emerged into the true light. So, also, the maidens in their search for the good that had been promised them, make use of the soul that had been perfected through beauty and speak to her as follows, 'Where has my little brother gone, O thou lovely among women?' [Cant. 6, 1]. Once they have been instructed through aforementioned signs that he is white and ruddy and the other things by which the beauty of him that is sought is outlined, they inquire where he is. Therefore they say, 'Where has my little brother gone and what way has he looked?'

Once they have discovered where he is, they wish to prostrate themselves towards the place where once his feet stood, and once they have discovered which way he looked, they may station themselves there, so that his glory may be seen by them. His appearance is the salvation of those that behold him, as the Prophet says, 'Let the light of thy face shine upon us and we shall be saved' [Ps. 79, 4].

Cant 6, 2

The instructress, not unlike Philip, who said, 'Come and see', guides the maidens to the apprehension of what they seek; but instead of saying 'Behold' (as he did), she points out the place where the one they seek is, and where he looks. She says, 'My beloved has gone into the garden to the beds of spices' [Cant. 6, 2]. So far his place is sufficiently indicated by the text. Thereafter what he sees and where he looks are revealed in the text by their teacher, when she says, 'He pastures [sc. his flock] in the gardens and gathers lilies.' This, then, is the bodily guidance of the word for the maidens. So they can learn where he is and whither he looks.

436.1. But we must at all costs discover by means of spiritual understanding the usefulness of this inspired piece of Scripture.[35] When, therefore, we hear that 'My beloved has gone down into his garden' we understand by these words the mystery of the gospel, where each of the names reveals to us a mystical meaning. The God who became manifest in the flesh through his rising from Judah 'to shine on the gentiles that sit in darkness and the shadow of death', [cf. Luke 1, 79] is termed beautifully and appropriately 'beloved' by his sister of the tribe of Judah that is wedded to him by a perpetual bond. The expression 'has gone down' is used because of the man 'that went down from Jerusalem to Jericho and fell among robbers' [cf. Luke 10, 30], the Word comes to the aid of him who had fallen into the hands of the enemy. All of this displays the condescension (*synkatabasis*) to our lowly state which proceeded from such unspeakable greatness.

Through the mystery of the garden, we learn that the true gardener plants his own garden. We human beings are his garden. For we are, as Paul reminds us [cf. 1 Cor. 3, 9] 'his field'. It was the Word at the beginning who cared for the human plant in paradise, which the Heavenly Father had planted. For this reason, after the wild boar had laid us waste, that is the garden, and defiled the heavenly planting, he (sc. the Word) came down in order to make the desert a garden once again, adorned with the flowers of virtues, irrigated, as such plants demand, by the Word itself with the pure and divine spring of his teaching.

437.8. 'The bowls of spice' [Cant. 6, 2] in the description of his beauty are taken to imply the praise of his cheeks by which the spiritual food is ground down for the benefit of those being nourished. It is here that the place and dwelling of the bridegroom is said to be by the Scripture and from this we gather that the groom does not lodge within a soul that is bereft of virtues and should anyone become, after the fashion we have traced out, a jar of ointment producing perfume, such a one becomes a bowl of wisdom and receives in itself the divine and pure wine, which brings joy to whoever receives it.

437.17. The following text tells us in what pastures the flocks of the good shepherd [cf. John 10, 11] are fattened. He does not drive them out to desert thorny wastes to gather grass for food. Instead, their food is the spices that come from the gardens; in place of grass there is the lily, which is said to be collected by the shepherd for the sustenance of the sheep.

In this way he teaches us that the nature and power which surrounds and embraces all things makes as its own place and surrounding the purity of those that receive it. Therein, the garden that has been variously cultivated by the virtues, is adorned with the blooms of the lily and abounds with fruitful spices. The lilies are a symbol of the shining and pure intelligence; the sweet scent of the spices is a symbol of the absence from the soul of the foul stench of sin.

So it is, as Scripture says, that the lord of the rational sheep behaves, leading them to pasture in gardens, and also cutting and gathering the lilies for the sustenance of the sheep. This truth he puts before his sheep through the great Paul, who out of the divine storehouse lays before us sustenance from the lilies. This is what he says, 'Whatever is true, whatever is honourable, whatever is just, whatever is pure, whatever is pleasing, whatever is commendable, if there is any excellence, anything worthy of praise' [Phil. 4, 8]. In my opinion this is the meaning of the lilies, with which the flocks of the good shepherd and teacher are nourished.

Cant. 6, 3

439.3. What follows is the speech made by the pure and spotless bride, 'I to my beloved and my beloved to me' [Cant. 6, 3]. This is the standard definition of perfection in virtue. By these words we are taught that we should have nothing other than God within us and that the purified soul should look to nothing beyond itself. It ought to be so cleansed of every filthy deed and thought, and be completely transferred into the world of intellect and immateriality and so to transform itself into the most exact reflexion of absolute beauty.[36] And even as anyone who beheld a sketch on a tablet, which is made to reflect as accurately as possible one of the archetypes, would say that the shape of both is alike, namely that the form of the image accurately reflects that of the model and that the model is clearly visible within the image. In the same way, she who says, 'I to my beloved and my beloved to me' confesses that her own beauty, the primal blessedness of our nature, has been transformed into Christ, made lovely in the image and likeness of the first, only and true beauty (Rom. 8, 29; Gen. 1, 26).

It is the same sort of thing that happens with a mirror. If it has been properly made and in conformity with need, when its surface is clear it provides an accurate reflexion of the face that appears in it. In like fashion the soul, once it has prepared itself appropriately and cast aside all earthly filth, expresses in itself the form of pure loveliness. This then is what the mirror that is both free and lively says [cf. Wisdom 7, 26], 'Since with all my soul I behold the face of my beloved, therefore all the beauty of his form is seen in me.' These words of hers are imitated by St Paul when he says that although he is 'dead to the world he is alive to God' [cf. Rom. 6, 11] and again that, 'Christ alone is alive in him' [Gal. 2, 20]. For he who says 'To me to live is Christ', intends by this to say that no human or earthly passion lives in him, neither pleasure nor grief, neither anger nor fear, neither cowardice nor terror, no cherishing of evil, no jealousy, no revengeful disposition. Such a one lives without craving for money, fame or honour or any of the other things that defile the soul through their form (σχέσις). Only someone who is none of these things is the only one who is as he should be. Only when I have filed away whatever does not belong to his nature, only then do I have nothing in me, which is not in him. For this reason he says, 'For me to live is Christ' [Phil. 1, 21]. So too the bride says 'I to my beloved and my beloved to me'. He is holiness and purity and incorruption

and light and truth and all the rest. He pastures my soul, not on grass
or on dry sticks, but among the brightness of the saints.

441.6. The nature of the lilies unlocks its meaning for us by
means of the shining character of its colour. It is for that reason,
therefore, that 'he who pastures his flock among the lilies' leads his
flock into the meadows of lilies, that 'the brightness of the Lord our
God may be upon us' [Ps. 89, 17]. Indeed, that which is nourished
agrees with the form of the nourishment. What am I driving at? Let
us imagine a hollow vessel made of glass, in which whatever is
thrown shines through, whatever it may be, soot perhaps or something cleaner or shinier. So, by putting the brightness of the lilies
within the soul, he makes the souls bright through their presence, as
the form that has been introduced into the soul shines through to
the outside.

441.18. In order to express my idea with greater clarity, I mean
that the soul is nourished through virtues. He terms virtues lilies in
symbolic language. Whoever's life is filled with virtues through their
good conduct displays the special nature of each particular virtue,
through their general character. Let self control, justice, bravery and
prudence and, as the Apostle says, 'Whatever things are true, whatever things are noble, whatever things are lovely, whatever things are
holy, whatever things are of good report, if there is any virtue, if
there is any praise' [Phil. 4, 8], let all these things be the lily. For
when all these things occur within the soul, they are revealed in the
purity of a life, adorning whoever possesses them and themselves
adorned through him who receives them.

Cant. 6, 4

442.10. Once she has dedicated herself to the beloved and been
adorned with his beauty in her own form, let us hear what she has
been thought worthy of by him who glorifies those who glorify him
[cf. John 17, 22]. And this we shall discover from the sequence of
thought in what is now said. For the Word says to the bride, 'Thou
art lovely, my near one, my glory, lovely as Jerusalem, terrible as
those drawn up for battle' [Cant. 6, 4].[37] Within the hearing of the
shepherds, glory rises up from the heavenly army to God in the
highest, for his favour (εὐδοκία) to men [Luke 2, 13/14] when they
saw peace born upon the earth. Jerusalem, further, is called the city
of the great king, by the lord of all creation [cf. Matt. 5, 35]. For
both these reasons it is clear to see, for anyone familiar with the

114

words of the gospel, what loveliness the Word acknowledges in the bride, by the comparison both with Jerusalem and with the grace of God.

443.6. It is clear that the exact intention of the text is as follows. It refers to the completed ascent of the soul to Himself and its subsequent stretching forward to the wonders of her Lord. For if God dwells 'in the highest' [cf. Luke 2, 14], the one 'who dwells in the bosom of the Father' [John 1, 18] is mingled with flesh and blood beyond the grace of men, that there may be peace upon earth. It is evident that she who moulds her own beauty in accordance with this grace (*eudokia*) imitates Christ himself in her endeavours and so becomes that to others, which Christ himself became to human nature. So it was that Paul, the imitator of Christ, acted in separating himself from this life [cf. ?Gal. 2, 12] in order that he might purchase the salvation of Israel in exchange for his own suffering. So he says in his prayer, 'I prayed to be accursed by Christ for the sake of my own people, my kindred according to the flesh' [Rom. 9, 3].

443.19. With reference to this, perhaps, what is said to the bride refers also to this. The loveliness of your soul is such as was the grace of our Lord for our sake, who 'emptied himself taking the form of a servant' [Phil. 2, 7], gave himself in exchange for the life of the world [cf. John 6, 51]. So, too, 'though he was rich he became poor for our sake, in order that we might live in his death and be rich in his poverty' [II Cor. 8, 9] and 'might reign' [cf. Rom. 5, 17] in the form of his poverty.

444.7. Her size and the similarity of her beauty to that of Jerusalem, clearly indicate the Jerusalem above, who is free, and the mother of those that are free [cf. Gal. 4, 26], the very city of the great king whom we have 'learnt about from the voice of the master. For she who embraces within herself him who cannot be circumscribed, so that God dwells and walks about within her [cf. 2 Cor. 6, 16] is adorned with the loveliness of him that dwells within her and so becomes the heavenly Jerusalem [cf. Heb. 12, 22] by receiving her (or his) (? ἐκείνης or ἐκείνου) loveliness within her.[38]

444.14. The beauty of the city of the king and its loveliness are in every respect the beauty of the king himself. To him belong, in the words of the psalmist, loveliness and beauty, and to him the prophecy refers which says, 'In your beauty and loveliness stretch out, ride forth and rule, for the cause of truth and gentleness and justice' [Ps. 44, 4/5]. With such marks as these is the divine beauty distinguished, I mean with truth and justice and gentleness. The soul, therefore, which is fashioned in such beauties, becomes as lovely as Jerusalem, adorned with the loveliness of the king.

445.4. So far we have dealt with the praise of the beauty of the bride and this has been achieved by a comparison with both grace and Jerusalem [cf. Cant. 6, 4; Luke 2, 13/14; Heb. 12, 22]. That what follows is to be thought of as a praise of the bride is beyond question. The underlying meaning, in the light of which such praise is accorded her, is far from clear. The text runs as follows, 'A wonder, like those drawn up for battle' [Cant. 6, 4]. One might perhaps suppose, following the line of our previous exegesis, that the praise of the bride was enhanced by comparing her to the celestial nature. There are the (powers) in order, where the authorities (*exousiai*) are ever in control, the lordships forever rule, where the thrones are totally stable, the rulers abide in submission to no one, where the powers bless God without ceasing, where the flight of the Seraphim never rests and the rest never changes, where the Cherubim never cease in their possession of their high and exalted throne, where the ministering spirits are forever doing their work and hearing the words.

446.1. The powers have been ordered by God and the arrangement of the intelligible and supracosmic powers abides undisturbed forever, without any evil upsetting their harmony.[39] Therefore the soul that is like them in all things does everything in order and fittingly and consequently induces that wonder which exists among the heavenly powers in their array. The meaning of wonder is amazement and we shall not be mistaken in understanding by amazement the wonder of the truth.

Cant 6, 5

446.11. The following verse [= Cant. Cant. 6.5] has a twofold reference. The words, 'Turn away your eyes from me, for they have disturbed me' could refer both to the one who speaks them and the one to whom they are addressed. To some it seems that they are addressed by the master to the pure soul, but I think that the reference of the words is rather to the bride. It is to her, above all, that the precise meaning of the language of the Word applies. The reasons for my opinion I shall now set forth.

447.3. I have frequently heard the inspired Scripture attributes wings to God. So the prophet says [Ps. 16 (17), 8] 'You will hide me in the shadow of your wings' and again [Ps. 90 (91), 4] 'You will find hope under his wings'. Moses expresses the same thought in his great song [Deut. 32, 11] when he says that 'He (sc. God) spread out his wings and received them'. There is also the saying of the Lord to Jerusalem [Matt. 22, 37] 'How often have I desired to gather your children even as a bird gathers together its young under its wings'. This being the case it would not be out of place for us to investigate the sequence of thought.

447.13. Holy Scripture, in accordance with some hidden reason, attributes wings to the divine nature. On the other hand, the first creation of man witnesses to the fact that our nature was initially 'in the image and likeness of God' [Gen. 1, 26] and thereby insists that he who was created in all respects in the image of God must have been in every respect like the archetype. Now Scripture informs us that the archetype was winged; therefore human nature also was created with wings. It follows, therefore, that in its wings also it should be like the divine.[40] And it is further clear that we must allegorise (τροπικὴ θεωρία) the language of wings in some sense befitting God. By the expression 'wings' are understood power, blessedness, incorruption and suchlike epithets. As long as man was in every respect like God, these qualities too belonged to him. However, his lapse into sin deprived us of these wings, for once we had left the shelter of the wings of God, we were denuded of our own wings. It was for this reason, therefore, that 'the grace of God appeared enlightening us, in order that we might put aside impiety and earthly desires and so might through piety and justice, again grow wings' [cf. Titus 2, 11/12].[41]

448.16. If what we say is not entirely devoid of the truth, it follows that it is entirely fitting that the bride should confess the grace that is hers coming from the eyes of God. For once God had looked upon us with the eyes of his love for humanity, then immediately we were equipped with wings in accordance with the grace we once had. I believe that Scripture communicates the same truth when David in his prayer in the sixteenth psalm says to the Lord, 'Let thine eyes see whatever is straight (εὐθύτητας) (by which he means my straightness), Thou hast tried my heart, thou hast visited me by night, thou hast tested me and no wickedness was found in me' [Ps. 16, 2/3]. For to say, 'Let thine eyes see the right' means the same as, 'Let not thine eyes see the opposite' (sc. of the right). For he who has looked upon what is straight (εὐθές), has not seen what is crooked, and again whoever has not looked upon what is crooked, has always contemplated what is straight. Therefore, through the removal of the opposite only the good is seen by the eyes of God and through them the soul once again sprouts wings, which had lost them through the disobedience of our first parents.

449.15. The same truth is communicated through the following words, 'Your eyes turn away from the opposite, when they look upon me, for they will not behold anything in me, which is opposed to me. Therefore from your eyes do I regain the wings I once lost and through virtue do I resume once again the wings as of a dove and through them the power of flight, to fly away and be at rest' [cf. Ps. 54, 7], by which is clearly intended 'the rest, with which God rested from all his works' [Gen. 2, 2].

450.4. After these expressions the outline of the bride's beauty is followed by a list of the different qualities that contribute to her loveliness, with aid of Scripture's use of appropriate imagery. The beauty of her hair, the order of her teeth, the flower on her lip, the sweetness of her voice and the blush on her cheeks, each is praised in its turn. The praise of each of the items mentioned is expanded for the bride by means of a comparison and juxtaposition of each with something else. Her hair is likened to the flocks of goats that appear on Galaad, while the shorn sheep rejoicing in their twins express by that likeness the praise of their teeth. The lip is likened to a rope stained with scarlet and the cheek is like the skin of the pomegranate. This is how the text reads: 'Your hair is like the flock of goats that have appeared on Galaad, your teeth are like flocks that have been shorn and washed, which have all born twins and none of them is barren (?bereaved); your lips are like a scarlet thread, and your voice is sweet. Your cheek is like the skin of a pomegranate, except for your silence' [Cant. 6, 5–7]. But since we have already examined these (sc. in homily 7) it would be quite superfluous to repeat my discussion yet again and so produce fatigue in the hearer. Even so, should there be anyone that would like to discover what was then said, through not having already heard our exegesis of the text, we shall briefly expose the sense of the riddling passage.

451.4. The hairs of the body have a function quite distinct from the rest of the body. Every body is governed by sense without which it can no longer live, (it is the body's life). Only hairs are at the same time parts of the body and yet are without perception. This is indicated by the fact that although other parts of the body are pained by burning and cutting, this is not the case with the hair. Again, seeing that, as Paul says, 'the hair is the glory of a woman' [cf. 1 Cor. 11, 15], hair that by its tresses adorns the head, we are taught

118

by the praise of the bride's hair, that those who are contemplating the head of the bride (by which is meant the Church), must hide their senses through wisdom and so rise superior to them. This is the meaning of Proverbs [10, 14], 'The wise will hide perception.' Sight for the wise is not the measure of what is beautiful, nor is the good discerned by taste, nor is the judgment of beauty determined by smell, touch or any other organ of sense. It is only once every organ of sense has been mortified that we may be able, through the soul alone, to touch and stretch out to those goods that are discerned by the mind alone. So do they glorify the woman, the Church. They are not inflated by honours nor are they constricted by littleness of soul, when distress occurs. Instead, should they need to be cut in half because of their faith in Christ, or perhaps handed over to the wild beasts or to fire, even so they will display the insensitivity of the 'hair' in their painful experiences.

452.7. Such was Elijah, when he came out of Gilead, his body hairy and filthy and covered with a goat skin, yet in no way terrified at the threats of the tyrant [cf. 4 (2) Kgs. 1, 8–17]. So, too, are all those who, in imitation of the noble nature of the prophet, raise themselves above the whole world despite 'their deprivations, persecutions and hardships, in mountains and caves and holes of the earth, of whom the world was not worthy' [cf. Heb. 11, 37/38]. All these, like a flock, are seen round the head of all, and so become the glory of the Church and mount upwards to heavenly grace together with the man from Gilead (sc. Elijah).

452.17. The goat has been added to the praise of hair for one of two reasons. It is perhaps because the nature of such an animal is somehow related to the growth of hair, so that the puzzle of the beauty that comes from hair becomes identical with the animal who is naturally shaggy with hair. It may also be that the same animal climbs without slipping on the rocks and moves around over the tops of mountains, making his way courageously through inaccessible and steep places. Such activity is not unnaturally connected with those who spend themselves on the rough path of virtue. Even further, one might say, that the goat contributes to the praise of the head by reason of the frequent use made of him in the priestly law by the law-giver [cf. Lev. 4, 23; Num. 7, 16].

453.7. I also know that in the puzzles of Proverbs [cf. Prov. 30, 29; 31], among the four beasts with stately stride, there takes his place the he-goat that leads the flock. We may perhaps conjecture the meaning of this in the following way. Every activity that begins through one person is spread abroad among many. Scripture informs us that metal work originated with one man, Tubal [cf. Gen. 4, 22], who discovered the art. After that anyone who is busy with the handling of metal refers his art to him. In like manner Abel was the first to be a shepherd, and Cain to till the field [cf. Gen. 4, 2]. Likewise, Scripture attributes to Nimrod the art of hunting [cf. Gen. 10.9], to Noah that of viticulture [cf. Gen. 9, 20] and to Enoch hope in God [cf. Gen. 4, 26]. Holy Scripture teaches us many similar lessons which show that through the expertise of one man a particular practice entered into the world through imitation of him.

453.21. So in the matter of zeal for God, Elijah's zeal led the way. Whoever imitated his zeal, followed in the footsteps of his prophetic freedom of speech and so became the flock of him, as it were, that led them in such a life as theirs. Such as these became the glory and praise of the Church, drawn up for the glory of the hair, leading a life separate and quite distinct from the life of the senses.

Cant. 6, 6

454.5. With similar means the text fills out the praise of the teeth. These refer to those who nourish the body of the Church through themselves. By it the text implies that they must always appear clean, as if they had just come from a bath, and in no way encumbered, as though they had only just been shorn. As far as the production of virtues goes they (sc. the teeth) are to become the parents of a double purity, that of soul and body. By this is meant that whatever is unproductive in the realm of what is better is exiled from these 'teeth'.

Cant. 6, 7

454.13. The cord that is laid across the lips indicates in the riddle the measured service of the word. By it the prophet refers to the 'guardian' and 'door' of all comprehension, when the mouth is opened at the right time and closed at the right time to speech. From the prophecy of Zachariah [2, 5] we know that 'cord' is a way of saying 'measure', because there the angel that speaks in it has in his hand a measuring line. The word (sc. of God) is particularly connected with measure, when it happens to be covered with a red dye. This is a symbol of the blood of the one who ransomed us. If anyone has, then, in the words of Paul, Christ who redeemed us with his own blood dwelling in him, he has on his mouth the measuring line made lovely by being dipped in blood. [cf. 1 Pet. 1, 18/19; 2 Cor. 13, 3].

455.5. The subsequent verse explains the mystery; the scarlet cord is termed 'timely speech' and the meaning of this is again whatever is both hourly and measured. For that which is exact and timely makes its appearance at precisely the appropriate moment, neither unpunctually nor outside the correct time. When the text likens the 'apple of the cheek' to skin of the pomegranate, she bears witness to the bride's perfection in good things. It shows that in no other thing is her treasure to be found, but that she herself is her own treasure and that she contains the preparation of all good things in herself. Even as the edible portion of the pomegranate is contained by its outer skin, so too is the inner treasure of the bride enclosed by the visible loveliness of her life. Such is the hidden treasure of our hopes, the particular fruit of the soul, which is protected by the virtuous life, as by the skin of the pomegranate.

456.1. The next expression, 'outside your silence', has the following meaning, namely that praise is not one of those things that arise from what we can see and so tell of. Rather, it arises from such things as are hidden in silence and so manage to escape verbal proclamation. And, as one might understand silence as 'beyond words', so one will not be mistaken in interpreting the Word as being 'outside silence'. For we are silent about such things that we are incapable of expressing through words.

456.8. If, therefore, silence is supposed to be outside him, then it follows that we must suppose that the Word is itself beyond silence. Whoever, then, uses the expression 'outside silence', clearly has something like the following in mind. Those things that language is capable of expressing are indeed lovely and mighty, and these things are 'outside silence'. But those things that are beyond expression are the things that are shrouded in silence, things that escape word and expression and are greater and more wonderful than those things that come to expression.

Cant. 6, 8

456.16. Let us now hear the praises that come next, the meaning of which is like that of the well in the Old Testament account, where a heavy stone laid on the mouth of the well prevents the shepherdesses from sharing the water. Jacob, however, removes the stone from the mouth of the well and filling the drinking troughs with water, enables the flocks to quench their thirst with the water from the spring [cf. Gen. 29, 2–10]. What is it that we are to liken to such a well as this?

457.3. 'There are sixty queens and eighty concubines and maidens without number. My dove, my perfect one is only one, the darling of her mother, flawless to her that bore her' [Cant. 6, 8/9]. Who will roll back for us the stone of this unclarity (ἀσάφεια)?[42] Who will draw out the water of the thoughts that lies so deep as to be inaccessible to human understanding? It seems to me fair to inform you that the knowledge of such matters belongs only to such as the Apostle addresses when he says, 'In every way you were enriched in him in all speech and knowledge' [1 Cor. 1, 5]. But our own poverty is incapable of grasping the riches of the word that lie before us. In order, however, to be free from the charge of idleness, we shall not shirk the labour of pouring out a little sweat on these verses also, for the sake of him who bade us 'search the Scriptures' [cf. John 5, 39].

457.17. We hold, then, that the philosophy contained in these words, which are devoted to the praises of the bride, presents us with teaching of the more subtle kind. And this is the teaching. Things are not created and recreated with the same order and sequence. When at the beginning created nature came to exist, in every separate case there was no interval between the beginning and the end. The passage from non being to being took place at once and perfection appeared at the very beginning. Now human nature is among the things that are created and, like everything else, it did not progress to perfection with the passage of time, but at its very first creation it was perfect. For Scripture says, 'Man was made after the image and likeness of God' [Gen. 1, 26]. This means the highest and most perfect of goods, for what could be found higher than likeness to God himself?[43]

458.10. In the first creation, then, there was no interval between the end and the beginning and our nature began with perfection. But when through its close connection with evil, our nature by death fell away from its abiding in good, it failed to regain its primal perfection all at once, after the manner of its first creation. Instead it progressed gradually in a certain order and sequence gradually shedding all its natural attraction to what was contrary (sc. to the divine image). For in the primal creation there was nothing to prevent the concurrence of the perfection of nature with its inception, as there was no vice; in the case of the second reshaping, however, there was a temporal distance to be traversed by those who hastened toward the first good.

459.1. For that reason our intelligence, bound through vice to its bodily inclinations, is stripped bit by bit, through the agency of its more refined behaviour, of its fellowship with the lower self. Hence, we have learnt that 'there are many mansions with my Father' [John 14, 2], So, in proportion as each of us has a relationship with the beautiful and a separation from what is worse, in that measure shall we receive recompense for our behaviour [cf. Rom. 12, 6]. Someone in the beginning of his attempt to share in the better life, is like a man swimming up from the depth of a life lived viciously, to share in the truth. Another goes even further in his desire for good things; yet another is halfway in his ascent of the heights and another goes beyond the halfway mark. There are still others who raise themselves above these; others surpass even them and yet others go beyond these in their upward striving. So God accepts each in their several ranks according to the varied choices of all, allotting to each and every according to their just deserts, and giving to the higher a just exchange of good and measuring out fairly a reward for those of lesser grade.

460.2. [Cant. Cant. 6, 8–9] Such, in our opinion, is the hidden sense of the forgoing verses which make distinctions for our benefit among the various souls that look towards the bridegroom. Some are termed 'maidens', who through their numerousness surpass the very nature of number. Others are called 'concubines' and others again 'queens', there being eighty of the former and sixty of the latter. But, above all these, the text exalts the perfect 'dove', who is to be thought of as being quite single and alone. She is also said to be alone for her mother and chosen for her who bore her.

460.12. The following is what we are led to think of through these divine oracles. The maidens are like people who have just escaped from profound deceit, as from a womb. They are 'newly born' [cf. 1 Pet. 2, 2] and because of the irrational character of their assent of faith are incapable, as yet, of a fully articulate response. There are a vast number of such persons. Though they suppose themselves to be masters of the saving word of the mystery, in fact they fail to possess within themselves the truth which rests upon knowledge and experience of the word. These are they who are called 'maidens', because their spiritual age is still young. Begotten though they were by the word of faith, they have not yet become by appropriate increase mature enough to be ready for marriage and to

123

advance 'to perfect manhood, to the measure of married stature' [cf Eph. 4, 13]. As yet they are incapable of becoming pregnant in the fear of the Lord, and so bring forth the spirit of salvation into the world. Instead, in the childish and incomplete state of their minds, their lives are conducted in an irrational manner. Yet even these belong to the company of the saved, even as the prophet says, 'You will save men and beast, O Lord' [Ps. 35, 7], by 'beast' meaning the less rational part of those who are saved.

461.7. We are also taught by the same text that there is a distinction we must make among those who, by means of appropriate attention, have increased in understanding and left their childhood behind them. Both types of soul become, as it were, of one body with the word. But some become attached by a passionate disposition of soul, as were the souls of David and Paul, the former saying 'It is good for me to cleave to my God' [Ps. 72; 28], while the latter proclaims, 'No one will separate us from the love of God, which is in Christ Jesus; neither life nor death nor things present nor things to come nor indeed anything else' [Rom. 8, 35].

461.16. Others, however, take flight from the adulterous experiences through fear of punishment. These, too, remain in incorruption and holiness, but they avoid evil under the tutelage of fear rather than desire. The former class, through their more perfect disposition, mingle with the divine purity in their passion for immortality. These are called 'queens', therefore, because of their membership of the kingdom. The others, however, are termed 'concubines' by the text, because they practise virtue through fear of punishment. None of them is as yet capable of becoming mother of the king and companion of his glory. For how should anyone possess such a power, who had yet to receive within himself the independence and self mastery of a virtuous disposition, being kept from fellowship with evil only by servile fear?

462.9. Examples of what has been said in the case of the queens are to be found in the case of those who are deemed worthy of a place at the right, to whom the king says 'Come, you blessed of my Father, receive the kingdom prepared for you' [Matt. 25, 34]. They, however, would belong to the second and lesser rank, to whom the Lord says, 'Fear him who has power to cast you into the hell of fire' [Luke 12, 5].

462.16. This distinction of rank seems to me to be further mysteriously indicated by a numerical distinction. What is my meaning? There are six commandments by which the kingdom is prepared for those on the right. Now let us suppose that each of these is a talent from the Lord [cf. Matt. 25, 35/36], which the good and faithful servant is to increase by his labour tenfold. In this way 'he who had been found faithful in few things has been established over many and so enters into the joy of his Lord' [cf. Matt. 25, 14–21]. The soul, then, through these six commandments, gains fellowship in the kingdom and the perfection of service in each case increases the command ten times, as the good servant says; 'The *one* talent that was yours has produced ten' [Luke 19, 16]. As a consequence we find that the one queen is extended among sixty. The one, therefore, becomes many divided up by the plural and distinct nature of the commands and, further, is shaped specifically by each of them. In this way, therefore, the one queen is divided up and numbered among sixty in accordance with the various nature of the commands. So the bride shares in the kingdom of Christ. The one bride becomes a whole race of queens and is numbered according to the honour she derives from her observance of the commandments.

463.19. If we are correct in assuming that through the sixty queens we are being told of the sixfold command which is nurtured in one soul in a tenfold manner, it follows that through the eighty (sc. concubines) the mystery of eight is being displayed by means of a similar riddle. With reference to this we may say that those who are being instructed by fear are separated from companionship with evil. We discover this from the psalms, which are inscribed with 'the eighth'. The words (sc. in such psalms [so Ps. 6, 1; 11; 12, 1]) spring from those who are being tortured and try to turn the divine ear to mercy in their fear of future punishments.[44] 'O Lord, rebuke me not in thy anger, nor chasten me in thy wrath. Be gracious to me O Lord, for I am weak; heal me, O Lord, for my bones are troubled' and all that follows in the pleas made to the impartial judge. Among these he complains that there is no remembrance of God in death [Ps. 6, 2–6]. (For how could it be possible for those condemned to weeping and gnashing of teeth [cf. Matt. 8, 12; 13, 42, 24, 51] to enjoy the memory of God, especially with the words of the prophet the memory of the Lord causes joy [cf. Ps. 76, 4 LXX 2 only]. Other things like this are put forward by the one who fears the eighth, who on becoming aware of his share in the divine mercy, says, 'The Lord has heard the voice of my complaint' [Ps. 6, 9].

464.21. But since there are many blessed fears revealed to us by Scripture it should be possible to discover a tenfold increase, as it was in the case of the six commands. The result would be that he who has been taught the fear of the Lord by the psalms 'by avoiding evil and doing good' [cf. Ps. 33, 15], should be able to increase by labour the value that comes from the fear of the Lord, as if it were some man or talent [cf. Luke 19, 16]. Such a soul that does good out of fear rather than out of love takes second place after the royal soul until she arrives at the number eighty, displaying in her life without confusion and, quite separately, every shape of virtue that may be achieved through fear. After this fashion is the number eighty arrived at by multiplying eight by ten. So it happens that the soul approaches The Good more in servile fear than in bridal love and she becomes a concubine rather than a queen. Her virtue has been achieved through fear (sc. of the eighth day), increased tenfold and so coming to the number 80.[45]

465.16. It is for this reason that the Old Testament account bids the concubine serve (sc, the groom) for a time with illegitimate, rather than legitimate, offspring. She is not, however, to live permanently with the queen, on the grounds that the queen's inheritance is not of like kind to that of the offspring of the slave, above all in comparison with the free offspring. For Scripture says, 'Cast out the slave girl and her son; for the son of the slave will not inherit with the son of the free woman' [Gen. 21, 10; Gal. 4, 30]. If anyone thinks that the interpretation offered of the numbers in the text seems somewhat forced, he should remember that at the outset we warned him that it was impossible to arrive at the truth in such matters simply by skating on the surface and passing by matters that require exercise of the mind for their understanding.

Cant. 6, 9

466.5. However, if 'love perfectly expels fear' [cf. 1 John 4, 18] as is written, and if fear, once transformed, becomes love, then what is saved will be found to be the unity (*monad*) of all those who are united among themselves in accordance with the perfection of the dove, all growing towards The Only Good. Something like this we gather from the following verse, 'My dove, my perfect one, is only one, the darling of her mother, flawless to her that bore her' [Song 6, 9]. A clearer expression of this can be discovered in the gospel, through the voice of the Lord himself. Having handed over to his disciples all his power, he then entrusts all other good things to his saints in his words to the Father. Finally, in addition, as the climax of all his gifts, he prays that that there be no difference of will or opinion among them in their judgment about the nature of the beautiful, but that instead 'all should be one' in their attachment to the one and only good. 'Bound together, therefore, through the unity of Spirit in the bond of peace' as the Apostle says [cf. Eph. 4, 3/4], all are to become one body and one spirit through one hope into which they have been called.

467.3. It would perhaps be better to put forward for inspection the divine words of the gospel one by one. 'That they may all be one, even as thou Father in me and I in thee, in order that they may be one in us' [John 17, 21]. The glory is the cohesive power of this unity and no one who looked at the words of the Lord carefully would deny that the Holy Spirit was the glory. For he says, 'The glory you gave me I gave to them' [John 17, 22]. He truly gave his disciples such a glory when he said to them, 'Receive the Holy Ghost' [John 20, 22]. He had received this same glory, which he who was girt about with human nature always had before the world began, and once that had been glorified by the Holy Spirit the spread of the glory of the Spirit was divided among all human beings, beginning from the disciples. Wherefore he says, 'The glory you gave me I gave them, that they may be one, even as we are one, I in them and thou in me, that they may be made perfectly one' [John 17, 22/23]. He, therefore, who grows and increases from childhood to perfect manhood finally comes to the measure of intellectual age. Instead of being a slave or a concubine, he shares in the dignity of kingship and receives the glory of the spirit through self control (*apatheia*) and purity. Such is the perfect dove at which the bridegroom looks when he says, 'My dove, my perfect one is only one, the darling of her mother, flawless to her that bore her' [Cant. 6, 9].

468.4. We are not totally ignorant about the mother of the dove, knowing as does the tree from the fruit. In our search for the mother of the flawless we will suppose her to be none other than the dove herself, for the nature of the parent is discerned in the child. Since that which is begotten of the spirit is spirit [cf. John 3, 6] it follows that, seeing that the child is a dove, the mother of the child must also be one, and is the very same as the dove that flew down from heaven at the Jordan, as John witnesses [cf. John 1, 32].

468.15. The maidens bless her [sc. the dove]; the concubines and princesses praise her. All souls from every rank share in a common straining to such happiness as this. Therefore, the text reads, 'Thy daughters know thee and bless thee; thy queens and concubines will praise thee' [Cant. 6, 9]. It belongs to every nature to strain, full of desire, to that which is happy and praised, so that if the daughters bless the dove, they desire themselves to become doves. Further, the very fact of the praise of the dove by the concubines and queens is at the same time a proof of the enthusiasm they have for the object of their praise. The end will be that those who are at one in the object of their desire, themselves form a unity, without any trace of evil being left among them. Finally, God will become all in all, [1 Cor. 15, 28].[46] Those who have been joined to each other in unity by their sharing in the common good in Christ Jesus Our Lord, to whom be glory and power for ever and ever, Amen.

5

EPILOGUE

ON TAKING LEAVE OF GREGORY OF NYSSA

It is undeniable that Gregory of Nyssa never occupied in the minds of his contemporaries of the later Roman Empire, or indeed among the theologians of East and West, quite the same position as that occupied either by his brother, Basil, or by their common friend, Gregory Nazianzen. No luminous halo surrounds him. The *Acta Sanctorum* assign his feast day to 9 March but, that apart, he has, unlike them, no universal feast day in the modern Roman calendar, while they are celebrated together on 2 January. In the Greek liturgy he is remembered on 10 January, though no elaborate liturgy is provided. By contrast, 25 January is kept more solemnly as the feast of Gregory 'The Theologian'. Neither was he 'canonized' to the same degree as they. Basil and the other Gregory became, along with Athanasius and Chrysostom, the great Eastern Fathers, not unlike the four Latin Fathers, Ambrose, Augustine, Gregory and Jerome.

He was not a monastic legislator like St Basil. He never acquired quite the name for orthodoxy which led Gregory Nazianzen to be styled 'The Theologian' although the emperor Theodosius, as we have seen, did appoint him commissary for the civil diocese of Pontus, to oversee the implementation of the decrees of Constantinople. Evidently his Origenist teaching on *apokatastasis* had not yet roused suspicion.

His greater speculative boldness and his greater indebtedness to the Platonic tradition have made him a subject of great fascination to many. His undoubted formal indebtedness to Plato in his *On the Making of Man* and in *On the Soul and Resurrection*, to the *Timaeus* and *Phaedo* of Plato respectively, and his material dependence on Plato's *Symposium* in his *On Virginity* and *Commentary on the Song*, far

129

outweighs anything of the sort in the writings of either Basil or Nazianzen, of Athanasius or Chrysostom.

Ironically, also, we now possess better texts of Gregory of Nyssa than we do of either of the other two Cappadocians, an advantage we owe to the activities of Werner Jaeger and his successors, and this fact has made Gregory the subject of much secondary writing since then. Yet what claim does Gregory have upon our current interest?

Part of the intriguing nature of Gregory of Nyssa as a writer lies in the fact that he compels us to ask the sort of questions about his literary character, his originality and self consistency, which we ask of any great author. What, we ask, was his 'centre', what distinguishes him from other authors of the same period or earlier, and ultimately, the most difficult question of all, why is he either important or interesting for us now? In other words, is Gregory simply an interesting fossil from a theological cabinet but of no permanent interest, or has he something of interest and value to say to us now?

To take the last point first. Gregory does indeed belong to a world and an intellectual climate very different from our own. Even to list some of the differences is instructive. He lived at a period when the basic teachings of Christianity were in the crucible of formation. The nature of the personal union of God and man in Christ, the deity of the Holy Spirit, at least up to 381, had yet to be defined and were, in the fourth century, the subjects of lively debate, which may strike us as strange.

Again, the value of ancient wisdom, above all the philosophies of Plato and Aristotle, was something that called for discussion. How much of it could be incorporated into the Christian scheme of things without endangering the centre of the faith? Indeed, had the faith a centre anyway, an essence, from which its accidental trappings could be removed without fear of dismantling the heart? Now some of these issues, although not all of them, seem very foreign to our anti-doctrinal age, though the need to find a *modus vivendi* with new scientific discoveries and more empirical philosophies still challenges the Church. It may be the case that the study of Gregory's coming to terms with his age may shed light on the way we might come to terms with our, in many ways, very different age.

But how great in practice is the divide, if such it be, and is it capable of being in any way surmounted? To take the general question of culture first. The barbarian invasions in the East and West, although to some extent heralded by events like the Battle of

Adrianople of 378, when Valens was defeated and killed by the Goths, were in fact events of the future. In the event, the Goths and the Vandals showed more interest in the West than the East. East Rome at that date did not attract the greedy spirit of the Barbarian, although Old Rome itself was sacked by Alaric the Goth in 410 and nearly so by Attila in 451. The City, as Constantinople came to be called, was spared. The break between the classical past and the medieval/modern world came much sooner in the West than in the East. The pontificate of Gregory the Great (590–604) is often thought of as the watershed in the West. But, even in the West, Latin continued to be used, right up to the time of the Reformation and the growth of nation states. It needs also to be remembered that in the West until 1965 and in the East even today, the language of the liturgy was respectively the language of Cicero and Augustine, of Plato and Chrysostom.

The gradual erosion of the Eastern Empire by the continuous onslaughts of the armies of Islam from 632 onwards was still a thing of the future and took a long time. As Norman Baynes has pointed out; 'As one studies the later developments of Hellenism one cannot but be struck by the hold it continued to possess over the minds of the Greeks of East Rome.'[1] Above all, Greek continued to be spoken. For the East, the decisive moment came on 29 May, 1453, with the sack of Constantinople by the Ottoman Turks.

Even so, this sad event was not without advantages. The sack meant the transference to the West of much culture and language, which we associate with the Renaissance and with the cry '*Ad fontes*', back to origins. So, although it is true that Greek is no longer a *lingua franca* in the western hemisphere, something of its spirit survives, in the search for form and understanding and clarity and in the critical spirit of Socrates. Even today there exists the twin heritage of the desire to understand with the mind, and the parallel awareness that the mind is, at best, a useful instrument, and that words and definitions must surrender before mystery. It is precisely in this fruitful alliance between the search for exactness and the perils of such a search that we meet in Gregory of Nyssa.

Again, on a more strictly religious front, the intellectual temperature of those centuries was very distant from our own. Both Christians and pagans then shared a common belief in the existence of God or of gods. Religion, in various shapes, was still thriving, as St Paul had written, 'Gods many and lords many' (1 Cor. 8, 5). Religion had still to be marginalized. Deists would have been rare, except in

131

the imaginations of carping critics; atheists, in the strict sense, were non-existent. The Enlightenment, at least in the eighteenth-century meaning of the term, was a phenomenon of the future, as was the Reformation and biblical criticism. Even so, the Bible continues to be read and the creed continues to be recited, as a living reminder of our cultural heritage.

Does this mean that we are separated from Gregory and his world by a sort of cultural divide that may not be bridged? Not entirely, for reasons already given. If the cultural relativity were so great, it would reduce studies of this sort to mere antiquarianism, shorn of further relevance. It is the contention of this book that this is not so, although it must be admitted that any attempt to go against this claim must appear to be special pleading. What has been offered in this book is not simply a specimen of the way a particular Christian wrote and thought on a fairly limited range of topics towards the end of the fourth century, although it does at least offer some account of the actual background against which Gregory wrote.

Gregory is, at the same time, a good example of the way in which a gifted Christian individual, who was also a representative of his age, responded to challenges that were both particular and universal. The question hardly changes. How far can Christianity come to terms with the spirit of the age, without ceasing to be also the voice of the spirit of the ages? Further, if, from the Christian point of view, that age was peculiarly rich and significant, then surely it and he have something to tell us about ourselves as well as about themselves.

In the earlier part of this book an attempt was made to outline some of the areas in which Gregory wrote and to try to shape into a loose system the way he responded to particular challenges. In doing so, certain questions obstinately refused to go away. One of them was: Is he to be thought of as a rhetorician, or a thinker and philosopher, and are these mutually exclusive? The answer to this question clearly affects the degree to which we are prepared to censure or pardon him for supposed inconsistencies. In other words, how seriously should we take him? The extensive interest shown in him by scholars of all religious persuasions indicates that he is in some sense a serious person, and not to be written off as a theological lightweight.

It must be admitted, at the outset, that Gregory is a very elusive figure. He is both a rhetorician, using language to convince, to the best of his ability, while he is also a serious figure who believes that

132

he must treat such issues seriously. He is a rhetorician but only up to a point. And we need to remind ourselves that certain distinguished rhetoricians, like Maximus of Tyre in the second century, devoted much space in their Διαλέξεις to the discussion of philosophical issues.

Again, as we have seen, Gregory will on occasion use the arguments of Origen and Basil. Even so, he is not merely a slavish copier of their views; he modifies and will either silently distance himself from them or openly dissent from them. He is a traditionalist in his respect for the great Christian figures of the past, but he has also a mind of his own. In this respect, if in no other, his relationship to Origen is not unlike Plotinus' relationship to Plato. A respectful admirer, but with a mind of his own.

Most revealingly, however, can his originality and particular contribution to theology be gauged in his attempt to rework his inherited Platonism in order to make it a vehicle for the expression of a Christian vision. Gregory believed that these were serious issues, worthy of close attention. To treat him as simply a spiritual writer is to forget that he was, above all, a theologian as a large portion of his surviving works eloquently proclaim. Four particular areas suggest themselves as examples of this preoccupation.

1 As has been illustrated in his *Catechetical Oration*, he endeavoured to prove that the gospel met the highest demands of the critic. He did this mainly in the areas of Trinity and Incarnation by suggesting that the doctrine of the Trinity could be seen as midway between Greek polytheism and Hebrew monotheism. His attempt to 'rationalize' the Incarnation took the form, as we have seen, of showing how the doctrine meets all the demands of a rational doctrine of a God, who is wise, powerful, just and good.

2 In endeavouring to evade the charge of tritheism, he invoked the ideas of 'concrete universal' – a sort of uncomfortable amalgam of Platonist realism and Aristotelian abstraction – to suggest that membership of the same class did not, of itself, in any way entail plurality.

3 Again, he is, on the one hand, in many ways austerely rational in his approach, and in all his works, whether exegetical or dogmatic, he insists on the imperative need to look for the sequence of thought, the ἀκολουθία or εἱρμός – a conception he perhaps derived from Stoic logic and physics – yet, at the same time, he is quite convinced that such a rational approach cannot bring us

very close to the object of our search. Faith alone unites us to the object of our desire, and that object, God himself, is in any case always elusive.

Indeed in a passage in the *On the Life of Moses* (2.163), Gregory strikes a Lessing-like note in maintaining that the highest we can rise in our search for the knowledge of God is our awareness that complete knowledge of what we seek will forever elude us. So, too, Lessing would have preferred to be for ever searching for the truth rather than actually possessing it in his grasp. God is in some sense open, through his works, to the aggressive under-standing of man, but He is also supremely mysterious and may never be fully known or understood.

4 In a recent article Rowan Williams has sought to salvage the psychology of Gregory from the charge of inconsistency. He illustrates the point by an exploration of his *On the Soul and Resur-rection*. In parts of this work Gregory – or what comes to the same thing, his sister Macrina – suggests that the soul, on the model of the *Phaedo* of Plato, is simple, without the passions playing any part in its composition (cf. *MPG* 46, 49Bff.). Yet elsewhere, at 64 and 89, a different picture emerges. There the soul needs passion of some sort in order to realise its ultimate truth. Williams tries, not wholly successfully, to reconcile the two models and, in so doing, illustrates something of the perpetual problem facing Gregory in his attempt to make sense of the Christian revelation in philosophical terms. Passion is and is not part of us. 'Is' because we need to desire God and 'is not' because desire can be debased and become simply a search for the gratification of the lower appetites.

In making these claims for Gregory, I would not wish to be under-stood as claiming that he produced totally satisfactory or perma-nently valid answers to the problems he addressed. His appeal to a curious amalgam of Plato and Aristotle, for example, with which to 'solve' the problem of the Trinity is hardly satisfactory. Again, some of the attempts Gregory makes to 'tame' the Incarnation, by adapt-ing it to the moral idea of God he found in Origen, have every appearance of destroying its mysteriousness. But that it is hardly the point. He faces the problem, which the central Christian teachings create for the inherited rationalism of the age, and endeavours to reconcile them. Where Gregory has much to teach us is less in the answers he offers than in the effort to face the challenge, and in his laying bare of the problem of the integration of faith within philosophy.

The peculiar interest of Gregory for philosophical theology lies in the fact that despite all this rationalism, there lies in his vision a conviction about the nature of God, which is certainly not at all rational, and of which, perhaps significantly, he makes no mention in his *Catechetical Oration* – the divine infinity. This immediately raises the question of his position within the Platonist tradition, for which he clearly felt great sympathy. What he seems to be doing in general is harmonizing two related, but *prima facie*, incompatible positions, a tension which emerges more clearly in his ascetical works than in his strictly dogmatic writings. On one hand, we are and must be like God. All we are comes from him, we participate in him, we are made in his image and likeness,[2] he is the ultimate source of all our life, above all our mental life and, at the same time, he has left traces of his nature upon the works of his hands. Yet, he is also quite unlike us, being completely transcendent and above us in every respect. This tension in his thinking occurs at *Against Eunomius* 1.273, where Gregory situates the divine nature within the realm of intellectual beings and immediately afterwards insists on the distinction between God as the source of all the πηγή and on creation κτίσις as derivative from him.

There is therefore a fruitful tension in his thought between the two convictions that control him; on one hand, there is and must be an unbridgeable gulf between creature and Creator – a conclusion reinforced by the controversy with Eunomius – and yet, at the same time, we, by reason above all of our powers of thought and free will, are importantly like God. Gregory sees this apparent contradiction very clearly and one of his most important works, the *On the Life of Moses*, is largely devoted to overcoming it as best he may.

This tension is evident previously in the progressive self-revelation of God in the book of Exodus, where God is progressively 'He who is' [Exod. 3, 14], incomprehensible [Exod. 20, 21] and infinite [Exod. 33, 20]. The *On the Life of Moses* is peculiarly instructive in this regard, because it enables us to see Gregory applying his theological insights, generated by the Anomoean controversy, to the spiritual life. The discovery of a progressive revelation in Exodus seems to be original to him. It is certainly lacking in Origen's homilies on the same book. Further, it is a very good example of the way in which Gregory both appropriates the

Platonist tradition and yet does not allow it to determine the ultimate pattern of his thought.

THE ORIGINALITY OF GREGORY IN COMPARISON WITH ORIGEN AND AUGUSTINE

All three writers belong within what might loosely be called the Platonist tradition. But within that general rubric considerable differences emerge. Easily the most obvious is the fact that for Origen and Augustine God is primarily thought of under mental models. For Gregory, on the other hand, God, though indeed intellectual, is more importantly above mind (though never, as he is with Denis the Areopagite, 'above being') and uncreated. If this be accepted it would appear that by comparison with his great predecessor and intellectual mentor, Origen, and his younger contemporary, Augustine, Gregory has emancipated himself more effectively than them from the tradition of Greek metaphysics. For Plotinus, and for later Greek thought, as Dean Inge observes, 'there are no straight lines across the map of the universe'. Further, in traditional Greek thinking, we miss both any interest in, or stress upon, the centrality of creation. Indeed, for both Origen and Augustine, the body and the physical universe are treated much more negatively than they are by Gregory, for whom the bodily resurrection is absolutely central.

I do not wish to imply by this that either Origen or Augustine deny the doctrine of creation. Origen asserts the creation of material things quite explicitly, a point he underlines with great clarity in *On First Principles* II, 2.1, although his attitude to spiritual beings, whether angels or souls, is more ambivalent. They seem to be involved in the same sort of relational necessity which demands the existence of the eternal Son. So Origen argues at *On First Principles* I, 2.10 that, 'as no one may be termed father without possessing a son, . . . so God cannot be termed omnipotent, and not possess beings over which he exercises power; therefore, that God may be shown to be omnipotent, it is necessary that all things must exist'. Again, for Origen, God is indeed a personal being, but he is to be thought of as Mind. At *On First Principles* 1.16, God is 'defined' as 'intellectualis natura simplex . . . mens et fons ex quo initium totius intellectualis naturae vel mentis est', 'a simple intellectual nature . . . he (sc. God) is mind and source from which every intellectual nature and minds is derived'; God is primarily and essentially mental and so are we. With such a conception of God it is hardly surprising that

Origen has been termed by Charles Bigg 'the least mystical of divines' (*The Christian Platonists of Alexandria* (Oxford: OUP, 1913), p. 132). The reason is clear. It is by the exercise of the intelligence that we are to approach the supreme intelligence of God. It is true that Origen does indeed use the language of deification with which to denote human nature's supreme relationship to God, but by that idea he means 'knowing God' and in doing so he follows in the footsteps of Aristotle, who held a similar view, in whose *Nicomachean Ethics* we read that the aim of life is to become immortal and that this immortality consists of blessed contemplation (cf. *NE* X, 7).

In Augustine, too, as in Origen, it is through the mind that we mirror God's presence within us – a point made clearly by Augustine in book 10 of his treatise *On the Trinity*. Finally, the present and future bliss of the created spirit is not mystical absorption, not endless pursuit, in this world and in that to come, but face to face vision, leading to love and praise (cf. *City of God* 22, 30). Despite his endorsement of the doctrine of creation and his fairly consistent rejection of that of preexistence, his actual account of the fall and return of the created spirits in *Confessions* 13, 2 bears all the marks of his dependence on Plotinus, in whose writings the created and uncreated spirit are not divided by a great gulf (cf. *Ennead* 5.1.1).

Gregory, consciously or unconsciously, distinguishes himself from such a position. For him, in *Against Eunomius* 1.270, we do indeed share with God in the intellectual life. All spiritual beings, men, angels and God are part of the large division of things described as 'intelligible and intellectual nature'. But, and herein lies the significant difference, this identity masks a greater dissimilarity. God is both uncreated and infinite; we (and the angels) belong to the world of time, creation and limit. And this fundamental divide may never be crossed either in this life or hereafter. This perhaps accounts for the strange fact, that the language of deification rarely appears in the writings of Gregory.[3] And while for both Origen and Augustine we are made for ultimate understanding of God, for Gregory faith is that whereby, if at all, we grasp him.

For Augustine, death means an overcoming of the temporal divide that separates us from the vision of God. At death we become eternal and finally and for good transcend the limitations imposed upon us by the 'trailing consequence of days and nights'. The purpose of the Incarnation, he writes in his second *Tractate on the First Letter of John* (section 10), is simply this '*ut fias aeternus*', 'that you may become eternal'. For Gregory, on the other hand, the διαστημα (tension) that separates time and eternity, creature and creator, can never be bridged, either in this life or the next, either by angels or by men. We are committed, as created spirits, to the everlasting, upward striving, which is often referred to as '*epectasis*' which realises in us the likeness to God, which is our goal.

In answer, therefore, to the vexed question, 'Was Gregory a Platonist?', the answer must be 'It all depends on what is meant by Platonism.' Is it the Platonism of Plato that is meant, or something later and more clearly defined, like the amalgam of Plato and Aristotle which began to emerge in the first century BC with Antiochus of Askalon, or the second century AD system of Alcinous, in his *Handbook*?[4]

Again, if by the term is meant an ideology which simply aims at the vision of, or absorption in, the Absolute, then clearly Gregory hardly counts as a Platonist. If we mean by the term a hierarchical vision of the universe arranged in articulated grades, of the type we find in Plotinus, then it is clear that Gregory was no Platonist, preferring instead to stress 'the straight line drawn across the map of the universe by the fact of creation', in strong contrast to Plotinus on the one hand and, on the other, to both Origen and Augustine, whom, although they both modify Platonism, do so much less drastically than Gregory.

If, on the other hand, the term is taken to imply the restless upward movement of the created spirit towards the uncreated infinite spirit of God, who perpetually eludes our grasp, then Gregory is most assuredly a follower of Plato. This tendency is peculiarly marked in the spiritual treatises of Gregory. Finally, to say he was not much of a philosopher is a little unfair. He wrestled with problems and offered solutions, in terms of the philosophy he had inherited.[5] It is true he was not always successful, but the effort in such areas is what counts. He does not adopt the easy solution of informing us that all is mystery and leave us there.

LATER INFLUENCE OF GREGORY OF NYSSA

Much has been said in this book about the possible influences, whether Christian or Neoplatonist, upon the thought of Gregory and of the way in which he, at least to some extent, rewrote that tradition. His writings were never regarded with quite the same degree of reverence as were those of his namesake, Gregory of Nazianzus, who, because of his universal orthodoxy, was surnamed

'The Theologian'. Gregory of Nyssa's own views on universal salvation, both in his *Catechetical Oration* (sections 26 and 32) and the *On the Life of Moses*, caused considerable embarrassment to later editors who, as we have seen, did their best to edit the offending passages out of his writings, above all in the *On the Life of Moses* 2.82.

Even so, he apparently became known as 'The Father of Fathers' and although, as David Balas observes in his article on Gregory,[6] 'the later influence of the writings and theology of Gregory has never been systematically researched', something of the mark he made on subsequent theology can be traced in three very prominent later Greek writers, Denis the Areopagite of the late fifth or early sixth century and, through him, by Maximus the Confessor (580–662)[7] and, in the fourteenth century, Gregory Palamas (1296–1359).[8]

Gregory's influence upon Denis can easily be seen by comparing the use the pair of them make of the figure of Moses in Exodus. Both writers give the same treatment to the passage at Exod. 20, 21, which speaks of 'the darkness where God was'. The *On the Life of Moses* 2, 152–170, especially in section 162ff., treats the passage as evidence of the divine mysteriousness; while Denis, in his *Mystical Theology* 1, 3, speaks in this context of being united to God, 'by a complete unknowing activity'. It is to Gregory, above all, that Lossky, in *The Mystical Theology of the Eastern Church* (page 33) attributes the 'apophatic basis of all true theology'.

Much of Gregory's influence found its way into Maximus through the medium of Denis, upon whom he wrote an elaborate commentary. But, over and above this indirect influence, there is much of Gregory also in Maximus' anthropology, a point well illustrated by Andrew Louth in his discussion of the dogmatic tradition of Maximus on page 27 of *Maximus the Confessor*. Again, in his introduction to the translation of Maximus in the *Classics of Western Spirituality* (page 6), Jaroslav Pelikan sees Maximus' achievement in the rescue of Denis from Neoplatonic interpretations by situating him within the Cappadocian tradition.

The final important influence of Gregory can be found in the works of Gregory Palamas (1296–1359) who, on occasion, cites Gregory of Nyssa, to whom he owes the sharp distinction he makes between the inner nature and outward energies of God. It may, however, be doubted if the emphasis that Gregory of Nyssa lays upon the image of darkness is reproduced in his namesake, who prefers to use the language of light with which to discuss the goal of the spiritual life.

NOTES

1 INTRODUCTION

1 For an account of the religion of Cappadocia, reference should be made
to the introduction to volume 1 of the Budé edition of the *Letters of
Gregory of Nazianzus* by Paul Gallay (Paris: Budé, 1964), p. viii; more
recently, see volume 2 of Stephen Mitchell's *Anatolia, Land, Men and Gods
in Asia Minor* (Oxford: OUP, 1993), especially pp. 49–51. Mitchell offers a
useful reference to Gregory of Nyssa's account of a sect of 'Hypsistiani'
in his *Refutatio Confessionis Eunomii*, 38.
2 Gregory of Nyssa, *In Praise of Gregory Thaumaturgos* in *GNO* X.1.3–57;
Basil, above all, in *Letters* 28 and 207.
3 And this despite the paucity of quotation from, or direct reference to,
Origen in his (sc. Gregory of Nyssa's) writing; only twice in the Prologue
to the *Commentary on the Song of Songs* = *GNO* VI.13.3 and *In Praise of
Gregory* at *GNO* X.I.13.11/1.
4 Basil, *Letters* 204.6; 223.3.
5 For the family of Gregory see the introduction to the *SC Life of Macrina*
by P. Maraval especially p. 46ff.
6 *Life of Macrina* 6.
7 Gregory of Nyssa, *Letter* 13 and the extensive correspondence purport-
ing to exist between Basil and Libanius = Basil, *Letters* 335–359.
8 Basil's low esteem, real or affected, concerning the classical education he
had imbibed at Athens and Constantinople can be inferred from his use
of the term 'vanity', which brings with it overtones of Ecclesiastes 1.1.,
occurs in *Letter* 223.2 and *On the Holy Spirit* 3.5. Gregory is less dismissive
though he will, on occasion, attribute the errors of Eunomius to the
influence upon him of Aristotle, as at *Contra Eunomium* 1.46. But it needs
to be borne in mind that Aristotle was never a great favourite among the
Fathers, on which see the article by A. Meredith in the *Dictionary of
Theology* s.v. Aristotelianism.
9 Gregory of Nyssa's marriage can readily be inferred from his adverse
comments in *On Virginity* 3; his wife's name may have been Theosebeia,
cf. Gregory of Nazianzus *Letter* 197.
10 Basil's low esteem of his brother's competence in business can clearly be
seen in his *Letters* 58 and 100.

11 *Codex Theodosianus* XVI.1.3.; Socrates, *Ecclesiastical History* 5.10.

12 The three funeral orations of Gregory on the empress Flaccilla, the princess Pulcheria and bishop Meletius are all in *GNO* IX.439–490 with copious introductions and notes by Professor Andreas Spira.

13 The actual extent of Gregory's use of classical themes has been suggestively explored in a collection of essays by J. Daniélou *L'être et le temps chez Grégoire de Nysse* (Leiden: Brill 1970).

14 In this passage Gregory explicitly states that he is expressing his views with the help of scriptural citations in order to avoid the suggestion that his doctrines are merely pagan teaching flimsily covered with Christian trappings. Cf. *GNO* VIII.1.43.1–7. The fact of the need to defend himself implies accusations of some kind.

15 *Contra Eunomium* 3.10.41 contains a near verbatim quotation from Plutarch's esoteric treatise *On Isis and Osiris* 25 (360D–E).

16 H. F. Cherniss, (1930) 'The Platonism of Gregory of Nyssa' *UCPCP* 11: 1–92. Although old and one-sided this work is by far the most influential of all on this subject.

17 The Platonist tradition from *Republic* 617E resisted the temptation to assign responsibility for evil either to god himself or to some malignant power, or to give it any status in the real world, by insisting on human responsibility for it; αἰτία ἑλομένου, θεὸς ἀναίτιος, 'the cause lies with the one who chooses, God is guiltless'. So Origen insists on the centrality of freedom and its absolute necessity for virtue in *Contra Celsum* 4.3. Plotinus, too, at *Ennead* 3.2.7, contains the same idea and speaks of 'evil acts, entirely dependent on the souls that perpetrate them' and cites the passage from the *Republic* just referred to. Gregory himself argues for the relative unreality of evil at *Or. Cat.* 7 and *Eccl. hom.* 6.5, where his thought, if not his actual language, recalls that of Plotinus at *Ennead* 1.8.3.

18 *Or. Cat.* 5 (= *GNO* III.IV.20.5–25); *In Illud 'Tunc et ipse'* an exegesis of I Cor. 15.28.

19 *De anima et resurrectione, MPG* 46, 89D.

20 There is a useful edition of this attractive opusculum by N. G. Wilson (London: Duckworth, 1975).

21 M. F. Wiles, 'Eunomius: hairsplitting dialectitian or defender of the accessibility of revelation', in Rowan Williams (ed.), *The Making of Orthodoxy: Essays in Honour of Henry Chadwick*, (Cambridge: CUP, 1989).

22 H. Chadwick in a footnote to his 1964 translation of *Origen, Contra Celsum*, calls *Timaeus* 28C 'the most hackneyed quotation in all hellenistic literature'.

23 See Philo *On the Posterity and Exile of Cain*, 169 and Clement of Alexandria, *Stromateis*, 5.17.83.

24 Plotinus, *Ennead*, 5.5.6.14 speaks of the nature of the One as being ἀπλετος and in 6.9.6.11 of the ἀπερίληπτον την δυναμεως.

25 The expression 'ὁ ἐπὶ πάντων θεος occurs at *Contra Eunomium* 1, 163; 198; 199; 247; 248; 513; 516; in each case it is applied to the first person of the Trinity.

26 For τὸ θεῖον see Index 111 in Srawley's 1903 Cambridge edition of the *Catechetical Oration*, s.v. θειον and also at *On the Life of Moses* 2.162, where it

NOTES

is clearly treated as a synonym of 'ο θεος and seems to apply to the deity as such rather than to a particular person in the Trinity. See also in the same work 2.164; 165; 229; 234; 236. The expression is particularly frequent in the classicising dialogue, *On the Soul and Resurrection* where it occurs *PG* 46, 24C; 57B, C; 65A; 89 B, D etc.

27 For the notion of the divine incomprehensibility in Basil and for the problems the doctrine posed, see *Letter* 236. He developed in response the distinction between the divine essence and its energies, without, however, clearly explaining the relationship between the two or their connection with the three divine hypostases.

28 *Die Unendlichkeit Gottes bei Gregor von Nyssa* by E. Muehlenberg (Goettingen: Vandenhoeck & Ruprecht, 1966).

29 Despite the normal Plotinian elevation of the One above all personality, on occasion, as at *Ennead* 6.9.9., the One is referred to as god and personal and, at 5.1.6 and 7, the language of self reflection is applied to It. See the brief discussion by John Dillon in *Enneads* (Penguin: Harmondsworth, 1991).

30 H. Doerrie in *Gregor von Nyssa und die Philosophie* (Leiden: Brill, 1976), 'Gregors Theologie auf dem Hintergrund der neuplatonischen Metaphysik'.

31 A similar claim had been put forward by Basil in *On the Holy Spirit* XVIII.44, a passage which closely resembles Gregory's own language at *Contra Eunomium* 1.202.

32 Origen's near obsession with freedom, largely provoked by his antignostic polemic is discernible everywhere, above all in *On First Principles* 3.1. – a text which comes to us in Greek via the *Philocalia* of Basil and Gregory of Nazianzus.

33 Gregory's emphatic rejection of preexistence is clear from his implied critique of Origen's *On First Principles* 1.8.3. in his *On the Making of Man* 28 and *On the Soul and Resurrection PG* 46.112–113.

34 On the subject of satiety or κόρος see Origen *On First Principles* 2.8.3. Gregory's doctrine of the divine infinity enables him to reject this teaching, which he does at *On the Life of Moses* 2.232.

35 The centrality and absoluteness of πίστις is clear from *Contra Eunomium* 2.84–93. It is not there, or indeed elsewhere in Gregory, a stage to be passed through. Augustine's account of faith in his *De Trinitate* XV.II.2 is instructively different.

36 The clearest account of Augustine's own views on freedom occurs in the final chapter of the *City of God* (= book 22, 30).

2 DOCTRINAL ISSUES

Notes to *Against Eunomius* 1.156–182

1 Jean Daniélou's marked tendency to see Gregory, largely on the basis of his use of darkness symbolism, both as an innovative mystic (in contrast to Origen) and as foreshadowing the more explicit treatments of darkness to be found in the Pseudo-Dionysius, is well illustrated in his

own seminal work of 1944, *Platonisme et théologie mystique* (Paris: Aubier).

2   Hans Urs von Balthasar, *Présence et Pensée, Essai sur la philosophie religieuse de Grégoire de Nysse* (Paris: Beauchesne, 1942).

3   The literature on Eunomius is considerable. (1) *Eunomius, The Extant Works*, edited and translated by R. Vaggione in Oxford Early Christian Texts (Oxford, 1987); (2) L. Abramowski in *RAC* s.v. Eunomius (this has the slight disadvantage of using the numbering of the earlier 1920 edition of Jaeger's text of the *Contra Eunomium*).

4   Basil shows less inclination to offensive snobbishness in his account of Eunomius and his background and is more interested in his dogmatic deviations. His assertion as to the Galatian, as distinct from the Cappadocian, origin of Eunomius doubtless made in the interest of preserving Cappadocia's good name for orthodoxy, is demonstrably false. On this see p. 145, n. 3 of the *Sources Chrétiennes* edition of Basil's *Contra Eunomium* 1.

5   Thomas A. Kopecek, *A History of Neo-Arianism* in two volumes (Philadelphia, 1979).

6   R. Vaggione (cf. n. 3) has a useful introduction and account of the system of Eunomius in its various stages, together with a full and useful summary of *An Apology for the Apology* as recorded in Gregory of Nyssa's response, though he never explores in what sense, if any, Eunomius' views changed in the course of his interchange with the Cappadocians.

7   E. Vandenbussche, (1944/45) 'La part de la dialectique dans la théologie d'Eunomius, "le technologue"' *RHE* 40: 47–72. Cf. Basil, *Letter* 90.3, where he writes of Eunomius and his party, 'They are quibblers, not theologians.'

8   One of the central difficulties in assessing the value and precise character of Gregory's reply is the unclarity surrounding his use of the term οὐσία, which sometimes seems to bear the sense of 'individual' (= the Greek ὑπόστασις = Aristotle's first substance, the principal subject of all predicates) and on other occasions 'class' (= Aristotle's second substance, more like φύσις). On this apparent carelessness cf. C. G. Stead 'Ontology and Terminology in Gregory of Nyssa' in *Gregor von Nyssa und die Philosophie* (Leiden: Brill, 1976).

9   The structure of Gregory's reply 156–183:

   A   (156–160) Eunomius abandons the traditional language of Scripture and councils and substitutes for this his only peculiar (and deliberately misleading) jargon.

   B   (161–166) The *real* purpose of Eunomius' use of spatial metaphors of 'up' and 'down' is to deny the real existence of Son and Spirit.

   C   (167–171) Real goodness and power do not admit of more or less.

   D   (172–176) Essence is also indifferent to time.

   E   (177–179) *De facto* Eunomius is a crypto Jew.

   F   (180–182) There are no degrees of being ousia, either.

   G   (183–186) Consequence and conclusion – Eunomius is both impious and foolish.

10   Although Eunomius' *Profession of Faith* recorded by Gregory is highly and austerely philosophic in expression, the same may not be said of his

Expositio Fidei as recorded in his *Liber Apologeticus* 5, which is little more than an expansion of 1 Cor. 8. 6. 'For us there is one God, the Father, from whom are all things and for whom we exist, and one Lord Jesus Christ, through whom are all things, and through whom we exist.' It is the substructuring of this seemingly innocuous 'Credo' that causes the problem.

11 The 'natural' implication of 'Father/Son' language was explored for the first time in Christian theology by Origen, following Aristotle, *Categories* 7, with his doctrine of co-relatives, cf. *On First Principles* 1.2.2/10.

12 It is worth remarking again on the polyvalency of Gregory's use of *ousia*.

13 For *technologia* and the verb, *technologein*, cf. note 7, above, and CE 1.155 and 2.59; 65 etc.

14 The expression ὁ ἐπὶ πάντων θεός, 'the God who is over all' seems to have been as much a part of Gregory's normal language (cf. CE 1.163; 199) as was ὁ ἐπὶ πᾶσι θεός, 'the God who is above all Gods' for Origen.

15 τὸ κυρίως εἶναι, 'to kyrios einai' = real, as distinct from either unreal or lesser being.

16 Gregory seems here unfair to the argument of Eunomius, (a) by (?deliberately) confusing the two senses of ousia of existence and essence; (b) by giving to the word ἄνω, 'above' a spatial meaning, which it never had in the intention of Eunomius. Alas, we have no means of knowing how Eunomius actually replied to his critics.

17 The argument to the infinity of perfect goodness would have sounded strangely to Plato who regarded the forms as the principles of limit and order. Why should the divine goodness not be self-limited? Plotinus with his more mystical approach seems to have believed in the infinity of the One at *Ennead* 6.9.6.10; 17. On this whole subject and on Gregory's originality, see the monograph of E. Muehlenberg, *Die Unendlichkeit Gottes bei Gregor von Nyssa* (Goettingen: Vandenboeck & Ruprecht, 1966).

18 Temporal distinctions are irrelevant to the divine nature. The thought of the strict eternity of God seems to be in Plato's *Timaeus* and in Plotinus' *Ennead* 3.7.3.37; so, too, Philo's *On the Unchangeableness of God* VI.32.

19 These three sections raise the whole question of the debt owed by Arianism in general to Judaism, a problem explored by R. Lorenz in *Arius Judaizans* (Goettingen: Vandenboeck & Ruprecht, 1978).

20 Here, as elsewhere, Gregory argues both that his teaching is in accord with the bible and philosophy *and* that Eunomius meets neither of these claims cf. CE 2.9/10.

Notes to *Against the Macedonians* 19–26

21 C. R. B. Shapland, *The Letters of Saint Athanasius, Concerning the Holy Spirit*, translated with Introduction and Notes (London: Epworth Press, 1951). Serapion was consecrated bishop of Thmuis by Athanasius in 337, shortly after his return from his first spell in exile from 335–337 in Trier. The opening of the first letter tells us that it was written from the desert, and therefore must be dated to some time between 356 and 361 when Athanasius spent his third exile there.

22 On the connection between, and influence of, Athanasius on Gregory of Nyssa cf. A. Meredith 'The Pneumatology of the Cappadocian Fathers' (1981) *Irish Theological Quarterly*, 196–211, though Torrance (cf. n. 15) is probably correct in finding Gregory more influenced by a Basilian causal model than is Athanasius, who prefers more organic ones like sun and fountain, for illustrating the structure of the Trinity.

23 Eustathius was probably the addressee of Basil, *Letter* 1. For an account of Eustathius see the entry in vol. IV of the D. Sp. s.v. by Jean Gribomont OSB (Paris: Beauchesne, 1937), pp. 1708–1712.

24 Basil's 'economy' (οἰκονομία) or 'carefulness with the truth' is discussed and defended by Gregory of Nazianzus in his *Oration* 43.69 and his *Letter* 58 to Basil. It does not seem to be an expression used by Basil of his own attitude to theological discourse.

25 Above all in his *Oratio Catechetica* 2 and *Or. III, On the Lord's Prayer, GNO*, VII.239.15ff. Gregory's text of the prayer adds to the phrase 'Thy kingdom come' the words 'Let thy Holy Spirit come upon us and purify us'.

26 The connection made by Gregory between the baptismal formula of Matt. 28, 19 and the deity of the Spirit occurs also in Basil *Contra Eunomium* 3.5 and *On the Holy Spirit* 10.26; it may derive from Origen *On First Principles* 1.3.5.

27 Transformation (μεταπόιησις) is applied also by Gregory to the Christian at baptism (cf. *Or. Cat.* 40) and to the transformed elements of the Eucharist at *Or. Cat.* 37.

28 The exceedingly close connection drawn between faith, freedom and baptism also appears at *Or. Cat.* 33–36.

29 The Holy Spirit as the perfecter is a prominent idea also in Basil, above all in *On the Holy Spirit* 9, chapter ix, 22–23.

30 Ἐπὶ τοὺς ἀξίους = 'to the worthy' again, like Basil, Gregory seems to make the presence and action of the Holy Spirit conditional upon the actual worthiness of the persons receiving Him (*On the Holy Spirit* 22.53); Origen likewise at *On First Principles* 1.3.5, 'In eis autem solis esse arbitror opus spiritus sancti, qui *iam* se ad meliora convertunt.' (n.b. my italics), 'I think that the work of the Holy Spirit exists only in those, who already are converted to better things'.

31 Again the pattern of ascent from the Spirit through the Son to the Father and the opposite way round is not peculiar to Gregory. Basil also uses similar ideas, above all at *On the Holy Spirit* 9.23 and 18.47.

32 The odd and inconvenient conclusion from this language is that the Father alone is the archetype and he alone is infinite (ἀόριστος). This would appear to contradict the argument of the *Contra Eunomium* in which the whole divine nature is treated as infinite.

33 Sap. Sol. 1.7. Basil *On the Holy Spirit* 21.54 and by Gregory Nazianzus *Orat. Theol.* 5.29. For πνεῦμα εὐθές (straight Spirit) cf. Basil op. cit. 9.22.

34 The argument that there can be no participation in God, in other words no deification, unless this is accompanied by a belief in the deity of the Holy Ghost echoes, perhaps intentionally, a similar argument in Athanasius' *First Letter to Serapion*, section 24, and also Basil, *Against Eunomius* 3, 5. Basil, indeed, is insistent here and elsewhere that the power of the Holy Spirit to divinize rests upon his own natural deity. In *Against*

NOTES

Eunomius 3, 2, 'The heavenly powers are holy, through their fellowship with that which is by nature holy τὸ φύσει ἅγιον'.

35 It must be admitted, at least in the passage under discussion, that there is very little in Gregory's account that is striking or original. He is less adventurous than Athanasius, less spiritual than Basil and the characteristic thought of Gregory of Nazianzus, that the unity of the deity is a function of the primacy of the Father, although present is less forcefully expressed than it is by his namesake in *Or. Theol.* 5.14. This may help to explain the relative paucity of references to the teaching of Gregory of Nyssa in the otherwise extremely full account of Patristic teaching about the Holy Spirit offered by T. F. Torrance in *The Trinitarian Faith* in chap. 6 'The Eternal Spirit' pp. 191ff. (Edinburgh: T. and T. Clark, 1988). Torrance makes a valuable criticism of the whole Cappadocian enterprise on p. 238, when he compares their tendency to employ the concept of cause within the Trinity and the consequent idea of 'chain' of dependence, unfavourably with Athanasius' preference for 'the living will of God', at *Contra Arianos* 2.2 and 31.

36 The argument that 'co-worship' implies, as it does, the inseparability and equality of all three persons occurs also in Athanasius in his *Letter 1 to Serapion* 18–21; Basil has a similar argument in *On the Holy Spirit* 26, 64. It was finally 'canonized' in the creed of the 150 Fathers at Constantinople in 381 by the clause, 'who together with the father and the Son is both adored and glorified'.

37 The phrase ὁ ἐπὶ πάντων θεός, 'the God who is over all', which derives from Romans 9, 5 and Ephesians 4, 6, seems to have been a great favourite with Gregory, (cf. n. 14, chap. 1).

38 The final portion of the treatise does little more than repeat the previous arguments about the inseparability of the three divine persons. It must, however, be admitted that the last two chapters translated leave a strange impression. Gregory seems to be assimilating the reverence offered to other human beings to the worship offered to God and, further, to be claiming that to give men the former and to withhold the latter from God is quite inconsistent. But that by itself hardly counts as a defence of the deity of the Spirit. For if worship language is indeed applied to our fellow human beings, then the reception of it by the Spirit hardly proves his divinity.

Notes to the Apolinarian controversy: *Against Apolin(n)arius* 16–22

39 Although later in his life Basil denied any earlier friendship with Apolinarius (cf. *Letter* 129), it seems clear that there had been a friendship between them, and that the correspondence between them in *Letters* 361–364 is genuine. It seems that Basil's conversion to the cause of Nicene orthodoxy as expressed in the symbol 'consubstantial', was largely the work of Apolinarius. Basil's shrewd critique of his erstwhile friend's Christology is registered in 'his *Letter* 262.1, although he never mentions him by name, referring instead to the strange opinion of those

who claim that the deity changed into the humanity of Christ was turned into flesh'. In *Letter* 261.3 Basil distinguishes between the passions of the body which Christ did possess and vicious passions of the soul which he did not possess: 'He received our flesh with its natural [fusika] passions, but he did no sin.'

40 J. N. D. Kelly, *Early Christian Doctrines* (London: A. and C. Black, 1960), p. 299: 'Gregory of Nyssa thus tended to hold the two natures apart'. So, too, J. F. Bethune–Baker, *Introduction to the Early History of Christian Doctrine* (London: Methuen 1903), p. 251: 'Gregory is basically Nestorian in tendency'. A. Grillmeier, *Christ in Christian Tradition* (ET), (London: Mowbrays, 1965), devotes only ten pages, 367 to 377, to Cappadocian Christology for which he clearly entertains no very high regard. In n. 33, p. 368, with reference to section 5 of *To Theophilus*, he speaks of Gregory's embarrassment; and later, while admitting that Gregory of Nyssa is more dyophysite, that is, more inclined to stress the two natures of Christ, than his namesake, he also insists that his use of Stoic mixture language, *anakrasis* (in sections 21; 26; 51 and 55), points in quite another direction, especially when the simile of the drop of vinegar is employed, on which cf. n. 5 below.

41 Charles Raven, *Apolinarianism* (Cambridge and New York: CUP, 1923), p. 262ff. 'When Gregory states his own views he reveals his resemblance to Apolinarius', citing in evidence of this ss. 20 and 21 of the *Antirrhetikos*.

42 J. H. Srawley in *JTS* 7(1906) 'St Gregory of Nyssa on the Sinlessness of Christ' says that in Gregory's Christology the 'dominant conception is the exaltation of the human into the divine'.

43 The use of the drop of vinegar metaphor is frequent enough in Gregory and probably has a Stoic background. It occurs in Gregory in *Adv. Apolinaristas* 8 (*GNO* III.1.126.19); *Adv. Apolinarium* 42 (III.I.2019/10); *Contra Eunomium* III.3.68.

44 *GNO* III.1.171, 18–20; *Letter* 3.15 and the note of P. Maraval.

45 For a useful and more modern discussion of Gregory's doctrine of transformation cf. B. Pottier, *Dieu et le Christ selon Grégoire de Nysse* (Namur: Brepols, 1994), p. 243ff., where Pottier argues that Gregory advocates a more dynamic Christology, between the two poles of Antioch and Alexandria.

46 A. von Harnack, *History of Dogma*, (ET) vol. iv., p. 151, n. 3 (Edinburgh, 1894–1897).

47 E. Muehlenberg, *Apollinaris von Laodicea* (Goettingen: Vandenhoeck & Ruprecht, 1969).

48 Gregory often insists on the importance of free choice for virtue as at *Eccl. Hom.* 6, *GNO* V.379.21 and Origen, *Contra Celsum* 4.3. The importance of the idea is particularly marked in Gregory's *Commentary on the Song of Songs* at Hom. 1 (35/19); 2 (55/7); 4 (103/15); 7 (208/17); 9 (265/1); 10 (313/19; 345/21).

49 Origen frequently employs 1 Cor. 6.17: 'He that is joined to the Lord is one spirit with him' to suggest the ideal of union with God, realised in Christ and available also to us at *De Principiis* 2.3.7; 2.6.3 (bis) 2.10.7.

50 For an exhaustive discussion of the 'physical theory of redemption' cf.

R. H. Hubner, *Die Einheit des Leibes Christi bei Gregor von Nyssa* (Leiden: Brill, 1974).

51 Gregory quite often uses the language of joining together with which to describe the effects of the resurrection at *Ref. Conf. Eunomii*, 177; *Or. Cat.* 16; 35; *De Tridui Spatio*; *GNO* IX.294.1.

52 The language of 'mixture', *anakrasis*, is sufficiently common in Gregory and is used for three distinct purposes and owes, as is often the case with Gregory, much to Stoic influences channelled through Origen (cf. *De Principiis* 2.6.6):

(i)   It can refer to the union of body and soul as in *Or. Cat.* 6 (= *GNO* III.IV.22.1; 8; 11, 18);

(ii) Of the soul and God in spiritual union as at *Or. 1 in Cant.* Cant. (*GNO* VI.23.1) the mixture with the divine;

(iii) It is also used as in the text for the union of divine and human in Christ. It is worth noting that the language of 'blending' or 'mixture' was censured by Cyril of Alexandria (*Quod Unus sit Christus MPG* 75.1261) and by implication at the Council of Chalcedon with its insistence that the union of the two natures in Christ occurred without fusion (*asynkutos*), a further Stoic expression. The language of mixture in the first and third senses mentioned above also occurs in Gregory of Nazianzus; for (1) Or. 28, 22 (largely a series of unanswered rhetorical questions) and 38, 11 where man is described as a mixed worshipper and cf. also Or. 32.9. and for (3) Christ is also a mixture as 'Oh what an amazing mixture' at Or. 38, 13 and also in his letter 101, 46 to Cledonius, which deals expressly with the challenge of Apolinarius, he writes that Christ's human nature 'will be mixed with God'. Nazianzus appears not to use mixture language for the second sense of spiritual union.

53 Gregory's language of the 'rational hundred' at 152.3 is repeated elsewhere in his writings, at *Eccl. Hom* 2 (*GNO* V.305.2) as is the idea that the human race taken together is the solitary sheep (cf. also *In Cant. Cant. Or.* 2 (*GNO* VI.61.8)). Origen has a similar notion at *On First Principles* 2.1.1. Harnack *DG*, vol 2 (ET), p. 296, 'Christ did not assume the human nature of an individual person, but human nature.' A like interpretation of the 'rational hundred' is to be found in the *Symposium* of Methodius of Olympus, discourse 3, ss. 5–6. The influence of Methodius upon Gregory is well discussed and illustrated by J. H. Srawley in the introduction (pp. xxvff.) to his commentary on the *Catechetical Oration*, (Cambridge: CUP, 1903), and by L. G. Patterson on pages 186–196 of *Methodius of Olympus*, (Washington DC: The Catholic University of America Press, 1997).

At one place at the end of the fifteenth *Homily on the Song of Songs* he writes that all will become eventually a monad (or one) by their common and free concentration on the one and only good (cf. Hom. 15, *In Cant. Cant.* (466/5ff.). He speaks of a saved monad. A very similar thought occurs in Augustine, who holds that the creation of the human race was designed to fill up the gap created by the defection of the fallen angels, cf. *Enchiridion* 29; 62; *City of God*, 14, 23; 22.1.

NOTES

More recently, and more adequately, Professor Rowan Greer in 'The Leaven and the Lamb' (1985) admits that, 'The lost sheep is not a specific human being, but humanity taken in its entirety [cf. *Adv. Ap.* op. cit.; *Or. Cat.* 15 (*GNO* III.IV.45.13)]. On the other hand, The Nyssen can speak of "the Man" the Word assumed or "the Man who bore God" (*Or. Cat.* 16, *GNO* III.4.49.4) in the man that had been assumed.' By way of resolution of this seeming paradox Greer suggests that for Gregory the transformation of humanity in general is preceded by the transforming of the particular human nature assumed by the divine Word: 'When Nyssa distinguishes the humanity and divinity [that is before the resurrection] he appears to treat Christ's humanity as concrete and individual . . . and so in this perspective resembles the Antiochene Christology.' Greer concludes the first part of his discussion as follows: 'The technical dimension of Nyssa's Christology fails to explain the basic puzzle of Christ's humanity as both individual and corporate.' He then offers a solution to the difficulty by suggesting that human destiny is bound up with the Incarnation in as much as his humanity is the leaven which is gradually to penetrate the whole lump of human nature. For this he cites *Or. xiii. In Cant. Cant.* (= *GNO* VI.390–391) 'So long as this process is at work we may distinguish Christ's humanity from ours and treat it as a concrete individual. But once the process has been completed, the distinction between his humanity and ours disappears.' In other words, Greer wishes to argue that Gregory's account of Christ is a function of his account of human perfection.

The slight misgiving one may feel with this version of Gregory's thought is that it appears to elide unsatisfactorily two distinct elements: the dynamic structure of Gregory's treatment of the person of Christ, and the idea of human perfection. His theory should mean that at the Resurrection Christ becomes 'universal man' and the period of our own probation is at an end. If Christ is *now* in glory and transformed, he should be 'mankind' already. But the whole idea of human growth and of the leaven symbolism (cf. 1 Cor. 5.5–8) implies that we are both imperfect and distinct from Christ who is *already* glorified. The two stages in our development and in Christ's and the two senses of mankind, individual and corporate, seem not to fit.

54 This is a peculiarly opaque passage. It looks as if the text from Zachariah had been used by Apolinarius in order to prove that the sword had been employed by God against Christ, and that Christ, although God, was still, strictly, sinful and vulnerable. Gregory, by contrast, applies the text, not to the shepherd but to the flock, by synecdoche. Gregory's position here and throughout the treatise is that Apolinarius' theology demeans the divine nature, by reducing it to human terms.

55 The word used by Gregory at this juncture is *parapoiesis*, or distortion. It throws some light upon the controversial tactics of the period, in that it suggests that even Gregory could be accused of being not entirely honest in his portrayal of his opponent's case.

56 Gregory was the first to use the word *exanthropizo* with which to express the idea of bringing God down to our level. It is an unusual word and of the four cases adduced by Lampe (PGL) (Oxford: Clarendon Press,

1961) only one comes from outside Gregory. He uses the verb at *Against Eunomius* 3.2.19 and *Catechetical Oration* 4 (*GNO* III.IV. 14, 26).

57 In this passage Gregory assembles expressions in his account of the divine transcendence which are at home in widely differing philosophies; the spiritual conception of God as immaterial belongs to Plato, the thought of God as beyond limit, *aoristos*, is more Plotinian, while the thought of him penetrating through all things is more Stoic.

58 The expression, *logos tes ousias*, or abstract essence, is common in Gregory especially in *Against Eunomius*, for example 1.174.227.496. The generic feeling of the expression, that is that the three persons belong to the same class, gave rise to the accusation of tritheism, against which Gregory was at pains to defend himself, above all in his *On Not Three Gods*.

59 Apparently Apolinarius had used Phil. 2.7 'in the likeness of man' to argue that Christ was not really a man at all and did not possess a rational human soul. This treatment of the Pauline passage is in fragment 69 on p. 186.20.

60 Apolinarius was accused of teaching a doctrine of the heavenly man, perhaps based upon 1 Cor. 15, 47, which refers to the 'second Adam' as being 'the second man from heaven'. It is not at all clear if that is what he actually taught, but it clearly suited Gregory to argue that he did, as it allowed him to argue that Apolinarius taught some form of eternal body. Gregory of Nazianzus deals with the interpretation of the text in his *Letter* 101, in sections 30 and 31. J. N. D. Kelly in *Early Christian Doctrines*, p. 294 questions the Gregorian interpretation of Apolinarius, but hardly reckons with expressions like those reported by Gregory on p. 169.5ff. (= fragment 50).

61 Here we find Gregory wrestling with the same text and giving to it a modified sense as meaning simply that Christ is not in *all* respects the same as we are.

62 Here as elsewhere is an attempt to preserve at all costs the traditional doctrine of the divine impassibility, current at least since Origen.

63 The idea of the divine namelessness may perhaps be referred to the Jews and was certainly clear in later Platonism; Justin believes God to be both beyond expression and beyond name (*Apology* 1, 10 and 63).

64 We have a clear case of the doctrine of *'communicatio idomatum'*, that is the belief that epithets, which properly belong to the godhead may be applied to the manhood, and vice versa. Language such as this suggests that Gregory held a stronger, rather than a weaker, sense of the unity of Christ. Gregory's own preference for the language of mixture and transformation and of the active presence of God in Christ, when discussing the Incarnation, suggests that his doctrine was closer to that of Apolinarius than he would have liked to admit. On this cf. Kelly, op. cit., p. 300.

3 GREGORY AND PHILOSOPHY

Notes to *Contra Fatum*

1 For a (largely fictitious) account of the life of Iamblichus we have

Eunapius' account in *Lives of the Philosophers* 457–460 (= pp. 362–372 in the 1961 Loeb Classical Library translation by W. K. Wright, London). The 1966 Budé edition of the *De Mysteriis* of Iamblicus by E. Des Places, S. J. Paris is also valuable.

2 In a celebrated passage in *De Mysteriis* 2.11 Iamblichus explains the role of theurgy in uniting us to the divine as distinct from the role of the intelligence. Although he denies the power of the mind to unite the mind of the theurgist to the gods, he does not deny the power of the mind in the case of the philosopher.

3 Julian's *School Law* was enacted as a religious/political act in June 362. Even the pagan historian Ammianus Marcellinus, who had no great love of Christians, describes the event in his *Res Gestae* 22.10.7 as cruel and inclement.

4 *De dis et mundo* was brilliantly edited, translated and annotated by one of the greatest of modern scholars, A. D. Nock in *Sallustius – Concerning the Gods and the Universe* (Cambridge: CUP, 1926). There is also a handy edition by Gabriel Rochefort, Paris, 1960 in the Budé series.

5 Gregory's insistence both on the absolute centrality of freedom (cf. *Or. Cat.* 5) and on the universal salvation even of the devil is clear (cf. *Or. Cat.* 26) – they are held in unresolved tension.

6 D. Amand (de Mendietta) *Fatalisme et liberté dans l'antiquité grecque* (Louvain, 1945) for Gregory esp. pp. 405–439.

7 Basil, *Homilies on the Hexameron* 6, 5–7 edited by S. Giet, Sources Chrétiennes 26 (bis) (Paris, 1968).

8 The best modern text, upon which this partial translation is based, is that by J. A. McDonough, S. J. and may be found in *GNO* III.II.31–63 (= *MPG* 45.145–176).

9 The *Vita Macrinae* is also disguised as a letter as Gregory admits in the prologue; for a discussion see P. Maraval's Introduction to the SC edition of the *Life*, Chapter V, pp. 104ff.

10 The word *lexis* is a favourite one with Gregory and usually denotes place or position in the physical order. Among other places it may be found at *Or. Cat.* 6; *Hom. Op.* 17; *Contra Eunomium* II, 273; III.3.7

11 On the evidence of Lampe *PGL* s.v., *synexallassein* seems also to have been a favoured word with Gregory.

12 The Stoic term, *proegumenon*, means leading or cardinal thing; it occurs in Marcus Aurelius' *Meditations* vii.55; viii.49; ix.41.

13 This is a sentence of peculiar difficulty, perhaps reflected in the note at the foot. In general, it must be admitted that Gregory's Greek is much less perspicuous than is that of his younger contemporary John Chrysostom (cf. inf.) and of Gregory of Nazianzus, whose antithetical and, at times, jerky style reflects the manner of the current Atticism he probably learnt during his student days in Athens with Basil.

According to N. G. Wilson (op. cit. p. 23) Gregory of Nazianzus, alone of Greek Christian writers, was thought to rival classical authors in matters of style. In this connection Wilson notes, op. cit. (p. 32) that apart from the psalms, 'The other Christian text which won its way into the list of books known to Christian schoolchildren was the selection of sixteen sermons and addresses by St Gregory of Nazianzus (329–389).' The

Nyssen did not enjoy the advantage, either of an expensive education nor did his work later become an authoritative textbook. Even so it would clearly be wrong to write him off as uninterested in stylistic questions. *Letter* 15 is addressed to John and Maximinianus, apparently two pupils of Libanius. He exhorts them to show his recently composed *Contra Eunomium*, to their master, 'if they find anything in it is worthy of the sophist'. An illuminating discussion of the whole issue is to be found in *Scholars of Byzantium* by N. G. Wilson (London: Duckworth, 1983, 1996) on page 26 of which he notes that 'the simpler style of Chrysostom may have been more readily understood by the average reader.'

14 The usage and meaning of the terms '*akolouthia*' and '*heirmos*' have been fruitfully explored by J. Daniélou in chapter 2 'Enchaînement' of his collected articles *L'être et le Temps chez Grégoire de Nysse* (Leiden,1970).

15 It is instructive that Gregory at this point insists on the virtuous character of God, a feature which is well brought out in the passages of his Catechetical Oration translated below. It also serves to underline the point that, for Gregory, it is likeness to God in virtue, rather than absorption in him that constitutes the goal of the christian life. The influence of Plato, *Theaetetus* 176, is not far away.

16 Von Balthasar, *Presence and Thought* (ET), p. 33: 'The whole method of the treatise consists in reducing all appearance of qualitative difference in the movement of the stars to pure quantity which, in itself, is incapable of being the cause of several qualitatively different effects.' In his note, Von Balthasar compares Gregory with Philo *On the Making of the World*, 55–61. In that passage, Philo while insisting on the function of the heavenly bodies to do more than send light upon the earth, seeing that by looking at their conjunctions men 'may conjecture future issues' (58), also subordinates the influence of the stars to the 'laws which God has laid down' (61).

Notes to *Oratio Catechetica 19–24*

17 There is a very full discussion of the subject of Gregory's treatment of the idea of oikonomia by R. J. Kees in *Die Lehre von der Oikonomia Gottes in der Oratio Catechetica Gregors von Nyssa*. (Leiden: Brill, 1995). Kees rightly sees chapter 5 as the place where Gregory first addresses the new theme of the economy of the Divine Word in his human nature, as the centre of the whole work (cf. Kees p. 60ff.), though he attributes a terminological precision to Gregory which would be more at home in Gregory of Nazianzus. He cites J. H. Srawley's note on p. 20 of his 1903 edition/commentary on the text to the effect that oikonomia is 'used commonly in Patristic writers of the plan or 'dispensation' of God in the Incarnation.'

In his Index III Greek words, Srawley lists over fifteen other examples of the expression in *Or. Cat.* alone, as in chapters 10 and 12.

18 The importance constantly attached by Gregory in all his writings to the idea of logical progression and order, expressed above all as *taxis* and *akolouthia*, is well brought out by J. Daniélou in his article 'Enchaînement' reprinted in *L'être et le temps chez Grégoire de Nysse* (Leiden: Brill, 1970) pp.

18–50. The net result of this stress on the orderliness and predictability of God's action is to reduce the importance within it of the 'supernatural', though not of the otherworldly.

19 Here and elsewhere Gregory insists not only on the importance of freedom in the understanding of human nature but also on freedom as *the* reflection in us of the divine nature. This is particularly clear in chapter 5 of *Or. Cat.* where Gregory explains that, although in many respects we have acquired through the fall many characteristics that distinguish us from God, in whose image we were made, freedom is the root of the image and the cause in God and us of all our actions. It is only through the gift of freedom that we are capable of choosing what is right. He describes it at *Or. Cat.* 5 (Srawley 26.8 = *GNO* III.IV.19/20) as the gift of liberty and free will.

20 On several occasions, notably in chapters 6 and 15, Gregory insists on the unreal character of evil/non-being and warns at the same time that, although it is possible logically to contrast the two, one must be careful not to read into this verbal opposition the idea that evil has some sort of independent existence, cf. Srawley 6 (33.4–14 = *GNO* III.IV.23/15 ff.). The treatment of evil as an absence, or as a lack, reflects the teaching of both Plato, who has no idea of evil, and of Plotinus, whose discussion of the nature and origin of evils occurs at *Ennead* 1.8. and who concludes at I, 8.512 that evil is a deficiency, an *'elleipsis'* and that, although unreal, it is not utterly so (cf. 1.8.3.6.). Such a view of the 'nature' of evil renders any doctrine of the atonement difficult to embrace and helps also to explain Gregory's universalism. There can be no room for evil/non-being in the triumph of absolute being/goodness in the presence of the Incarnate Lord.

21 'Discoverer of evil' is a favourite designation of Satan both here and in other writings of Gregory. It also occurs at *Or. Cat.* 26, where the ultimate salvation of the devil is asserted, and at *Contra Eunomium* III.2.39., although he appears not to be the inventor of the phrase, as Lampe (PGL) (Oxford: Clarendon Press, 1961) s.v. cites passages from Methodius and Athanasius with the same sense.

22 A similar idea, namely to establish the divine justice, lies at the root of the so called 'ransom' theory of atonement. It is usefully discussed by Gustav Aulen in *Christus Victor* (ET), (London, 1931) above all, for Gregory on pp. 48 and 49. Origen, here, as often, provides the basic thrust, though not the imagery, of Gregory's approach. In a passage from his *Commentary on Matthew* 16, he argues that God's power must be conditioned by his justice. Origen's view is also discussed by Kelly, *Early Christian Doctrines*, pp. 185, 186. Augustine's *Enchiridion* 49 has the same sort of idea: 'Hence it was in authentic justice, and not by violent power, that the devil was overcome and conquered'.

23 The portion of Gregory's treatise above translated gives some idea of his rationalistic attempt to explain traditional Christian language about the atonement in and for a more philosophically alert audience. The assumption which dominates his treatment is of a god who conforms to the highest that philosophical presuppositions require in his goodness, power, justice and wisdom. Such a view will not permit God to act in a

way that fails to express these primary ideas. Above all, his power is not absolute or unrestricted by anything; he can only act 'fittingly'. He cannot act 'outside' or 'over against his nature', which itself owes much to the thought of human perfection.

24 *Phthonos*, or envy, is a characteristic of the devil in Gregory. In *Or. Cat.* 6 it is envy that makes the devil prey on Adam. Elsewhere in Gregory it appears as a sort of relic of paganism and means that malevolent power which deprives the world of its best citizens, as in Gregory's *In Meletium GNO* IX.443.12. In Herodotus' *Hist.* 1.32 it is also predicated of God, who resents the flourishing of human beings. Plato explicitly denied it of god at *Timaeus* 29E.

25 The sentence, which terminates here, occupies twenty six lines in the Jaeger text and is a good example of the difficulty and complexity of Gregory's style, alluded to above.

26 As Srawley notes on p. 89 of his commentary, the thought of the ransom paid to the devil was not an invention of Gregory, but occurs in Irenaeus, *Adv. Haereses* v.1.1., cf. also n. 22 above.

27 'Condescension', is a favourite expression with the fathers for the Incarnation, above all in Athanasius cf. *De Incarnatione* 8.

28 This argument for the disappearance of evil and non-being at the approach of death leads inevitably to a belief in the salvation of all, including the devil, whose negativities are done away at the approach and triumph of the good, cf. sections 26 and 32 of this treatise.

4 GREGORY AND SPIRITUALITY
Notes to *Against Eunomius* 2.84–96

1 The subject of the nature and originality of Gregory of Nyssa's mysticism has been much discussed, principally by J. Daniélou in his innovative work, *Platonisme et théologie mystique* (Aubier: Paris, 1944), which insists both on the novelty and Dionysian character of Gregorian mysticism. This has been contested by H. Crouzel in 'Grégoire de Nysse, est-il le fondateur de la théologie mystique? Une controverse recente' *RAM* 33 (1957) 189–202. He supports Origen's claim to be regarded as a mystic.

2 Proclus the Neoplatonist philosopher (412–485 AD) has a sentence which on the face of it appears to represent a despairing attitude to reason in his *Theologica Platonica* i.25, when he speaks of the 'faith in the gods' as exceeding all manner of *gnosis*; faith it is that unites the worshipper to the gods – language similar to, but almost certainly independent of, Gregory's remark at *Contra Eunomium* 2.91 to the effect that it is impossible to draw unto God without the medium of faith, 'joining (συνάπτουσα) the mind to the incomprehensible nature of God'.

3 Gregory is anxious in this part of his treatise to establish two separate but related facts, (a) that in his innermost nature God cannot be grasped by the human mind; (b) even so this need not lead to total agnosticism about God. Concepts have a relative importance, as pointing beyond themselves to the object of reference. So he is able to eschew a Platonic 'fundamentalism' about language, on the one hand, that treats words as revealers of natures, and total scepticism or agnosticism on the other.

4 In Gregory's mature writing, above all in his *Against Eunomius* 1, 315; 371; 2, 86; and *Commentary on the Song of Songs* 6 (*GNO* VI.183, 5/10) he departs from the Platonic and Origenistic usage (cf. *Against Celsus* 1.9) both of which regard 'faith' as a preparation for knowledge. The motives for this fairly uniform departure are by no means clear, but the influence of Scripture, above all of 1 Cor. 13.13, must be partly responsible.

Notes to Homily 6: *On the Beatitudes*

5 Various derivations for the Greek word, *theos*, were current in antiquity. Three deserve notice: (i) from *theein* = run because God is everywhere, (cf. Plato, *Cratylus*, 397D; and Gregory of Nazianzus *Or. Theol.* 4.18.); (ii) from *theasthai* = to see, by far the most popular, from the idea that God sees all things (cf. *Contra Eunomium* 2, 149); (iii) from *tithenai* = to set things in order (cf. Herodotus, *Histories*, 2, 52).

6 Basil clearly distinguishes between inner being and outer activities in *Letter* 234, 2 and *Contra Eunomium* 2. 13.

7 It is hard to know if the expression 'eye of the soul' is of purely classical Greek provenance or is also of Christian inspiration. It occurs in Plato's *Republic* 533D and in Plotinus at *Ennead* 1.6.8, and also in the Christian Platonist tradition in Origen at *De Principiis* 1.1.9, where it forms the basis for a doctrine of the spiritual senses. However, it may also be found used 'casually' by Clement of Rome in *1 Corinthians* 19.3.

8 For the idea that the vision of God makes us happy see especially the exegesis of Matt. 5, 8, above all in Origen, *De Principiis* i.1.9 and Plotinus, *Ennead* 1.6.7.2 and Augustine, *De Vita Beata* 4.25.

9 For ἀοργησία as a virtue and its effect on the idea of God, cf. M. Pohlenz *Vom Zorne Gottes* (Goettingen: Vandenhoeck & Ruprecht, 1909). It was a classical ideal, as we see from the opening of Marcus Aurelius' *Meditations* 1.1., 'From my Grandfather, Verus, I inherited a kindly disposition and sweetness of temper' (= *to aorgeton*). In his *Commentary on Romans* 1.16, Origen wrestles with the idea of the 'wrath of God' (= Rom. 1, 18) and concludes that the idea must be understood medicinally of God's desire to reform us.

10 The expression ἀνατμητικός appears to be a Gregorian invention. It is recorded neither in *LSJ* or in *PGL*. It may have a reference to Heb. 4.12, where the Word of God is described as alive, active and cutting τομώτερος.

11 For the idea that the devil is the inventor of evil see n. 21, p. 153.

Notes to *On the Life of Moses*

12 The idea that Gregory was advanced in years when he came to write the *On the Life of Moses* derives from a remark in part 1.2 when he refers to his 'grey hair'. He seems to refer to himself in similar terms at *Against Eunomius* 2.605, when he was, at most, 45. Again, *Letter* 11.7 datable (perhaps) to 379/80 also refers to Gregory's grey hair.

13 The expression applied to God far outweighs both here and elsewhere

NOTES

more personal 'titles' for God, cf. *Life* 2, 234; 236 (3 times) and 237. Srawley's index to his edition of the *Catechetical Oration* contains many cases of a like usage.

14 See n. 7 above.

15 The use of the burning bush as a symbol for the appearance of the Word (as distinct from the Father) occurs also in Philo, *Moses* 1.66 and Justin, *Dialogue with Trypho* 59, 2 and in Clement of Alexandria's *Protreptikos* 1.8., 'The Word appeared in the desert by the burning bush'. The significant difference between Gregory and his predecessors is shown decisively at this point by the fact that for him the Word is fully divine, for *them* he is less than the unseen, incomprehensible God and Father who from the nature of the case cannot appear in, or in any way be restricted to, a particular geographical spot.

16 This seems to be the first recorded instance of the burning and unconsumed bush being referred to Mary's virginity '*post partum*'. A similar thought occurs in Gregory's *In diem natalem salvatoris* (*PG* 46, 1136CD; = *GNO* X.2.III.247, 1ff.), 'She, [sc. Mary] is both mother and virgin; her virginity did not prevent her giving birth nor did the birth destroy her virginity.' Cyril of Alexandria in chapter 26 of his *Against the Anthropomorphites* has (? independently) a similar idea when he writes 'She [sc. Mary] gives birth to the light and is not destroyed [sc. by this].'

17 It is never quite clear in Gregory whether he is talking about the psychological state of 'not being deceived' or about the reality of the object of perception. Psychological perception and essential reality are not kept sharply distinct.

18 Easily the fullest and most satisfactory discussion of Gregory's teaching on this matter is to be found in D. Balas' Μετουσία Θεοῦ, *Man's Participation in God's Perfections according to Saint Gregory of Nyssa* (Rome: Herder, 1966).

19 'Condescension' is the *terminus technicus* for the Incarnation, at least by the time of Athanasius' *de Incarnatione* 8; 9; 46. Athanasius applies it both to the creation of the world by the Word and to its restoration by him. Although according to *PGL* the word was used occasionally in these senses before Athanasius, he seems to have given currency to the term.

20 *Metastoicheiosis*, best translated as 'transelementation', is used by Gregory in a variety of different, though connected, contexts: (i) It can refer to the change wrought in Christ's body as a result of the resurrection/ascension (*Antirrheticus, adv. Apolinarium* 25 = *GNO* 3.1.170.10); (ii) the effect of the Incarnation as worked out in the sacramental and moral life upon the lives of individual Christians (by far the commonest sense in Gregory) (*Letter* 3, 18; *Contra Eunomium* 3.3.69); (iii) the effect produced on the Eucharistic elements as a result of the words of institution (*Or. Cat.* 37). It means the same as μεταποίησις and in the case of Christ (= i, above) seems to imply the obliteration of specifically human characteristics.

21 Gregory uses the neuter τὸ and the masculine ὁ indifferently of the divine nature, and may perhaps imply by this his conviction that for him the Biblical revelation and philosophy of Plato are at one on this crucial point.

156

22 The popularity of *to theion* as a designation of God in Gregory has already been noted, especially in n. 13. It is also particularly common in Gregory's *Commentary on the Song* as the following references from *GNO* VI indicate; 22, 19; 28, 22; 108, 11; 109, 1; 133, 7; 11; 172, 23; 250, 15; 258, 14 etc.

23 The collocation of εἱρμός and ἀκολουθία also occur in Philo's *On the Posterity and Exile of Cain* 23.

24 It is the constant teaching of the Cappadocians that although the divine essence is beyond our reach, his activities reveal his 'outer qualities' or ἐνέργειαι, cf. *Against Eunomius* 2, 102; 3, 6, 8; and *In Cant. Cant.* 1 (*GNO* VI.37.1ff.). Basil has the same teaching in his *Letter* 234; he also distinguishes elegantly between the divine *ousia* and the distinctive properties of the three persons at his *Contra Eunomium* 2.29. Gregory of Nazianzus is less insistent on the divine impenetrability than the other two Cappadocians and attributes ignorance at *Or. Theol.* 2.12 rather to human frailty than to the infinity of God.

25 Gregory of Nyssa goes beyond Gregory of Nazianzus (as, for example, at *Or. Theol.* 5.15), here and elsewhere by insisting on the inaccessibility of God even to angels. Cf. also *Against Eunomius* 1, 307; 2, 86ff.

26 The fusion of religious and mystical language occurs in the prologue to Gregory of Nyssa's *Homilies on the Song of Songs*, *GNO* VI.22.17 and in Plotinus' *Ennead* 6.9.11.29.

27 Here and throughout the treatise an extremely close connection is made between the two lives of action (= morality) and contemplation, which are not treated in watertight compartments, but as leading to and reinforcing each other. In this respect, Gregory differs from Evagrius who seems to treat them as distinct moments, such that the end of the former, πρακτικη, is the beginning of the other.

28 The pattern of ascent in Plato's *Symposium* 201ff. is everywhere evident, as it is in Origen's *Commentary on the Song*, above all in his prologue 2, 22. Even now one of the best and most stimulating discussions of the whole issue of the place of ἔρως in the life of the Christian is by Anders Nygren, *Eros and Agape* (London: SPCK, 1932). Subsequent writers like Fr. Martin D'Arcy in *The Mind and Heart of Love* (London: Faber and Faber, 1945) may disagree, but they cannot afford to ignore Nygren's dichotomy. His discussion of Gregory's treatment of the love motif occurs on pp. 430–446. According to Nygren, mysticism is an expression of *the Eros motif* (his italics) and is everywhere evident in Gregory (cf. p. 431).

29 Origen is commonly supposed to have taught that the reason for the fall of souls from their primal blessedness was satiety caused either by the limited nature of God or, less probably, by being weary of the delights of paradise cf. *De Principiis* 2.8.3. It would appear that for Origen God was not Infinite.

30 For the importance of the cooperation of God with us in the *ascetica* of Gregory cf. *De Instituto GNO* VIII.45.3 and E. Muehlenberg in *ZNW* 68 (1977) 93–122, 'Synergism in Gregory of Nyssa'.

31 As Daniélou notes on this passage, here we find Gregory insisting on a paradox of stable mobility by which, on the one hand, he admits the

need for perpetual motion and, on the other, he rejects the Origenistic notion that mobility of itself implies declension from good to what is worse. Sand is a symbol of frailty even in Homer, as at *Iliad* xv.361ff. Gregory also uses the image of sand with which to illustrate the insubstantial nature of human achievement, in his first *Homily on Ecclesiastes* section 9 (= *GNO* V. 290.6). For the thought of Christ as 'perfect virtue' cf. *Gregory's Hom.5 in Ecclesiasten* = *GNO* V.358.9.

32 The last of Gregory's fifteen homilies on the Song of Songs deals with the first nine verses of chapter 6. It follows the text fairly faithfully, and at least purports to be a verse by verse commentary on the text. It must be admitted that both the language and the exegesis, particularly when Gregory deals with numbers, are both tortuous to the point of obscurity and in several places I have been forced to content myself with giving what I take to be the general, rather than the exact, sense of several passages. Although he frequently employs certain favourite ideas and motives, as for example those of εἱρμός and likeness, his adhesion to the line by line method of commentary forces him to give a less than pellucid account of his vision of the spiritual life. The final idea of the union of all spiritual beings in a communion of vision and love for God, owes much to the influence of Origen, as for example at *Principles* 1.8.3 (Greek text) and is, at the same time, the natural end of Gregory's interpretation of the Song.

33 This is a rather unusual version of John 1, 46. Gregory appears to replace the sceptical question of the gospel with an indication that Nathaniel, far from doubting the value of Philip's message, was quite aware of the scriptural tradition and was prepared to accept Christ for that reason. I follow in this the German version of Franz Duenzel at this point, (cf. *Fontes Christiani* Band 16/3 (Herder, 1994) p. 770, n. 13).

34 Freedom of choice is a key idea in Gregory's understanding both of the person of Christ and of the individual's spiritual progress, as indeed it was for Origen before him. It consorts ill with the so-called 'physical theory of redemption' which stresses the incorporation of the individual in Christ, above all through the Incarnation and sacraments as the source of our salvation. The subject is treated minutely and extensively by Reinhard Hubner in *Die Einheit des Leibes Christi bei Gregor von Nyssa* (Leiden: Brill, 1974). According to Franz Duenzl on p. 146 of his translation and commentary of the Song in the series *Fontes Christiani* (Freiberg: Herder, 1994), the word means both the God given ability to choose and the actual choice. Gregory's understanding of Christ, above all when defending himself against Eunomian objections, insists on the importance of free choice, as at *Ref. Conf. Eunomii* 177.

35 The conviction of the necessary usefulness of everything in Scripture seems to derive from 2 Tim. 3, 16, 'All holy Scripture is inspired and written for our instruction'. Philo held a similar view to Origen (cf. *Principles* 4.1.6) and in all three cases it led inevitably to allegory. On this, see my remarks in *Studia Patristica*, vol. XVI (1985), p. 423–427 'Allegory in Porphyry and Gregory of Nyssa'.

36 The idea of the transformation of the self into the likeness of absolute beauty is not peculiar to Christianity. It has its root in Plato and perhaps

earlier with the ideal of 'likeness' at *Theaetetus* 176B and of 'fashioning one's own image' at *Phaedrus* 252D, taken up by Plotinus verbally at *Ennead* 1.6.9.13.

37 The ingenuity and complexity of Gregory's exposition at this point make his actual point obscure.

38 Although the majority of the manuscripts at this point read ἐκείνης, it is hard to see what useful sense this makes; the natural meaning is 'his beauty' which the bride, on becoming herself the heavenly Jerusalem, receives into herself.

39 Although Gregory here and elsewhere admits that the heavenly powers are always capable of improvement, he does not admit that they can fall and in this respect he departs from Origen for whom, as Augustine shrewdly observes at *City of God* xxi.17, the spiritual order is in a perpetual state of instability and therefore of 'falsa beatitudo' (false happiness), for having fallen once already, there is, in principle, no reason why they should not do so again.

40 This is a difficult passage, suggesting, as it seems to, that although initially man was created both in the image and likeness of God, the loss of wings, consequent upon the fall, meant that we had to recapture the lost likeness. Such indeed is the teaching of Origen at *On First Principles* 3.6.1. Elsewhere, however, Gregory seems to hold the opinion that even *post lapsum* we were equipped with both image and likeness, both of which, as Srawley notes on *Catechetical Oration* 5 (Srawley 24.5; *GNO* III.4.18.7) are regularly identified by Gregory. Perhaps this is simply a christianized version of the old Greek maxim, 'Become what you are' familiar from Pindar onwards.

41 The language of 'wings' is a clear indication of the influence on Gregory of Plato's *Phaedrus* 246. It was popular in all forms of later Platonism. Plotinus uses it frequently as a metaphor of the soul's fallen condition, as at *Ennead* 4.8.1 while it was much exploited before Gregory both by Origen (cf. *Principles* 3.4.1) and even more by Methodius of Olympus, *Symposium* 8.1.

42 For unclarity or obscurity as an invitation to allegorize and therefore dig deeper cf. Porphyry, the disciple and biographer of Plotinus, *De antro nympharum* 4 (*On the cave of the Nymphs*), an elaborate exegesis of Odyssey 13, 102–112 'since the narrative is so full of unclarities, (*asapheia*) . . . we must assume that the author allegorised'.

43 Here is further evidence of Gregory's uncertain handling of the relationship between image and likeness.

44 Compare the more extended treatment of this text by Gregory at *Inscr. Psalmorum* at *GNO* V. 187–193.

45 This is a passage of extraordinarily difficult Greek and the translation is hardly more than a paraphrase. Gregory's characteristic search for a clear sequence of thought is evident here and at 447, 13 and 458, 10.

46 Gregory's more ample treatment of this text, sc. 1 Cor. 15, 28 occurs in his *In illud* etc. (*GNO* 111.2.3–28) and is a clear indication of his universalism. As Franz Duenzl, the translator of the *Fontes Christiani* edition of the Song, observes, the fact that Gregory's commentary ends here is not

accidental, but proceeds rather from a clear perception of his understanding of the text.

EPILOGUE

1 Norman H. Baynes, *The Hellenistic Civilization and East Rome*, (Oxford:
   OUP, 1946), p. 40.
2 Although Gregory insists, in line with Genesis 1, 26, that man was made
   after the image and likeness of God, he also – deliberately – refuses to
   make the distinction between image and likeness which we find in all
   writers from Irenaeus and Origen (*On First Principles* 3.6.1) onwards. Cf.
   Gregory, *Catechetical Oration* 5 (Srawley, p. 24, 5; *GNO* III.IV.18, 7).
3 The whole subject of deification has been the source of very fruitful
   discussion. J. Gross in *La divinisation du chrétien après les pères grecs* (Paris:
   Gabalda, 1938), p. 219, sees in Gregory a perfect expression of the
   Greek idea of divinization. Other writers, like I.-H Dalmais, in the *Dictionnaire de Spiritualité* vol. III, 1380–1389. s.v. divinisation, are less sure,
   for example, Dalmais writes, 'Grégoire est extrèmement reservé dans
   l'emploi de ce vocabulaire et de ce thème'.

   Gregory is quite unlike Athanasius who, at *On the Synods* 51 and elsewhere, argues for the deity of the Christ from the deification that he
   brings, and also for the deity of the Holy Spirit on the same grounds, at
   Letter 1 to Serapion 25. He is also, unlike Gregory of Nazianzus whose
   fondness for deification terminology is well discussed in *The Dynamics of
   Salvation* by Donald F. Winslow, in chapter VIII, $\Theta E\Omega\Sigma I\Sigma$. Gregory of
   Nyssa is remarkably reticent on the whole subject, although he does use
   the language of deifying with reference to the Third Person in chapter 25
   of *Against the Macedonians, On the Holy Spirit* (= *GNO* III.I.113, 16) as a
   proof of his deity.

   He does, indeed on occasion, use this sort of language at *On the Life of
   Moses* 2, 35 and at *Catechetical Oration* 25, but even there he never uses the
   strong language of his namesake. All he seems to mean is that our nature
   should become divine, not God himself. In chapter 5 of his *Oration* he
   writes, 'If man came into existence to participate in the divine goodness,
   he had to be fashioned in such a way as to fit him to share [*meteinai*] in
   that goodness' (*GNO* III.4.17.9–11). The language of sharing is clearly
   preferred to that of divinization. It is also a way of relating the inferior to
   the superior used on occasion, but not frequently, by Plato, when
   endeavouring to give an account of the relationship existing between the
   particular and the form of the ideal in his *Parmenides* 132D. This is
   perhaps an indication of the fact that he saw more clearly the implications for spirituality of the doctrine of creation and of the gulf between
   God and creatures entailed by it.

   It is also worth noting, as D. Balas does in his *Metousia Theou*, that
   Gregory steadily refuses to use the language of participation when discussing the relation of Father, Son and Spirit. God, Gregory insists, does
   not share in goodness or possess it, He is it. There is no participation in
   God (*Against Eunomius*, 1.276). We, by contrast, can grow in our sharing
   in the divine perfections, largely by our increase in moral excellence (op.

cit. 2, 70). Only in chap. 37 of his *Catechetical Oration* does he seem to go further, when he says that the sacrament transforms us (*metapoiei*) into itself, that is the body of Christ.

So, for example, an expression of the type we find both in Basil, *De Spiritu Sancto* 9.23, 'becoming God' and in Gregory of Nazianzus, *Oration* vii.23, 'becoming a son of God', indeed God himself, which both have a family likeness to Plotinus, *Enneads* vi.9.9.58, are nowhere to be found in Gregory of Nyssa. And, when Gregory does speak of divinization, it is largely through virtue rather than through knowledge that this takes place whereas, for Origen and Basil, divinization is closely allied to growth in knowledge. It is everywhere the imitation of the divine goodness that is paramount. So, in *Homily II on the Lord's Prayer* (= *GNO* VII.I.28.25) Gregory uses Matt. 5, 48 to enforce the need of 'likeness to the Father'.

4 A very full and fair discussion of Gregory's ambiguous adhesions in philosophical matters, especially in the usage of *ousia* language is to be found in B. Pottier, *Dieu et le Christ selon Grégoire de Nysse* (Paris, 1994), pp. 85–107.

5 Gregory of Nyssa's basic seriousness and distance from his namesake can well be illustrated by comparing his careful approach to the correlation of cataphatic and apophatic descriptions of God with the elegant juxtaposition of such epithets by Gregory of Nazianzus in his *Poemata Arcana* 3.41ff., usefully discussed by D. A. Sykes in his 1997 edition and commentary on the poems, above all, p. 127.

6 D. Balas 'Gregor von Nyssa' in *TRE* XIV, 173–181.

7 A useful account of the influence of Gregory may be found in the *Dictionnaire de Spiritualité*, vol. VI, column 1007, by Professor Canevet.

8 Heinrich Doerrie has some very helpful information in his article on Gregory III in *RAC* XII, 870–872.

BIBLIOGRAPHY

Note

Two of the most useful bibliographies of fairly recent work on Gregory of Nyssa can be found at the end of the English translation of Hans Urs von Balthasar's *Presence and Thought: An Essay on the Religious Philosophy of Gregory of Nyssa* (San Francisco: Ignatius Press, 1995). The first (pp. 183–187) restricts itself to items published before 1939; while the second, assembled by Brian Daley, appeared in 1988 and 1994/5. But recent though it is, it is still lacunose. For earlier work the reader is directed to *Bibliographie zu Gregor von Nyssa*, edited by M. Altenburger and F. Mann, 1988, Leiden, Brill.

To date the only complete edition of the works of Gregory of Nyssa is still to be found in *Migne's Patrologia Graeca*, volumes 44 to 46. In 1908, however, money was provided on the occasion of the sixtieth birthday of Wilamowitz, which was, with some misgivings, assigned by him to the production of a new, critical edition of the works of Gregory. The enterprise was entrusted to Werner Jaeger who, in 1920, produced the first fruits of this undertaking in the shape of a critical edition of the treatises of Gregory *Against Eunomius*. Since then there has been a steady flow of increasingly elaborate editions edited at Leiden under the title *Gregorii Nysseni Opera* (*GNO*).

GNO III.1 contains the smaller dogmatic treatises on the Trinity and on Christology, mostly directed against Apolinarius; *GNO* III.IV has the *Catechetical Oration*; volumes V and VI contain his sermons on Ecclesiastes and on the Song of Songs; VII.1 has the *On the Life of Moses*; volume VIII.I contains the *Ascetic Works* of Gregory and the 3 volumes of X are all sermons.

In addition to these editions there are also useful commentaries on several works in the French series *Sources Chrétiennes: On the Life of Moses* (vol. 1), the *De Virginitate* (vol. 71), *Life of Macrina* (vol. 178) and the Letters (vol. 363). There is also a very useful English text and commentary on the *Catechetical Oration*, by J. R. Srawley, (1903), in the Cambridge Patristic Text series. Finally, many of Gregory's writings have been translated into English in the Library of Nicene and Post Nicene Fathers by Moore.

The following short bibliography makes no claim to being comprehensive; only those works which may be thought to be of more general use have been included.

162

Armstrong, A. H., 'The theory of the non-existence of matter in Plotinus and the Cappadocians', *Studia Patristica* [= SP] 5, 427–429, 1962.

—— (ed.), *The Cambridge History of Late Greek and Early Medieval Philosophy*, Cambridge, 1967.

Balas, D. L., Μετουσια Θεου. *Man's Participation in God. Perfections According to St. Gregory of Nyssa*, Romae, Herder, 1966.

——, 'Gregor von Nyssa', *TRE* XIV: 173–181.

Canevet, M., 'Gregoire de Nysse', *Dictionnaire de spiritualité ascétique et mystique*, vol. 6, Paris, pp. 971–1011, 1967.

Cherniss, H. F., 'The Platonism of Gregory of Nyssa', *UCPCP* 11: 1–92, 1930.

Crouzel, H., 'Gregoire de Nysse est-il le fondateur de la théologie mystique? Une controverse récente', *RAM* 33: 189–202, 1957.

Daniélou, J., *Platonisme et théologie mystique. Doctrine spirituelle de saint Grégoire de Nysse*, Paris, 1944.

——, *L'être et le temps chez Grégoire de Nysse*, Leiden, 1970

Diekamp, F., *Die Gotteslehre des heiligen Gregor von Nyssa*, Munster, 1895.

Doerrie, Heinrich, 'Gregor III (Gregor von Nyssa)', *RAC* 12: 863–895, 1983.

Doerries, Hermann, 'Griechentum und Christentum bei Gregor von Nyssa' (a review of H. Langerbeck's edition of *GNO* VI), *TLZ* 88: 569–582, 1983.

Drobner, H., 'Gregor von Nyssa', *Die Drei Tage zwischen Tod und Auferstehung unseres Herrn Jesus Christus*, Leiden, 1982.

Fedwick, P. J. (ed.), *Basil of Caesarea, Christian, Humanist, Ascetic*, Toronto, 1981.

Grillmeier, A., *Christ in Christian Tradition*, London, 1965.

Hall, S. G. (ed.), *Gregory of Nyssa, Homilies on Ecclesiastes, An English version with Supporting Studies*, Berlin, 1993.

Holl, K., *Amphilochius von Ikonium in seinem Verhältnis zu den grossen Kappadoziern*, Tübingen, 1904.

Horn, G., 'L'amour divin. Note sur le mot "Eros" dans Saint de Nysse', *RAM* 8: 378–389, 1925.

Hubner, R. H., *Die Einheit des Leibes Christi bei Gregor von Nyssa*, Leiden, 1974.

Ivanka, E. von, *Hellenisches und Christliches im fruehbyzantinischen Geistesleben*, Vienna, 1948.

Jaeger, W., *Early Christianity and Greek Paideia*, Cambridge, Mass., 1961.

——, *Gregor von Nyssa's Lehre vom Heiligen Geist*, Leiden, 1966.

——, *Two Rediscovered Works of Ancient Christian Literature of Gregory of Nyssa and Macarius*, Leiden, 1954.

Kopecek, T., *A History of Neo-Arianism*, 2 vols, Cambridge, Mass., 1979.

Lossky, V., *The Mystical Theology of the Eastern Church*, Cambridge, 1957.

Louth, A., *The Origins of the Christian Mystical Tradition*, Oxford, 1981.

Macleod, C. W., 'Allegory and Mysticism in Origen and Gregory of Nyssa', *Collected Essays* (30), Oxford, pp. 309–326, 1983.

——, 'The Preface to Gregory of Nyssa's *On the Life of Moses*', *Collected Essays* (32), Oxford, pp. 329–337, 1983.

May, G., 'Die Chronologie des Lebens und der Werke des Gregor von Nyssa', *Ecriture et culture philosophique*, edited by M. Harl, Leiden, pp. 51–66, 1971.

Meredith, A., *The Cappadocians*, London, 1995.

——, 'Gregory of Nazianzus and Gregory of Nyssa on Basil', *SP* 32: 163–169, 1997.

——, 'Traditional Apologetic in the *Contra Eunomium* of Gregory of Nyssa', *SP* 14: 315–319, 1976.

——, 'Origen's *De Principiis* and Gregory of Nyssa's *Oratio Catechetica*', *Heythrop Journal*, January: 1–15, 1995.

——, 'Licht und Finsternis bei Gregor von Nyssa', *PLATON in der abendlaendischen Geistesgeschichte*, Darmstadt, pp. 48–59, 1997.

Meyendorff, J., *Byzantine Theology: Historical trends and doctrinal themes*, New York, 1974/1979.

Mitchell, S., *Anatolia; Land, Men and Gods*, vol. 2, *The Rise of the Church*, Oxford, 1993.

Muehlenberg, E., *Die Unendlichkeit Gottes bei Gregor von Nyssa*, Goettingen, 1966.

Norden, E., *Die antike Kunstprosa*, Darmstadt, 1981.

Nygren, A., *Eros und Agape*, Watson, 1932.

Otis, B., 'Cappadocian thought as a coherent system', *DOP* 12: 95–124, 1958.

——, 'Gregory of Nyssa and the Cappadocian Conception of time', *SP* 14: 27–357, 1976.

Pelikan, J., *Christianity and Classical Culture: The Metamorphosis of Natural Theology in the Christian Encounter with Hellenism*, Yale, 1993.

Pohlenz, M., *Vom Zorne Gottes*, Goettingen, 1909.

Sheldon-Williams, I. P., 'The Cappadocians', *The Cambridge History of Late Greek and Early Medieval Philosophy*, edited by A. H. Armstrong, Cambridge, Chapter 29, Part 6, pp. 432–456, 1967.

Spira, A., 'Rhetorik und Theologie in den Grabreden Gregors von Nyssa', *SP*, 9: 1906.

Srawley, J. H., 'St Gregory of Nyssa on the Sinlessness of Christ', *JTS* 7: 434–441, 1906.

Stead, G. C., 'Ontology and Terminology in Gregory of Nyssa', *Gregor von Nyssa und die Philosophie*, Leiden, pp. 107–127, 1976.

Voelker, W., *Gregor von Nyssa als Mystiker*, Wiesbaden, 1955.

——, 'Zur Gottes Lehre Gregors von Nyssa', *VC* 9, 1959.

Williams, R. 'Macrina's Deathbed Revisited: Gregory of Nyssa on mind and passion', *Christian Faith and Greek Philosophy in Late Antiquity*, Supplement to *Vigiliae Christianae* 19, edited by L. Wickham and C. Bammel, Leiden, 1993.

Wilson, N. G., *Scholars of Byzantium*, London, Duckworth, 1996.

INDEX

Printed in the United States
121969LV00002B/119/A